I WAS
SADDAM'S
SON

I WAS SADDAM'S SON

LATIF YAHIA

AND

KARL WENDL

ARCADE PUBLISHING • NEW YORK

FIRST ENGLISH-LANGUAGE EDITION

Library of Congress Cataloging-in-Publication Data
Yahyá, Latif
  [Ich war Saddams Sohn. English]
  I was Saddam's son / by Latif Yahia and Karl Wendl. —1st English-language ed.
    p. cm.
  ISBN 1-55970-373-3
    1. Yahyá, Latif. 2. Iraq—Politics and government. 3. Political corruption—Iraq.
4. Persian Gulf War, 1991—Personal narratives, Iraqi. 5. Hussein, Saddam.
6. Hussein, Uday Saddam. I. Wendl, Karl. II. Title.
  DS79. 7. Y34 1997
  956. 7044'2—dc21   97-2734

Published in the United States by Arcade Publishing, Inc., New York
Distributed by Little, Brown and Company

10 9 8 7 6 5 4 3 2

Designed by API

BP

PRINTED IN THE UNITED STATES OF AMERICA

CONTENTS

A section of photographs falls between pages 136 and 137

PUBLISHER'S NOTE

SADDAM Hussein has proven one of the most durable dictators alive, and he has shown himself ruthless and wily enough to remain on the world screen for years to come. Since his initial ascent to power in 1968 as the number two man behind General Ahmad Hasan al-Bakr, and especially since he officially succeeded al-Bakr in 1979 as the supreme leader of Iraq, he has thrived, while his opponents, both inside and outside Iraq, have strayed from power or died. Nothing has been able to topple him—not stalemate in the war with Iran or defeat in the Gulf War, nor embargo by the nations of the world, nor persistent rebellion in the north and south of his country, nor mutiny in his army, nor assassination attempts against him, nor threats to his authority from within his clan and his political party—yet George Bush, the leader of the Allied coalition that ostensibly vanquished Iraq, has retired in defeat, as has his coalition partner, the "Iron Lady," Margaret Thatcher. His archenemy, Ayatollah Ruholla Khomeini of Iran, is also long gone. Saddam has done more than persist in office. Though his ambitions have ruined and impoverished his country, he has made his personal survival and that of his regime a national triumph, thanks to the efficiency of his security apparatus and propaganda machinery. Incredibly, he has literally snatched victory from the jaws of defeat. For many Iraqis he continues to be a heroic figure, offering the hope of an era in which Iraq will become the new Babylon, a center of wealth and a new great power among Arab states.

The heir apparent to this master of survival has been his firstborn son, Uday Saddam Hussein. Already one of the most hated men in Iraq, Uday is no stranger to the worst crimes and appetites of humankind. He has repeatedly committed murder, torture, and rape, as well as other crimes, and his greed and depravity are notorious. He has threatened to be an even greater scourge than Saddam: "Just wait until I become president," he has promised his intimates, according to the narrative that follows, "I'll be crueler than my father ever was. You mark my words. You'll yearn for the time of Saddam Hussein."

I Was Saddam's Son is a unique insider's account of the workings of power in Saddam Hussein's regime, and a chilling portrait of the man who may succeed him. Born with an uncanny resemblance to Uday Hussein, the author, Latif Yahia, was forced to become his double, or *fidai*. A fidai is more than a body double: he is a bondman, a warrior and loyal follower, willing to give his life for his master. For the four years of his training and service, Latif Yahia gained access to the inner circle and was the privileged witness to excesses ranging from the horrifying and criminal to the absurd. He became familiar with the security apparatus and the members of the Saddam clan, as well as with the clique surrounding Uday. As Uday's stand-in, he took part in affairs of state, made public appearances, and, during the Gulf War, visited the troops on the front lines while Uday remained safely away. He witnessed murders committed by Saddam and Uday Hussein and at their behest. He was made to watch videos of tortures, and saw firsthand what goes on in Saddam's prisons. When Saddam's soldiers looted Kuwait, he was there, participating in the plunder on behalf of his master, and silently keeping note.

He was no innocent, as he admits here, and his motives in reporting what he saw and heard include some measure of vengeance and self-justification or self-absolution, clear-eyed or not. There is no doubt some manipulation of fact, in part clearly to protect those who have remained behind or may seek to return to Iraq. Nevertheless, when the TV news magazine *60 Minutes* ran an interview with Latif in 1995, the main lines of his story checked out with authorities in the Kurdish resistance and the American military. Whatever its impurities, his testimony in this exposé conforms to what is generally known about Saddam's regime, and is inescapably damning in its detailed accounts of the dictator and especially his psychopathic son.

Latif Yahia's co-author, the journalist who broke his story to the world, has added to this edition an epilogue updating the account with events in Iraq and within the regime since Latif's flight, culminating in the attempted assassination of Uday on December 12, 1996, and its aftermath. Whatever else the epilogue records, it points to the tight bonds between Saddam and his two sons and to the brutal lengths to which they will go to retain their grasp on power. It is still unclear how debilitating Uday's wounds are. He appears to have recovered from them sufficiently to resume his former activities and again be a dangerous man. Should he inherit Saddam's power, whether alone or with his brother, Qusay, he may prove to be more destabilizing to the region, and more of a threat to the world at large, than Saddam ever was.

· I R A Q ·

BLACK SEA

RUSSIA

GEORGIA

ARMENIA

AZERBAIJAN

CASPIAN SEA

Erzurum

TURKEY

Tabriz

Diyarbakir

Urmia

Tigris

Zakhu

Dahuk

Makok Mtns.

IRAN

NINEVEH

Salahaddin

Mosul

Arbil

SYRIA

Euphrates

Kirkuk

Sulaimaniya

Tikrit

Kermanshah

IRAQ

Ramadi

Baghdad

Zagros Mtns.

Fallujah

Tigris

JORDAN

Karbala

Kut

Hillah

Najaf

Hayy

Amarah

Qadisiya

Shatrah

Ahvaz

Samawah

Euphrates

Nasiriyah

Shatt

Abadan

SAHRA AL-HIJARAH

Rumeila

Basra

SWAMPLANDS

Safwan

al-Arab

BUBIYAN

Jahrah

★ Kuwait City

Hawalli

Ahmadi

NEUTRAL
ZONE

KUWAIT

PERSIAN
GULF

SAUDI ARABIA

al-Khafji

0	100	200 Kilometers

0	100	200 Miles

I WAS
SADDAM'S
SON

I

ON THE IRANIAN FRONT

MORNING, September 23, 1987. I was sitting in a black Mercedes limousine with tinted windows. My driver didn't say a word. The car had to be brand-new: the dark leather smelled acrid, fresh. Not a speck of dust, no stains. The carpet on the floor was clean and bright. The dashboard of rare wood shone impeccably, the air conditioner worked noiselessly, the purr of the engine was almost imperceptible. We glided majestically through the grounds of the Palace of the Republic in Baghdad, an area as vast as the downtown section of an average European city, containing ministries, ministerial apartments, athletic facilities, theaters, cinemas, hospitals, an airport. Sandwiched in between were fantastic parks and elaborate fountains, turquoise-colored swimming pools with marble rims. A city within a city. Saddam's secret nerve center.

I had no idea where I was being taken, and didn't dare ask. I felt scared, because a second black limo followed directly behind us. On the front I was never afraid, but now sweat seemed to spill from every pore. I dried my wet hands on my uniform and had to wonder, "Why me?" But the fact is, people disappear constantly in Iraq. They are arrested, tortured, sent to prison for life, or summarily executed. Nobody knows why. All we have are rumors and suspicions.

We're sure of only one thing: a wrong word, a careless joke about the president, or an obscene gesture referring to him or his family can be your death sentence. I was convinced that I had always demonstrated loyalty to the regime and was therefore blameless, yet my anxiety grew with each passing minute. *Could I have criticized Saddam somewhere, sometime*, I asked myself, *before friends at home or joking with colleagues on the front? Did I slip up and reveal how this war repulsed me, that I thought it was accomplishing nothing other than to rob me of my youth and time?* Maybe I'd just carried out an order badly, or somehow failed to carry one out.

I had been drafted into the Iraqi army nine months earlier, on January 6, 1987. The Iran-Iraq war was still going strong after seven years, and our forces had captured seven hundred square miles of Iranian territory. More than forty divisions were deployed in the border region around the Shatt al-Arab, the estuary at the confluence of the Euphrates and Tigris rivers in the south of Iraq. Yet, as a student, far away from the fighting, I took little notice of the war other than the occasional rocket that targeted Baghdad and recently had destroyed two downtown businesses. It simply didn't interest me.

I had finished my law studies at Baghdad University with grades of "excellent" — the best possible. It had been a joyous occasion for me and my family. I looked forward to nothing more than working in my father's businesses, but that wasn't to be, thanks to a law subjecting all males over eighteen who had graduated or discontinued their studies to the military draft.

According to the law, those who weren't equal to their studies or interrupted them for any other reason had to spend thirty-six months on the front. Graduates, Iraq's pride, were required — in principle — to serve only twenty-one months. But I knew that my twenty-one months of military service could easily balloon into ten years. Laws in Iraq can be changed any time at the whim of the president. If Saddam Hussein lacked soldiers on the front, the tour of duty was simply extended with the explanation that "your fatherland needs you." And at that time there was no end in sight to the Iran-Iraq border conflict for anyone, let alone an ordinary citizen like me. We knew only that Saddam wanted the waterway because it was "of vital importance for Iraq," and because the Iranians also coveted it.

For years, friends of my family had participated in the war against Iran. Few had not sacrificed at least one son. War victims were everywhere in Baghdad: young men with burnt faces, amputated legs, amputated arms, desperate people with empty souls and expressionless eyes. Beside them were healthy young men with Kalashnikovs hung around their necks, waiting for buses to take them back to their units.

Though I never stopped and spoke with any of the young soldiers while driving through Baghdad, I had the impression that most felt no further desire to fight. They were compelled to, whether they wanted or not, because the penalty for disobedience or desertion was death. This had been Saddam's directive since the beginning of the war. Thousands of deserters had already been put to death in the al-Ameriya camps, in Prison No. 1, and in the al-Rashid camp in Baghdad. Mass executions were carried out not behind prison walls or in secluded chambers out of public view, but live, on television, for the benefit of all Iraqis.

Saddam's goal was to strike fear and intimidate. That was why he ordered public executions — and staged them in front of the young victims' desperate families. Mothers, fathers, sisters, and brothers were forced to watch as the "traitors to the fatherland" were publicly hanged, so that they would experience the torment of their children and brothers, feel the suffering in their own bodies. So that they were covered in disgrace.

But this torture was not enough: the mourning families also had to pay a penalty to the state as restitution for their sons' "guilt." More than that, they were forbidden to bury their dead honorably. "A deserter has failed before the president and Allah," the authorities mocked. "He has lost his

honor and doesn't deserve a decent burial." Saddam termed
his treatment of the youth of Iraq "just punishment for
godless people."

I was assigned to a commando training unit made up of
university graduates. Our instructors were told to make officers of us privileged recruits as quickly as possible. Within
four months we had to be ready to assume command positions within the army.

My ID number was 23. Our course was named "Saddam
the Arab" and began January 16, 1987, at the al-Rashid barracks on the outskirts of Baghdad. For a whole month we were
drilled, drilled, drilled, until we were ready to drop. Twenty-
four hours of brainwashing: we were roused at 4:00 A.M., had
roll call at five, then daily orders: fitness training followed by
drills followed by fitness training. Bare-chested, wearing only
our uniform pants, we were chased by our instructors all over
the dusty barracks enclosure. Pushups, marching double-
time, deep knee-bends. We crawled over the asphalt, clambered over the obstacle course. The worst instructor was
Salem al-Juburi, a powerful, dark-haired man from southern
Iraq. He swore at us, struck us with a wire cable if we were
sloppy in our drills, treated us like animals. We hated him for
it, but he was evenhanded, treating everyone alike. He drilled
the two hundred Moroccan soldiers, our Muslim brothers
training in Iraq, until they were ready to drop.

Lunch was at 2:00 P.M. Then more of the same: military
drill, exercises, political education. No pause, no idling, not
a second to think about anything other than the army and
the soldier's duty. Those who didn't want to submit were
harried around the oven-hot barracks enclosure until they
couldn't move. Our instructors had one goal only — to
break our personalities in order to make mindless fighting
machines out of us.

During our training, we were prohibited from calling our
relatives and friends. Even letters were strictly forbidden. No
distractions were allowed. Only after a month did we receive

two days of leave. Forty-eight hours away from the relentless programming, forty-eight hours to be a human being.

Then came the second part, the actual military portion of the training. We joined the al-Saeka company to learn the use of light weaponry, especially the automatic rifle. How to take apart a Kalashnikov, how to load the magazine, how to clean the weapon, how to remove a stuck cartridge. Monotonous repetition: Take it apart, clean it, assemble it. Take it apart, clean it, assemble it. We practiced until we could assemble and use the weapons in our sleep. Then came an intensive course in karate and self-defense. We were taught the tricks of hand-to-hand and street combat, how to approach the enemy without a sound.

At the end came survival training: hours, days without food and water. Our instructors marched us to a huge hall that could have held a thousand people. As we entered, the stench was nauseating — a penetrating stink of urine, human excrement, sweat, and decay. Many, we had heard, had been driven to such despair here that they stopped being able to function normally.

Five hundred of us were locked in the hall. Our instructors sat on a kind of platform, like tennis judges. The floor, of pounded earth, was dotted with puddles containing dead dogs and cats. The cadavers were half carrion, some already almost skeletons. Cockroaches, beetles, and mosquitoes were everywhere. The military even brought in loads of snakes and tipped them over onto the floor.

We had to survive a week in this room. The instructors forced us to eat cockroaches, to throw ourselves in puddles with the animal cadavers and, once down, to stay down. Those who refused were beaten and kicked by their comrades as part of the drill. Solidarity and friendship ceased. It was a struggle to endure, which some of us barely won.

Sattar, a tall, thin, sensitive recruit I knew from college, nearly cracked under this ordeal. As an instructor screamed at him from his platform, "Sattar, stuff the creatures down your throat! Catch them and stuff them down your throat!" he took several matchbox-sized cockroaches in his hand. He squeezed them until a milk-white liquid seeped out of their hard backs. "Put them in your mouth and chew — I want to hear them crunch!" But Sattar couldn't do it. He began to retch, suppressed the urge to vomit, clamped his lips shut. His thin face became flame red, and the veins on his forehead grew thicker as if they were about to burst. He managed to control his nausea twice. His body convulsed, tears flowed from his eyes. Then he lost it. He sank slowly to his knees, gagged, puked, gagged. "Pick him up!" screamed the instructor. "Pick up that piece of garbage!" And we knew what to do. Two of us grabbed Sattar under the arms and lifted him up while he was still vomiting. The third held his head, and the fourth put a cockroach in his mouth, even as he continued to retch. "Bite through it. You are an Iraqi soldier, bite through it," came the shrill command from the platform, and it sounded as though the instructor was enjoying the humiliating spectacle. Sattar chewed and threw up, and they stuffed the cockroach back in his mouth. There was a crunch as he chomped down again, and Sattar's body trembled from head to toe as he forced the insect down his throat.

Although that course brought me to the brink of exhaustion, I know today that basic training helped me develop and made me into a man. I was in top physical condition afterward. Because the army had forced my brain to turn off, my body was on autopilot: An order found obedience, nothing else. At the end, even forty-mile marches in full gear were hardly a problem because each muscle, each fiber of my body reacted completely automatically, and my brain was able to form no resistance.

We became warriors, and the harsh training hardened our will to fight. "Our goal is to make you brutal and inhuman," our instructors told us, "like beasts. Even the Israeli secret service fears you, and that's something you can be proud of. The world must fear you, and you must forget your own fears."

We considered ourselves special, and the system continually stoked our self-confidence. "You're a team," they told us. "You're privileged young men who were allowed to go to college, which makes you the chosen few. Everything has prepared you to become what we want you to be. You have a unique opportunity to serve your country as few can. For now, you're only raw material for your ultimate duties, but when we're finished with you, you will be the best-qualified soldiers in the world."

Basic training ended on April 5, 1987. We were granted four days' leave, during which I traveled into Baghdad to visit my family. Father was proud, because I acted as if the hardships hadn't bothered me, as if I had enjoyed myself. But really I was of two minds: Though deep down I resented and opposed the war, I was also fascinated by the weapons with which it had brought me into contact. In the Arab world, weapons are part of every man's life. A weapon is more than an instrument of death; it is also an expression of strength and determination, of power and wealth. It is customary in Iraq for every man to carry a firearm. No home or family is without one, whether it be a pistol, a rifle, or a Kalashnikov. A weapon is part of a man, and if he doesn't have one, he's no man. That is what we were taught.

In talking with my father, I offered little detail about the past weeks and discussed instead the next month of training. Parachute jumps were coming up in the program. Within thirty days we were expected to be able to jump from planes and carry out guerrilla attacks behind enemy lines.

Our chief instructor was rough and tough, thoroughly imbued with the regime's ideology but also a soldier's soldier. Because of him, we didn't dread the first jump, and he constantly reminded us that we were among the elite. We weren't permitted to think about anything but our job. "You have to become familiar with fear," he told us in a fatherly way. "If you don't get to know fear now, you won't be able to deal with it later."

A jump platform towered nearly 400 feet high in the middle of the barracks compound. The iron rungs to the top seemed endless, but the instructors harried us ruthlessly all the way up. Stopping once meant two lashes with a thick cable. I recoiled when I stood on top for the first time with the practice chute on my back. I was scared but had no choice. "Whoever refuses to jump repeats the whole course," our instructors threatened. The jump instructor yelled at me through the loudspeakers affixed to the top of the tower, "Don't be afraid. Be strong, concentrate!"

I tensed my muscles, took a deep breath, screamed, "al-Saeka," and plunged into the void.

"Saddam the Arab" ended on May 9, 1987. Sixty of the five hundred men who had started with me had given up before completion. They were eliminated as officer cadets or made to repeat the course.

We attended the graduation ceremony in fancy dress uniforms. Lined up in blocks of two hundred on the drill square, we listened as an army band played the Iraqi national anthem. No less a figure than army commander Abd-al-Jadbar Shanshal came to hand us our commission diplomas and announce that we were full members of the Iraqi army.

This was a proud day for me — twenty-three, and already an officer.

Thus I took the first career step within Iraqi society, which considers military prowess, along with money, as the most desirable attribute in a young man. I felt happy, content with myself, and liberated, and to top it all off I was accorded four days of leave. Again I visited my parents, but this time the days at home weren't as carefree as before. I knew that after this brief holiday I'd have to go to the front: I had received my marching orders at the same time I was decorated for the successful completion of officers' training.

May 13, 1987, was a real scorcher. We were transported

by army bus from Baghdad to Moussa Ibn Nassir, the 35th Division. The unit was located east of Basra, in southern Iraq. Its commander was Mohammed Taher Tavfik, an affable man whom I knew personally because he came from the same Baghdad suburb as I did. When we arrived, I was nervous, exhausted, unsure what to expect. Mohammed Taher Tavfik took it all in, but now was not the time for comforting words. "You have twenty-four hours to rest up from your trip, then you'll be transferred. To the front," he thundered, and made no further comment.

The barracks descended several stories underground, similar to a subterranean garage. I slept poorly that night. The heat, the mosquitoes, the dull thudding of shells, which we could hear even down there, bothered me greatly. I was listening to the sounds of war for the first time in my life. As our side returned fire, I could feel the vibration. I even imagined I could smell the war. I was part of it. There was no turning back.

The next day I was transferred to Observation Post No. 5-2 in al-Aazir. The post was situated in a region of marshes. Our Iranian enemies — we called them Khomeinis — were no more than a mile and a half away. When the wind was favorable, we could hear them talking in their positions, threatening to cut our throats when they overran our lines. Sometimes they sent cries of *"Jays May Akram!"* in our direction.

May Akram was a cabaret singer who performed in some of Baghdad's worst establishments. Even in dissolute Iraq, where alcohol, bars, and nightclubs were as common as in the United States and Europe, she had a sordid reputation. May Akram was a whore. The Iranians' taunts meant "You're a godless army of whores."

My job held nothing of the romance of war constantly evoked for us during our training. My orders were "observation of the enemy troops and radio transmission of the encoded observation results to the unit." My post was a covered platform supported by six iron legs and reachable only by boat. The swamp extended in every direction. Inside were two tiny benches that doubled as beds, a table on which we kept our radio, and a tiny cooking area. The whole platform was no bigger than three square yards. This is where I was to hold out; this was the glorious war against the devil Khomeini.

My team consisted of radio officer Ismail Taha, a hardboiled warrior, not much older than I, but already a veteran of several years on the front; Mohammed Mottasher, a simple soldier from a Baghdad suburb; and a cook. I was charged to hold this position for twenty-two days, which we filled with a monotonous regimen of constant observation. Boredom made it difficult to maintain concentration, yet even the slightest change in the enemy positions had to be reported immediately to my unit, which responded with heavy artillery fire. We personally had only light weapons and therefore no chance of responding effectively to any attack. Should one come, our orders were to pull back calmly and quickly.

For weeks nothing happened. We waited, observed, waited. Hours passed, days. Then sudden, short, intensive artillery battles broke the monotony. Of the enemy I saw little more than the small trucks used to bring food to soldiers on the front and not even those normally, but just the dust thrown up by the trucks. Sometimes, particularly at night, the Khomeinis seemed so close we could hear them breathe. Then came days when we heard and saw nothing of them, although we knew they were out there. It was simultaneously spooky and unbelievably tedious. The front had become mired down in a kind of trench warfare that could go on forever.

It wasn't long before I had more than enough of my assignment of sitting and waiting. Deep blue skies above us, murderous heat around us, water and more water before us, the swamps of the Shatt al-Arab. As an officer, I supposedly had it better than the common soldiers, but did being an officer really improve my lot? I ate what the others ate, slept on the same wooden benches, and, like them, was only a tiny cog in the machinery of this incomprehensible war. I saw no reason to fight — I didn't hate my enemy, couldn't hate him because I didn't know him. It would have been easier to hate him had there been some kind of murderous dynamics to the war. But like this? We simply had too much time to think about things. Ninety-five percent of our duties consisted of waiting. Absurd.

The only advantage I enjoyed as an officer was that I received seven days' furlough every three weeks. After twenty-two days I could finally leave my position and go home to Baghdad, city of my dreams. My father was impressed when I told him about the front. Still, he couldn't help but see that I was searching for some reason the war was being fought. "Look at our house, Father. We have everything. The people in Iraq have it good. Why do we have to die on the front, why?" He avoided my questions and met each of my arguments against the war with the same explanation: "Military duty is duty toward the fatherland, and desertion is punishable by death." There was no other way, I had to go back. Concern for my family forced me to "do my duty."

Two days later, on June 10, 1987, came my baptism by fire. The Khomeinis attacked from all sides in a bid to roll over the 35th Division and cut it into pieces. Quickly I ordered my radio officer to establish contact with headquarters. He screamed the alarm into the airwaves, and the response came back from the commanding officer: "Abandon the position. Pull back." But it was already too late. As we clambered into our boat, we spotted Iranian helicopters coming at us, first two, then a whole group, providing a wild pyrotechnic display. A shell hit our observation post and blew the primitive iron structure to smithereens. A few minutes earlier and we would have been goners, but the danger hadn't passed. Although our artillery units rained shells on the enemy, he continued to advance. We felt hemmed in, with no chance of breaking through. Nevertheless, we were able to fight our way to another base, but in vain: The commander there was forced to surrender almost immediately.

The whole company was taken prisoner. Officers and common soldiers were separated. The Khomeinis bound our hands, herded us into a crude cellar, and beat us. Only six men were assigned to guard duty, because outside the fighting continued.

Ghassan Hamoud, commander of the Tenth Armored Company and a much-decorated war hero, had begun his counterattack. His assignment was clear — to secure our freedom and drive the Iranians back — and he was successful. After two hours the Khomeinis were back where they started. They left behind all their equipment and fled on foot, wading through the swamps, our guards among them. A crazy war.

Hundreds of Iranian soldiers were captured by the men of the Tenth Armored Company in the counterattack. What began as a rout became a day of triumph for the Iraqi army, and Saddam Hussein deployed his entire propaganda team — television crews, newspaper reporters, photographers — to record the victory. We were feted as though we had won the war. Our whole unit received special decorations, and I was promoted to first lieutenant.

I should have celebrated that day, but I felt miserable. Nassem Tibn, a young soldier from the Anbar district of Baghdad who had gone through basic training with me, was gravely wounded during the counterattack, not by a bullet while fighting, but by an Iranian soldier who had been taken prisoner. The Iranian was lying facedown on the ground with his hands on the nape of his neck, and Nassem Tibn was supposed to be guarding him. Suddenly the prisoner leaped up as if driven by a steel spring. In his hand he held a stone, which he smashed into Nassem Tibn's face. My friend screamed and collapsed, bleeding from a large, ugly-looking wound to the head. His blood poured out into the sand.

One of my men promptly levered a cartridge into the

breech of his rifle and shot the Iranian prisoner point-blank. It was the first time I saw a person die. The Iranian took the bullet in the chest, fell forward, crawled a few yards, and slumped on his face. I heard the death rattle and watched his body convulse. Then he lay motionless in his worn-out, faded uniform. It seemed somehow inhuman and base to watch this youth die, but deep down I felt glad. He deserved it.

A few days later, on July 25, 1987, I was transferred to an artillery formation, Unit 954. Like my previous posting, Unit 954 lay on the foremost front line. We were well armed. All of our equipment came from the Soviet Union and included the most advanced 85-mm mortars, with a range of about two miles. To my satisfaction, I was serving under experienced officers: Troop Commander Mohammed Ghaleb, a nice guy who had already carried out hundreds of attacks in the war; and First Lieutenants Nassir Baker and Saad Ahmad, both from good families in Baghdad and more modern in their thinking than any Harvard MBA, both tall, slender, in excellent condition, and sporting the obligatory mustaches.

Soon I became their friend, although at first I couldn't see why they should accept me so quickly and warmly into their group. I was present when situation reports were discussed. I took my meals with the other officers in the command post. Our position consisted of a subterranean system of passages supported by wooden pillars and protected by sandbags. The command post, a smallish bunker, felt close and stuffy, but radiated a certain charm. A few small tables, stools, a cooking area in a corner: everything was spartan, but I felt good here.

Suddenly I had access to the glorified upper circles of the military, a world so full of itself that reality, the horrors of war, seemed remote. For the first time I had influence, felt powerful, belonged to those who gave the orders. The protocol was clear: Issue orders mercilessly, while taking extreme care not to go too far. Never make a mistake, never give offense to those who really have the say in Iraq — the members of

Saddam's clan. Not even the most harmless joke must pass your lips, no thoughtless remark about the president, no criticism of his family and their hangers-on and lackeys.

It wasn't until Mohammed Ghaleb let the secret slip one day that I finally understood why I was accepted with such ease, why they gave me the feeling of being someone special. We were drinking a glass of tea and making small talk. Ghaleb drew me toward him in a fatherly way, took my right hand, smiled at me while taking a sip, and said, almost in a whisper, "You have good connections to the influential circles in Baghdad. You're one of them. . . ."

I said nothing, smiled back, took a sip, wiped my mustache with the back of my hand, nodded. What was going on became instantly clear. All this time they'd believed I was a member of Saddam Hussein's family because I happened to bear a close resemblance to his son, Uday. Of course, none of them really knew what Uday looked like — they had seen him only in newspaper photographs and on television, and these images weren't of the best quality. And since none of them had direct access to the president, there was no way they could check out my credentials. Ghaleb was so convinced I was a member of the Clan that he even suggested I become the unit's political leader — a singular honor for a young officer, which, however, I was obliged to turn down because I wasn't a full member of the Ba'ath party. In the army hierarchy, party members outranked simple military personnel. Instead of me, a young lieutenant sent by Baghdad got the job.

I didn't care, especially because I had no time to be angry. On September 20, 1987, pure excitement gripped the officers of our unit. A secret and urgent dispatch had arrived direct from the president's office, an unusual event. And the dispatch concerned me, the first lieutenant who appeared to be the spitting image of Uday Saddam Hussein.

Ghaleb summoned me and asked excitedly, "Yahia, did you do something wrong? Did you break the law?"

I was surprised. "No, never. Why?"

Ghaleb grinned in a superior way and then said with a warm, paternal air, "Yahia, you must go to Baghdad by the quickest means possible. It has to do with an important secret mission."

I wanted Ghaleb to explain, but he dismissed me with an elegant, self-important wave of the hand: "No questions, Yahia, my friend. Go," he said, grinning broadly as if he knew what was going on. He had no clue, but I didn't know that at the time.

Twenty-four hours later I found myself at military headquarters in Baghdad. It was 6:00 P.M. I was still wearing my uniform from the front, and was sweaty and covered with dust. Party member Kaiser Harb al-Tikriti greeted me in the headquarters reception area. He seemed to be expecting me and told me to sit down for a minute, my car would be coming soon. We waited in silence for ten minutes, and he asked me only one question: What was it like on the front? "Great, fascinating. I'm proud to be part of it," I lied, because lying is a necessary form of self-protection in Iraq. Everybody lies. The Lie has become part of our society.

Ten more minutes passed, and then the black Mercedes arrived in front of the entrance. I climbed inside, the driver accelerated, and we sped off in the direction of the palace grounds, only a short distance away. Even as I got in, I noticed that a second Mercedes limo had pulled up behind my car. I glanced back as we drove off and saw that it was following us. Three men were sitting inside, their faces grave, and I knew that something serious was going on because normal arrests don't happen this way in Iraq.

So what had I done? We had been gliding along for five minutes, an endless time. I asked the driver for a cigarette, but he had none. My whole tour of duty as a soldier flickered before my mind's eye. Question after question sprang up: When did I complain about the war? With whom had I spoken about the president in any way? Surely my father, with whom I discussed my problems during leave, hadn't let slip a wrong word, sometime, somewhere, to anyone? No, no, that couldn't be! I was certain no one in my family could have done such a thing, at least not on purpose. But the eyes and ears of the Clan are everywhere. Why had my commander, Ghaleb, always steered the conversation toward the president's family? Were they testing me, verifying my loyalty? Had the references to my similarity to Uday only been a trick to fool me? Had they been probing my stability?

I couldn't come up with a satisfactory answer. I felt like asking my driver if he knew where we were going, but he just kept his eyes on the broad paved road. In the seat diagonally behind him, I pressed myself against the door and fixed him with a stare. He showed no reaction beyond smoothing his thick mustache when he glanced at me in the rearview mirror. Our glances met again. I wanted to ask the question, but held back. *Maybe it's all a mistake,* I thought, calming myself. *The driver would have dropped a hint otherwise. I'm sure he knows every one of the rumors and accusations that circulate here by the thousands. Everyone in Baghdad knows them; he must, too.*

It's no secret, I told myself indignantly, that over and over innocent people are accused and executed to pay for the mistakes of the president's family, or to carry out their cruel wishes. Only a few weeks earlier, in a TV broadcast we picked up on the front, I had watched throngs of curious people push their way onto Rashid Street, Baghdad's main promenade and shopping boulevard. The crowd gaped at four men, flanked by heavily armed soldiers and chained hand and foot, who were being exposed to the people's wrath. For almost an hour, hysterical women screeched at them, pulled their hair, and spat in their twisted faces. Then the miserable victims were led away — directly to the gallows. They were Baghdad merchants sentenced to death on Saddam's orders. At the time, Saddam proclaimed that "these base creatures have harmed the people with their rapacity and sold goods at extortionate prices," and everybody knew it was a lie. Saddam's family just wanted to eliminate rivals who had interfered with their business interests and who complained that the Clan had a Mafia-like chokehold on the whole country. The merchants represented a scream of protest, nothing more.

Their execution showed only too clearly how much Saddam feared the people. But the people also feared Hussein. We all feared each other, and I, idiot that I was, thought that I had learned to live with that.

I hadn't. Suddenly my world had been turned completely inside out, and I sat in the middle of a vortex sucking everything downward. I had become a protagonist in the bloody theater piece called Iraq, my homeland.

Someone's confused me with another person, I thought to myself, in an effort to buck up my courage. Then I noticed that my lips were moving. My forehead was clammy with sweat, my short-cropped hair felt damp, my undershirt clung to my skin. *So do I have to pay the price for someone else's crime? Is that my end?*

It was just the beginning.

The Mercedes came to a halt in front of the Nissr-Baghdad Palace, the place of business of Uday Saddam Hussein, the president's infamous son. I recognized the building, although neither I nor anyone else in my family had ever been here before: I'd seen it hundreds of times on television and in the newspapers. Yes, this was Uday's palace. That had to be it. What did Uday want from me?

My driver got out and opened the door. Again he uttered no word, avoided my gaze, kept his face expressionless. Two men in uniform took me inside. I waited for five or six minutes, standing in a kind of foyer. A large mirror hung on the wall, beside it white leather furniture decorated with gold. All at once the door opened, and he was standing in front of me, grinning, a fat Cuban cigar between his index and middle fingers — Uday Saddam Hussein. My first thought: *He's hardly changed. We're still like twins.*

2

PARADISE IN HELL

I'D known Uday for years. We had been schoolmates and attended the same class at the Baghdad School for Boys at the time when his father was still Iraq's vice president. Uday is only four days younger than I. He was born on June 18, 1964, and I on June 14. During my childhood, I didn't know much about him or care about his existence one way or the other. I had an excellent home life. My family lived in a big, stately house in the al-Azamiya district, one of the best residential areas in the capital. My parents were well off. My father, Yahia al-Salihi, owned a factory and three flourishing stores in Baghdad that sold electrical appliances and stoves. He also dealt in marble and other stone. We belonged to the upper class, though I couldn't appreciate that as much in grammar and high school as I did later. I knew only that I was the eldest son, the pride and joy of my mother, Bahar al-Midjani, and a good Muslim. I could have what I wanted, as could my brothers Jotie, Robie, and Omeed and my sisters Galalha and Juan. We had it all.

We lived as in paradise, and at the time Baghdad itself was still a paradise. I liked going to school, and my father encouraged me and worked to develop my talents. He taught me, supported me, honed my skills. I believe my father loved me most of all his children, but of course that would be the natural impression of the oldest son. During the summer holidays he took me with him to his stores and showed me how to deal and sell. He always said, "You have to become like me, a good merchant," and I didn't disappoint him. I finished the first six years of school with the best possible marks. I was at the top of the class, and my teacher, Madame Fauzya, told my father, "Your son is very talented. He'll make his way."

My biggest thrill was to observe how the workers in my father's stores took apart the appliances — tape recorders, televisions, VCRs — then repaired and reassembled them. I craved learning. I wanted to know everything, every detail. I also had a talent for painting. I made large, gaudy, realistic paintings with strong, bright colors, depicting mosques, houses, trees, the Tigris River, my teacher, my siblings. For some reason it was easy for me to draw things from memory.

Back then, the Baghdad School for Boys was the upper school for Iraq's elite, as it remains to this day. It caters to the rich and well-to-do, the sons of politicians, top officers in the military, people of influence. Children from ordinary families weren't allowed to attend unless they'd received excellent marks and recommendations from their previous school or displayed some outstanding talent worth developing. This was the training ground for the urbane young men destined to propel the leading people of the Arab world even further ahead of the pack.

The physical plant of the school consisted of a main building and two smaller ones, and stretched over grounds spanning nearly two and a half acres. Beneath it lay a sophisticated system of bunkers that had been built by the Americans and offered protection even against nuclear attack. There were rooms upon rooms, endless passageways with bowling alleys and Ping-Pong tables, and storage chambers full of food supplies. The school doubled as a military base in addition to being a training center for the elite.

The teachers were just as carefully selected as the students. Saddam took a personal interest in seeing that only the best were hired. We were Iraq's showplace, the cream of a system in which the privileged enjoyed every possible advantage and those beneath them socially had virtually no chance to rise: a topsy-turvy form of socialism that bore more than a passing resemblance to developing capitalism.

We were insulated, shielded, protected. The ordinary people, the plebes, were given no opportunity to distract us from the high standards set by our educators. Thus the school fell more or less under the protection of the Jehaaz al-Amn al-Khass, the most exalted of the six Iraqi secret service organizations. Gardeners, caretakers, the cleaning staff, were all employed by this branch of the secret service. The government built checkpoints all around the school in al-Azamiya district, as near as only a few hundred yards from my house. Guards were perpetually on watch, monitoring everything. It was impossible for outsiders to trespass on the grounds without being detained. Anyone who tried to smuggle in an unauthorized companion would be expelled irrevocably.

We lived in a glass schoolhouse, where we were constantly observed and controlled, inmates in a system that had only two goals: to provide young men with the best possible education and simultaneously to make them perfect party soldiers. Nobody asked for individuality; the only important thing was "one thousand percent" observance of the rules.

A special commission made sure that the teachers were ideologically unassailable and selected from the highest ranks of the Ba'ath party. The chairman of the commission was our principal, Fasaa. A powerful, fierce-looking man, Fasaa weighed at least 220 pounds, was about forty-five years old, and had — everyone noticed this immediately — a huge head on a fit and trim body. He had once been a boxer, advancing to become a national champion. Everyone suffered under him. He was brutal, evil, an animal, but well connected, and this is why we and the teachers had to endure him. He was likely a loyal party rank-and-filer who had been given the job through patronage.

The teachers passed on the pressure from Fasaa to the students. Each of us had to become a member of the party by the age of twelve. There were no exceptions. The party was the most important subject of study. How was its hierarchy structured; what were its basic tenets, goals, and programs? We learned that the party was the greatest element of society; without the party you were nothing. Our fundamental textbook was the party's program, *The Central Report of the Ninth National Conference of the Ba'ath Party*, which also gave its history from the founding to the present. Everybody in Iraq had to memorize every line, every word, of this book. The *Central Report* eclipsed even the Koran in importance.

All of this was unexceptional for me. I was only twelve and knew nothing else. Because all of us were subject equally, I didn't consider it harassment or a special burden to be drilled two hours a week about the Ba'ath party. Our teachers made certain that we knew our catechism a hundred percent. We were quizzed, and those found lacking received extra work as punishment. If the same children remained unprepared, they were promptly thrown out of the school. We thus immersed ourselves in the party program as if it were the holiest of the holy, which, in effect, it was.

The first level of the party hierarchy is that of the sympathizer. Beginning as a common sympathizer, you become an active sympathizer, then a pioneer, and finally a full member. Once you are an active member of the party, you can advance to company leader, department leader, and last, executive member on the community or supra-regional level.

To me, much more rewarding than inculcation in the ways of the party was getting to know my outstanding contemporaries, for instance, Ali Mohammed Saleh, whose father was party leader, a prestigious post in Iraq, or Vamied al-Saadoun, whose father was an officer in the al-Khass. Oussama Kahtan came from the family of the Iraqi Central Bank director. Above all, there was Siad Michel Aflaq, whose father shared the credit for introducing, propagating, and making a success of the Arab Socialist Ba'ath party in Iraq. He was one of the country's leading thinkers and Saddam's most influential political counselor.

Siad was a pleasant young man with perfect manners. He was exceptional, something one noticed immediately from the erect and elegant way he walked, from his deportment, and from the way he spoke and acted. At fourteen he was as mature as others were at thirty — an almost fully developed personality.

I considered it crucial to gain his friendship, and worked hard at it — slowly, carefully, because I didn't want anybody to notice that I desired nothing more than to become his friend. I sought him out during recess, smiled at him once in a while during lessons. One Monday in November 1978, just after we had completed a difficult essay, he approached me and suggested that we meet outside school, at the al-Alvia Club.

The al-Alvia Club lay directly behind the Sheraton Hotel and was an emanation of the other Baghdad, the exclusive, rich, cosmopolitan city of fantasy. Iraq was still the darling of the West then. Investments were being negotiated, trade flourished, billions of dollars poured in. Few major western businesses could make do without a branch in Iraq; international hotels were sprouting from the ground, Sheraton, Hilton, and others. Baghdad was the center to which everyone gravitated, the businessmen and arms traders, soldiers of fortune and pleasure-seekers from our brother Arab countries. For Baghdad was western, and everything was available: nightclubs and bars, alcohol and women — beautiful women for little money. Oilmen and weapons dealers of all nations and colors lived here and threw their money around as if it were only printed paper.

I didn't dare ask Siad what membership cost, because the amounts I had heard spoken of were so enormous that I knew my family couldn't possibly pay them: supposedly $2,000 to $3,000 a month.

Siad picked me up on a Friday afternoon in a Mercedes that he drove himself, although he was only fourteen, like me. For the upper class in Iraq, there are few prohibitions or inviolable rules. Children of the rich and powerful do what they want, for nobody, not a single police officer, would dare run a check on members of this class, let alone stop them and ask to see a driver's license. The system is so feudal that those on top can fix things as they like.

I had put on my finest suit. Siad wore a lightweight Armani suit, an Yves Saint Laurent tie, and Gucci shoes. He smelled of a heavy, sweet, expensive perfume.

Even the entrance to the club was imposing: a large gate fronted by two bodyguards who scrutinized everyone driving in. Siad had a sticker on his windshield identifying him as a member. Immediately after the entrance came the parking lot with its armada of cars, none cheaper than a Mercedes. No car was dirty, let alone dented. Everything shone here; the bright chrome bumpers gleamed like silver in the dazzling sun.

There was more security after the parking lot. Siad casually showed his membership card, a photo ID bearing his name and address. I was nervous when the security people asked me for mine, but Siad solved the problem elegantly, as was his style, by taking my arm and telling the guards I was a friend, and that was enough.

Then the club itself, a paradise unlike almost anything in the West: a concentration of restaurants and gigantic arcades with computer games, videos, pool tables, everything. There were also party rooms that seemed as big as St. Peter's Square in Rome or St. Stephen's Square in Vienna, which could be rented for posh gatherings with lush decorations, for weddings and birthdays. Some wealthy socialites might reserve a ballroom at the al-Rashid Hotel, the Sheraton, or the al-Mansur for such occasions, but those who really wanted to shine in Baghdad society came here.

Cleverly integrated into this system of game rooms and

restaurants were a number of terraced swimming pools. Beside them extended polo grounds, a cricket field, and two basketball courts.

Siad seemed to know almost all the young men in the club. I kept to the background that day, tried to stay out of the small talk, sought shelter behind Siad's perfect demeanor. I listened with interest while he talked with his father's friends, when the newest cars were discussed, and when the conversation turned to the absolute ne plus ultra of Iraqi society, the al-Said Club.

The al-Said Club was even more elegant and fashionable than the al-Alvia, however impossible that may have seemed to me. Only members of Saddam Hussein's family and the families of his advisers, friends, and government ministers had access. The club was located in the exclusive al-Mansur district.

Siad raved about the first time he'd accompanied his father there. "It's paradise, absolute paradise," he said, and we stood around him and listened as if he were a prophet. "Al-Said isn't Sunset Boulevard, or Ocean Drive in Miami Beach. It's far more." He gestured dramatically with his glass of gin and tonic on the rocks. "The grass is green, but not a normal green. When you look at this grass, you think of the best golf courses in England and you feel like crying. Dark, thick, juicy lawns. Life, the sun, the stars, the universe — all of that is al-Said."

Siad gesticulated like Bing Crosby wooing Grace Kelly in *High Society.* "And then there are the swimming pools. There are winter pools and summer pools, both inlaid with mosaic tile, and the water is as blue as a sapphire. Fabulous." The conversation became a monologue, with Siad spinning his tale almost without interruption: "Only ministers show up there. Security knows almost every ID card, every name, every detail by heart."

And he launched into a story. "Once, a Mercedes 500 SEL drove up. At first I couldn't see a driver, but there had to be one, because not even a Mercedes drives itself. And then he got out."

None of us dared interrupt. We waited, without breathing, for the punch line. "It was a twelve-year-old boy in a white tuxedo. He had a gun on his hip, and four bodyguards accompanied this child. He was a minister's son.

"If you create the least disturbance in the club, you're thrown out without a second thought. It doesn't matter who your father is, or how much influence your family has. If you cause the slightest problem, then your father won't even *want* to see you again, because they'll mess up your life completely. For good."

One of us posed the logical and simultaneously ridiculous question: "What about chicks?"

Siad took a deep breath, grabbed his head in exaggerated shock, and let the words tumble out. "What an idiot! Chicks are completely off limits. Look the other way if they smile at you and want to get to know you. Stare at the ground, glance to the side, look up at the sky. Do something. Walk more quickly, start whistling a tune, but for God's sake, don't approach them. Those girls are untouchable, unattainable, from another planet. Even for me!"

He took another deep breath, pursed his lips for a moment, and intoned, like an instructor in a survival course, "Have fun, play pool or basketball, but keep your hands off the girls. They're watched constantly, and if you talk to them you'll start being watched too, and then all of a sudden you're in the hands of the secret service, and at some point those hands will tear you to shreds. You'll lose your future, your hope, your life. You'll lose everything. The demons will never let you go, especially if one of the girls is Uday's."

By the end of the day, my mind was in a whirl. I was elated, confused, deeply impressed, and upset at the same time — the club, the stories, lunch with Siad, this fine young gentleman. I was convinced that you could become someone in Iraq only if you were a member here. As Siad prepared to drop me off, I asked him to stop the Mercedes on a side street and let me out there. I didn't want him to park directly in front of our house, because although it was large and impressive, I suddenly felt inferior and small.

He called after me as I climbed out, "Latif, I'd be happy if you became a member too." Two days later I was a proud member of the al-Alvia Club. Siad got me a card, fee free. I never asked him how he'd managed to do it, but doubtless his father had intervened. Siad accepted me as his friend, and from then on we spent every spare minute in the club.

Once, on a Friday afternoon when we were playing basketball, five-on-five, we suddenly heard the crack of shots, salvos from a submachine gun. They were coming from the direction of a terraced swimming pool. We ran over and saw several guys in dark brown djellabas, the traditional robes, standing near the cash register. One of them was standing directly in front, waving the submachine gun in one hand and a receipt in the other. Beside him were several older men. The men bargained, argued; the young guy with the submachine gun screamed and fired several bursts in the air.

I asked one of the waiters who the younger one was, and he hissed, "It's Uday Saddam."

So this was the infamous son of Saddam Hussein, I said to myself, and although I saw him only in profile, I noticed immediately how much alike we looked. The eyes, the nose, the hair. He was like me.

I made no mention of this incident to either my father or my brothers. I also made a point of not finding out why Uday had fired. I remembered Siad's warning on our first day in the club: "If you notice something, look away, ignore everything, appear uninterested. Never try to make contact with them or to find out anything about them, because they are stronger and more powerful than you and your parents. They are Iraq."

A year later, at about the middle of the school year, our teacher announced the arrival of a new student. "The young gentleman comes from the al-Mansur High School, and he's going to be your classmate."

It was Uday Saddam Hussein. Uday's father had selected our class for him because we were the best and most active. None of us had bad marks; none of us had problems in the political courses.

His first appearance at school was like a scene from a bad movie: The door flew open, and Uday, fifteen like the rest of us, strode in, head high, without a word of greeting. Two powerfully built bodyguards took up positions beside the door, two at the other end of the classroom, and a fifth sat beside him and held his notebook.

The whole class was brimming with excitement. None of us could concentrate, including the teacher. The spectacle of his entrance was repeated every day in the following weeks and months. First came the bodyguards, then Uday, usually in a T-shirt and jeans, like a cowboy. His hair was longer than ours, and he wore it in an Afro, like Jimi Hendrix.

After a few weeks, we finally got used to the daily performance. Uday was never friendly, never normal, never conventional, and actually I found him repugnant from the very first. He had no respect for the teachers or anyone else who tried to tell him what to do. He couldn't care less about tests or homework — or anything. There were twenty-four of us in the class, and while everyone else worked hard to succeed, Uday wasn't interested. If a teacher tried to call him to the blackboard, Uday would throw chalk at him and order him to change the subject or simply to leave him alone. He came when he wanted to, left when he wanted to, and basically did whatever he wanted. He never took his textbooks home with him — and nonetheless he received the best grades at the end of the school year.

Uday observed no rules. He drove his Porsche into the schoolyard and went so far as to break the strictest taboo of all: girls.

One day he brought his girlfriend to class with him.

Salva Ahmad al-Sabty had thick black hair, light skin, and green eyes. She looked wonderful in her dress. None of us said anything; there was embarrassed silence. Uday sat down at his usual place, and Salva sat beside him. She looked annoyed, as if he had forced her to come along. You could hear a pin drop when our teacher entered. We waited tensely for his reaction, for thunder and lightning, for a screaming match, but all he did was to approach Uday, bow, and say quietly, "Mr. Uday, you can't do this. . . ."

We felt how humiliated he had to be, how he must be boiling inside and struggling not to lose control. Uday enjoyed his helplessness, cut him off, and hissed, in a commanding tone, "You do your work, I'll do mine. Continue teaching!" Then their eyes met briefly.

During the class, Uday lounged in his seat, played with a gold fountain pen, laughed, grinned, and held his girlfriend's hand, while she tried to make herself small beside him. Uday knew the teacher had no authority to do anything, and the teacher knew it as well. He started his lecture as if nothing had happened. After about half an hour, Uday jumped up, took his girlfriend by the arm as she smiled in embarrassment, and disappeared without saying another word. He just stood up and left. We could hardly believe what he had done, but it was true, and we experienced for the first time the power that Uday wielded. He was the son of Saddam Hussein, who, in the meantime, had become president of the Iraqi Republic.

The teacher who had dared to question Uday about the presence of his girlfriend was gone the next day. None of us ever saw him again or found out what had happened to him.

One room in the school was reserved for art class. We spent two hours a day there, and for me they were the most pleasurable lessons, because drawing was my passion. My first pictures at the School for Boys were taken from nature. I drew scenes from Kurdistan, where I had driven during the summer with my father in his white Volvo, to Sarsang and

Shalava. My grandparents came from this beautiful region in northern Iraq. My grandfather had left before the birth of my father and opened a business in Baghdad, but we still had numerous relatives there, and I enjoyed my summer holidays. I captured that feeling in my large, colorful pictures.

Our art teacher was so enthusiastic about our class's work that he put a room at our disposal for a special exhibition. The show was a complete success. My pictures drew the most attention, and a painting of Kurdistan won the prize for best picture.

All my friends congratulated me, and so did Uday. He came over after the exhibition, embraced me, patted me on the shoulder, and said, "I want you to paint a picture for me: a portrait of my father, the president. I want to give it to him as a gift."

That was in 1980. Saddam Hussein formally assumed office as the head of state and of the government on May 16, 1979. At the same time he became secretary-general of the Ba'ath party and supreme commander of the armed forces. He succeeded President Ahmad Hasan al-Bakr, who had died of a heart attack. That, at least, was the official version. Everyone said privately that Saddam had had him liquidated — with poison. Al-Bakr's wife and his oldest child had apparently also been liquidated shortly before he was. They died in a suspicious car accident, when a truck smashed into the limousine in which they were riding.

Saddam Hussein had been planning for a long time to take over from al-Bakr and had been the de facto president for years. He was always on television, and the people of Iraq saw in him their savior, the direct descendant of the Prophet, and a god who could make the nation great and strong again, a new Babylon. Again and again in his speeches, Saddam told us that Iraq was the modern-day successor of Nebuchadnezzar's fabled kingdom.

Although the new president had dozens of people executed — my father called them putschists — we hardly noticed. More important, according to my father, was the fact that Saddam had declared war on illiteracy and granted women the rights that were denied them by Islam in other countries. Besides, he had increased oil production, and we, the people, benefited from the oil industry's profits.

When Uday asked me to paint his father's portrait, I recalled the day Saddam came to power: All of Baghdad, all of Iraq, was astir. Like all my friends, I ran through the streets of the city, screaming "Saddam, Saddam," and millions screamed with us. People embraced. Everyone was joyful. Even my father, normally a sober man, was ecstatic: "Everything will be better now, and Iraq will take the lead among Arab nations."

We were all fooling ourselves, but nobody had any inkling of that then.

Now I knew only that the son of this magnificent man had done me a great honor. Saddam Hussein had dozens of court painters. Every artist in the country was keen to cash in on his bizarre personality cult. Large, gaudy pictures of Saddam sprang up everywhere, on every street corner, in barracks, on public buildings: Saddam the soldier, Saddam the farmer, the president, the powerful strongman. Saddam everywhere.

Though surprised, I played the whole thing down. "Okay," I said. "I'll do it."

Uday brought several photographs of his father from his car, which, as always, was parked in the schoolyard. "I'll need four days," I said, and Uday nodded.

Three days later I was finished, and the portrait looked really good. I brought the picture to school and gave it to Uday after class, and he showered me with compliments. "Perffffect, Perffffect," he lisped. He had slightly protruding teeth and a light speech defect as a result, but nobody dared mention it to him.

I reaped the rewards of my work a few days later. Uday had contacted Sael al-Juburi, a party functionary, and ordered him to promote me to the next level of the party hierarchy. Up till then I had been on the lowest, Majeed, level. Now I advanced to Nassir.

But that wasn't all. Uday sought out my company, chatted with me every day, wanted to spend time with me, even promised that I could have whatever I wanted from him, he would make the arrangements.

For my part, I remained cool and remote. First there was the similarity in our looks, about which I felt so uncomfortable that I turned aggressive every time one of my classmates mentioned it. "Look, here comes Uday," they would taunt me, and you could feel the envy in their words, for many of them courted Uday in the hope of favors. Second, my parents advised me to avoid him because his escapades had become more and more notorious. "Be friendly," my father warned me, "but distant."

After graduation, I registered initially at the technical university, since my goal had always been to become an engineer. I changed my mind after Uday also chose technical studies and enrolled instead to study law. After that, I lost track of him and heard only occasionally about his excesses.

3

THE BONDMAN

SUDDENLY I faced him again. He looked little different from the time when he'd asked me for that picture of his father: his big brown eyes, the distinctive eyebrows, the straight nose, the two days' growth of beard. The only noticeable change was that his hair was shorter. Instead of the Jimi Hendrix afro, it was cropped short and kept in place with glossy cream.

Holding his fat Cuban cigar in his right hand, Uday laughed demonstratively and offered me a seat on an upholstered green couch. He himself sat down on a thronelike white leather armchair. Above him hung a gigantic mirror with a golden frame.

Uday acted friendly and asked me in a conversational tone of voice how I was doing, and my nervousness began to dissipate, although I still didn't know why I was sitting there, why the cloak-and-dagger return from the war.

"How do you like it on the front?" he asked with apparent interest, adding, "I hear you've become a good soldier."

I kept my answer brief, and concentrated on not saying the wrong thing, because I remembered Uday's fits of rage from our time together at school. He was a powerful man; he could crush me, destroy me, and nothing and nobody could prevent him. "I like what I'm doing," I told him modestly. "Two, three more years, and I'll go back to my father's company. My father imports machines from Europe to build gas stoves. It's a good business."

Of course, not a word about how skeptical I'd become about the sense of this war in which more than half a million men had already died, nor about the dead and wounded I'd seen. Iraq is great, Saddam is great, and so is his family.

I shared my career plans with him, because the mood was so friendly and pleasant that, even if the friendliness was false, being completely open seemed to be the safest bet. Why should I lie and say that I was interested in pursuing a career in the army?

Uday seemed to approve: "Nice, great. I'm a business-man, too, although you probably didn't know that, and couldn't know it. I appreciate independent entrepreneurs."

He leaned back and took a drag on his cigar. He didn't inhale, but blew out the bluish smoke immediately, looked deep into my eyes, and said with a superiority that left no doubt about our respective roles in this conversation, "Don't try to gloss over anything. Don't try to hide anything. I know everything about you, everything, do you understand?"

His tone of voice was razor-sharp, and right away I thought of Mohammed Ghaleb, my commander, and the elegant Nassir Baker and Saad Ahmad, the two perfect party soldiers. They had referred repeatedly to my resemblance to Uday and always wondered if I came from the Family. They had spied on me, eavesdropped, tested me. They had to have been Uday's minions, secret agents working for their boss in Baghdad.

"Would you like an orange juice?" Uday asked incon-gruously, jerking me back to reality.

"Yes, yes, please," I answered, and what happened next was strange. Uday didn't say a word, didn't push a button, didn't pick up the phone. Yet suddenly a door opened and a servant clad in black trousers, a white jacket, and white gloves brought in a glass of freshly squeezed, unsweetened orange juice. Like my driver, he too said nothing, set the glass down, and disappeared quietly, still without saying a word, his head lowered as a sign of respect. I noticed again that none of Uday's employees dared to look the boss or his guests in the eye. Any inadvertent eye contact resulted in the servant looking away immediately.

The conference room where we were sitting had lovely pastel-colored wallpaper. No kitsch in bright colors, no cramming the room with superfluous displays of wealth, but rather, in everything, understated elegance. The carpets were thick and expensive, the furniture European, the flowers refined and chosen with restrained taste.

I drank a swallow of orange juice and held on to the glass. Uday remained silent. I looked at him and he at me. I had the feeling we were thinking exactly the same thing: Both he and I shared this lightly curled, thick, black hair, expressive brown eyes with long eyelashes, and thick, dark eyebrows whose crescents arched into our foreheads. Then there was the shape of our heads: slightly oval, no jutting jawbones, no special characteristics.

Uday took another drag on his cigar. His upper lip was hardly visible, because, like me, he wore the same bushy, thick mustache that all Muslim males grow at age sixteen. A beard is the symbol of our dignity, our alter ego. I was accustomed to wearing a full beard, well-kept and trimmed, but that became impossible in the army since you can't slip a gas mask over a full beard so that it sits really tightly, and gas attacks were a constant possibility. Our arsenal and that of the Iranians were full of mustard gas and other chemical weapons.

His slightly protruding teeth were less noticeable than during our school days, concealed as they were by his beard and the cigar in his mouth. *He's a little bit bigger than me*, I reflected. It was something I noticed as soon as he greeted me. *Did he shake my hand at all?* I wondered. I couldn't remember.

"Latif," Uday said, breaking the silence, and the corners of his mouth rose to form a peculiar grin, "I'm a straightforward person and don't want to beat around the bush too long." He jumped up, walked a few steps, then leaned on the back of the armchair with his left hand: "I want you to work with me."

"Work with you?" I repeated. The phrase irritated and frightened me, but I remained outwardly calm and answered, "I'm not talking to the son of the president now, am I? I'm talking to my school friend, the one who was so enthusiastic about my picture. Do you still remember?"

My attempt to evade the question annoyed him. "Yes, yes," he hissed, and asked me straight out, "Do you want to work with me?"

"We can be frank," I replied, pausing for a moment before asking, "What do you want from me?"

"I want you to become my fidai."

"Fidai?"

The word sent me reeling. I'd been brooding the whole day. My mind had been churning. Everything was closing in on me, and I had the feeling that something terrible was about to happen. Everything I saw, heard, and felt contributed to my anxiety: the man waiting at party headquarters, the two Mercedes, the mute driver, the elegance of the palace grounds, the quiet hum of the motor. I wanted to run away, swim, watch the clouds float by, sweat out my uncertainty until I no longer registered the sticky sweat on my uniform shirt.

And now this. *Fidai.* The word reverberated in my skull.

A fidai is more than just a double. A fidai is everything. In the Arab world, a fidai is a true follower, a warrior and a partisan, a bondman always ready to give his life for his lord.

Saddam Hussein had had two doubles, two fidais. Everyone in Iraq knew that, as did the western intelligence agencies. This was no big deal. From time immemorial, dictators had doubles almost by custom. Saddam, however, was uncanny in his use of them. Whenever he smelled the risk of attack, he had a fidai stand in. A Saddam double had already been assassinated in 1984. Now there was only one, Faoaz al-Emari, again something that all Iraqis knew, even though they might not be familiar with the details of his excruciatingly prepared appearances. I remembered my commander, Ghaleb, asking me once, "Do you know Faoaz?" and I shook my head and thought him crazy. I didn't even know what to make of his brash question.

Uday asked again whether I wanted to become his fidai, and I hesitated briefly to gain time so that I could gather my thoughts. I was shaking like a terrier. "I don't understand your question. Do you want me to protect you, or what?"

Uday tipped back his head, inhaled deeply through his nostrils, set the cigar down in the ashtray, and spread his arms wide like an actor unable to make his voice dramatic and who therefore gesticulates too much. "You should be honored to be the son of the president under my direction," he intoned solemnly. He collected the cigar and again took a deep puff.

"But we're all sons of the president," I answered, using a tired phrase left over from my political education.

"That's not going to help you. You've been under observation for a long time. We know everything. I know where you go, who you talk to, what your parents do. I've seen your father and mother's bank accounts, and I've seen your bank account. Everything, do you understand, everything. I want you because you're the right one for the job."

"I could protect you, I am —" I replied, but he cut me off.

"You don't have to protect me. I want you to *be* me. Everywhere, always."

Uday's expression changed instantly when I hesitated again. He struggled not to lose control, and screamed at me, "What? You don't want to be the son of Saddam Hussein?"

The question was a threat that cut me to the quick.

Up to this point, doubles had always been chosen from among the members of the president's family. A relative, whose resemblance stemmed from shared blood ties, would be engaged for the job. Only for Uday had they been unable to find a suitable candidate, and that was why I, his school chum, had been selected: Latif Yahia, eldest son of a respected Baghdad family, was the "chosen one."

As far as Uday was concerned, my selection was a great distinction, an honor he was according me. Everyone in Iraq wanted to become a member of the Issaba — the "Gang" — that surrounded the president. I, however, felt like a victim, because I knew that I had no choice and that my fate was sealed on this September 23, 1987. To resist would be useless, for Uday tolerated no contradiction. His wishes were Allah's wishes.

Feeling cornered, I fought for words. Uday was my executioner, master of life and death, prophet. "You demand that I eradicate my name, my personality, to become Uday Saddam Hussein?"

His response sounded like the *"Rien ne va plus"* of a croupier: "Exactly!" he retorted, and stuck his chin out at me.

That was it. My fate was decided, yet I dared appeal to him as my schoolmate. "I'm honored that you chose me to work with you, but I can't be someone other than myself."

"Give yourself time," he offered generously. "You don't have to make up your mind this instant."

He paused for two or three seconds, then added, "I'm going to leave you alone to think about it. By the time I come back, I want a straight yes or no."

Although Uday's ultimatum was plain, my fear abruptly vanished. It felt like a morning when you wake up and suddenly you're a new person. Uday's menace, the whole situation, his demand that I become him, had shaken me to the marrow, and it was clear that I couldn't accept his "honor." On the other hand, the stifling sense of oppression had lifted to the point where I was curious to find out what would happen if I refused. How was he going to deal with that?

He could do whatever he wanted. He had graduated from high school and college though he could hardly write, producing Arabic characters that looked like the scratchings of a paraplegic. He was incapable of reading high Arabic, couldn't compose a sentence without making at least one error, and probably had never opened a book on his own, let alone read one through.

"What if I say no?" I asked.

He hardly reacted, saying only, "That I'll let you know later," and disappeared into an adjacent room, leaving me alone and completely confused.

Nothing happened for ten endless minutes. I sat on the couch as if paralyzed, staring blankly ahead of me, stroking my mustache, and thinking about Uday's face. He looked like a nice person for some reason. But I'd already seen how ordinary people can do horrible things to one another. I remembered Sattar and the cockroaches, how we shoved the vermin into his mouth until he vomited, how we didn't stop because we were under orders, and you can't disobey an order. Or can you?

My body refused to sit still anymore. I crossed my left leg over my right, then the right over the left. I felt like smoking but decided not to because that wouldn't be good manners, although in fact the room already reeked of Uday's thick Cuban cigar.

I stood up, rubbed my hands together, and began to pace. The door through which Uday had disappeared opened almost simultaneously. A servant appeared and asked if I desired anything.

"A glass of water, please," I said.

The servant brought me one straightaway. I emptied the glass, set it aside, and paced up and down the room. One two three, one two three . . . back and forth I went, then stopped before the mirror, crossed my arms, stretched, yawned, examined my complexion, and reflected that I really should do something about it. Uday had such smooth skin. I considered my reflection again, without once thinking that someone might be behind the glass.

Uday had said he'd be back in ten minutes, but an hour passed without him showing himself. Waiting was apparently part of the game. People who wait lose their self-respect after a while, especially if they know they have no choice but to wait. Making someone wait means wielding power.

After another half hour Uday finally returned, grinning, striding in with long, firm steps. "Why so uneasy, my friend?" he asked. I realized for the first time that he must have been observing me pace back and forth, to and fro — with a camera, through a mirror, in some way.

"What if I say yes?"

"Then you're my brother and you'll have everything you want. I'll give you that in writing. You'll have the most beautiful life on earth, each of your wishes will be granted, everything that's mine will also be yours. Do you understand? You're going to be my brother."

"My lord, that would be wonderful, but I just can't. I'm an officer in the army and still have a year to serve, maybe more. But after that, I want to be a merchant. I cannot accept this task. It's too much for me. My lord, please understand. . . . I can't accept."

Uday stalked to the door after I refused, tore it open, paused for a moment, turned around, and hissed, his face hard and determined, "That's also no problem. We'll remain friends anyway."

He slammed the door with a bang. Only a few seconds elapsed before two bodyguards, Azzam al-Tikriti and Salam al-Aoussi, burst in.

They came right at me, grabbed me by the arms, and ripped off my two-star shoulder tabs, then blindfolded me, dragged me outside, and shoved me into a car. I remember thinking there was a good chance it was the same Mercedes

I'd arrived in. The interior smelled like new, and the leather seats were soft and smooth. The driver started the motor, and the door shut only after we had begun to accelerate. That solid slamming sound — it could only be a Mercedes door.

We drove for a long time, maybe half or three-quarters of an hour, but I couldn't escape the feeling that we were just going in circles. The sound of other cars or of blocks of houses whizzing by was missing, as if we were simply driving around the palace grounds, and we didn't stop once, which we would have had to, if we had passed through one of the palace gates. Saddam's center of power is surrounded by an electrified barbed-wire fence.

The palace is in the Karada Mariam district, near al-Karkh, on the bank of the Tigris River. It covers an area of more than a square mile. The Tigris forms the natural boundary to the east and south between the palace and the city. We couldn't be near the river now, because I surely would have heard the sound of flowing water or river traffic. But the occasional sound of tires reflecting back in short intervals meant that we must be passing the big mansions belonging to the president's family.

The architecture of these houses was first-class. I'd seen them when I was being brought in. While millions fought against the Khomeinis on the front, Saddam had his castle renovated from top to bottom by a French company and equipped it with the most sophisticated security, including protection against threats from the air. Iran's rockets occasionally reached Baghdad, and Ayatollah Khomeini's top goal was to murder our godless president.

The palace compound has four main entrances, which are guarded in rotation by the third, fifth, seventh, and ninth units of the Republican Guards. The first is on the western side, near the suspension bridge. Known as the Family Gate, it serves as the private entrance for Saddam and his family, as well as for his ministers and their families. I was whisked in through this entrance.

The second is near the Republican Bridge, on the northern side of the palace. The Baghdad Gate is reserved for the members of the Revolutionary Command Council and the National Committee.

A third entrance, connecting the eastern and northern wings, is reserved for palace personnel, and the fourth entrance, the Lion's Gate, for the director and members of the intelligence services Jehaaz al-Amn al-Khass and Jehaaz al-Mukhabarat al-Amn.

The four gates lie nearly a mile from Saddam's quarters and are so thickly armored that even a tank would have trouble breaking through. About nine hundred yards behind them are metal tracks embedded in the asphalt. Driving over them in a car, you feel a slight bump and hear a soft "thump-thump." Hidden within are bands of steel spikes that shoot up at the push of a button, making it difficult for a suicide bomber to approach the palace in a vehicle laden with explosives. These nail-studded traps are also used by our engineers on the front.

If we had passed over them in the car, I would have felt and heard it, which seems to confirm that we kept away from the main entrances.

Between the gates and the street is a buffer zone, a kind of no-man's-land. Earlier there were foreign embassies here, but after Saddam assumed power, all buildings near the palace were taken over by the intelligence services. They had even commandeered the Ibn-Sina, a hospital. Previously private and of modest quality, the Ibn-Sina had been thoroughly revamped by European and American companies, which outfitted it with the most advanced medical equipment. All the doctors and nurses who had worked there were let go and replaced by ideologically trained personnel. Since then, the hospital has functioned as Saddam's private clinic.

My driver stopped suddenly. I had lost my orientation and couldn't tell where we were. Azzam al-Tikriti and Salam al-Aoussi, the bodyguards who had bound my eyes, ordered me to get out, gripped my arms, and led me first up some steps, then through several rooms and doorways, and finally down a couple of steps and through two more rooms.

When they removed the blindfold, I found myself in a tiny chamber, not much bigger than a shower stall, no more than three by five feet. No window, no bed, no toilet, not even a bucket for waste. Everything was red: red walls, a bright lamp giving off a dazzling red light, red cement floor, and on the floor a dark red woolen blanket. The ceiling was unreachably high and red.

The two bodyguards locked the door behind them without comment. I was a prisoner.

One hour, two hours. *They want to make you color-blind,* I thought. I closed my burning eyes, opened them wide again, as wide I could, and that hurt even more. I pulled the blanket over my head but continued to see the red ceiling, the red floor. Red, red, red. Everything was red.

I pressed the balls of my hands against my closed eyes and kept them there for a long, long while. I saw stars, jagged sparks, patterns of light large and small. I removed my hands and first saw black, then again the horrible red.

I had no way of telling time. I couldn't tell how long I'd been squatting there, whether half a day or longer. I didn't know whether it was night or day. I didn't know where I was, except alone in a timeless room without a toilet, without water, without anything except pervasive red. I thought of my comrades on the front, my parents. But what was the point? They had no idea where I was, what I was doing, what was going on here.

Suddenly I heard steps, then voices and the rattle of keys. *Damn it, get away from the door!* I huddled in a corner, my heart beating in my throat. If I had had a gun at that instant, my finger would have been on the trigger. The gun would have been cocked, and head and gun would be pointing in the same direction, the way they taught us.

The door opened partway. I could see the rough outlines of Azzam in the red light. He had a tray in his hand, gave it to me, and said only, "Eat something."

Then he withdrew and locked the door. I squatted again and forced down the food.

This went on for days. I wasn't able to stretch out and lie down. My legs hurt. I huddled in the corner and vegetated, one thought chasing another. At some point I started talking to myself. Not in real sentences but just babble, like a baby, an infant. I moved my lips and made noises until the guards came again and brought me food and drink. When they did that, I knew it was lunch- or dinnertime.

At noon I was given bread and water. Warm sticky rice and water in the evening. I tried to control my waste during the first forty-eight hours, urinating only once and then briefly. When I saw the urine making its way toward my blanket, I forced myself to stop.

I held back my feces until my intestines felt like bursting. I screamed, ranted, pounded the walls with my fists, and begged and pleaded with them not to humiliate me in this way. But nobody reacted, and at some point my honor, my training, stopped mattering to me.

I defecated in a corner so that I wouldn't have to lie in my feces. It stank so terribly my eyes burned. I discovered dried blood on the walls, and knew it couldn't be mine because I wasn't that far gone yet. The blood spots had to have come from someone else. *It's probably only a matter of time until everyone here starts mutilating himself,* I thought. But I swore by Allah and my father that Uday wouldn't drive me to that point.

I always saved half a glass of water to be able to wash myself at least a bit. In the end I just huddled in my corner. In the opposite one were my feces, which I'd buried under the blanket, already so soaked through with urine there was no way I could use it for cover. At least then I didn't have to look at my own excrement.

They brought me bread and rice seven times. That's how

I knew I'd spent a week in this kennel when Uday himself appeared in the doorway. I didn't see him, only heard his mocking tone: "Hello, Latif, how are you?" His bodyguards bound my eyes again; we went up a few steps, through two doors, a number of rooms, and down the stairs to freedom.

I felt the hot September sun, grass under my feet. Then without warning they ripped the protection from my eyes. It was as if a bolt of lighting had struck me. I couldn't see, held my hands in front of my face, pressed the balls of my hands into my squeezed shut eyes, just as I had done in my cell. I stood like that for ten or twenty seconds, then carefully removed my hands, squinted, tried briefly to see. Everything was red. The grass, the trees, the whole garden. Uday was red, too. His shirt, his trousers, his face, his protruding teeth, were red.

"Did you think about my suggestion?" he asked. I noticed indistinctly that he, too, had not shaven. He had grown a beard. To look even more like me?

"You've changed your mind, haven't you?" He knew what I'd gone through. He must have been familiar with this cell. They'd probably finished off hundreds there while sadistically enjoying the way they could break their victims — that proud men could reach the point of lying in their own filth, and even rolling around in it, because there was no alternative, the cell was so small.

My eyes were watering. I still couldn't see properly, but my rage exceeded my good sense: "Officers of the Iraqi army cannot be confined without the knowledge of the Defense Ministry. That's the law. I haven't murdered anybody, I haven't dragged your family through the mud. . . . The ministry has to —"

"Has to do what? A thousand officers like you aren't worth one pair of my shoes."

You ridiculous son of a bitch, I said to myself, but uttered nothing. My power of sight was slowly returning. I squinted, distinguished the outlines of the trees, the meadow. I looked at my uniform. It was covered with excrement, hard, dried excrement. *I must look terrible.*

"I'll sic my dogs on you and your sisters if you say no again," Uday screamed at me. I realized then that it was useless to resist any further. Uday was prepared to do anything. It wouldn't be the first time he set his killer dogs on someone. I recalled an incident I'd heard about during my college years. One day, Nahle Sabet, a pretty girl studying architecture like Uday, simply disappeared. The story was that Uday had had her abducted and taken to his property north of Baghdad, which was camouflaged as a farm. In reality, it served as a training site for his killer dogs: Rottweilers, Great Danes, Dobermans, huge terriers made wild with beatings and raw meat. For weeks, Nahle Sabet was beaten, maltreated, raped, and her will broken. After Uday lost all interest in her, he had her locked in the kennels with his hungry dogs.

4

TRAINING TO BE UDAY

OUR drive lasted only fifteen minutes, during which my eyes gradually adjusted to the daylight. Our small convoy of four cars wasn't stopped when we left the palace by the Family Gate. The cars slowed only briefly as we drove over the security tracks, and the Kalashnikov-toting guards waved us through when they recognized Uday's cars. Then we veered left onto an avenue and after about a half-mile turned toward Project No. 7, one of Uday's numerous private residences. My companions were again the two bodyguards and the driver who'd brought me from headquarters a week ago.

I felt empty, burned out, betrayed. I still wore my filthy uniform. I felt as though I were living in a nightmare or a horror film. What was happening didn't seem real, but I knew I'd agreed to become Uday's fidai, and had thus sold my soul to a sinister human being whom I despised. When I gave in, Uday had flashed a disgusting grin and said magnanimously, "See? As of this moment, you're not only my friend but also my brother."

His brother, what good was that? Couldn't I have held out any longer? No, suppress the thought. It was useless to dwell on this further, for Uday might well have eliminated me and my family, had I said no. Saddam's clan had already had thousands killed. Their victims disappeared from one day to the next. Nobody in Iraq knew where to, but there was no doubt they had been liquidated.

My car stopped in the driveway leading to Project No. 7. In front of the house were several parking spots, hidden from view of the street. Alongside them was a well-groomed lawn with short, thick grass, and behind that a massive wooden gate with heavy double doors decorated with a larger-than-life Iraqi eagle in green, black, and white — our heraldic animal. Over the eagle, black stars, an inlay of ceramic mosaic tile. To the left and right of the door, automatic cameras hummed electrically. We were being observed.

There was no name on the door, only an intercom in a wall niche, protected by plate glass.

The double doors opened automatically and noiselessly, and my two guards led me inside the two-story building. From the outside, it looked nondescript, hardly out of the ordinary. There were thousands of houses like it in Baghdad, for Baghdad is rich; the upper class lives in feudal excess and loves to display its wealth.

But behind the mundane façade spread a broad oval courtyard, dominated by an imposing swimming pool. Six wide, spreading steps led to the pool, which was trimmed with black marble. On the right side stood a sickle-shaped bar, also made of the polished black marble with fine white veins running through its surface. Next to the bar were several chaise longues of white bamboo with white cushions bordered in gold thread. Rooms radiated from the swimming pool like the points of a star.

They brought me first to the room at the extreme right of the pool, Uday's office. Again, I couldn't help but be impressed by his taste. His office was generously appointed, but there was no hint of Oriental kitsch: no plush velvet, no gold, no playful Arabesque patterns, no soaring and scalloped stucco on the walls, and not the usual surfeit of furniture and objects. The room was linear, clear, and bright. In one corner sat a massive desk with a dark, shiny work surface, next to which were two armchair-like stools upholstered in lightly colored fabric.

Behind the desk was a bookshelf full of Arabic literature. "Pure decoration," I told myself, amused. I'm sure Uday never touched any of those books. Several folders lay on the desktop, along with a Cartier fountain pen, a Dupont cigarette lighter, and a black electric cable. The cable was thick, round, and about two and a half feet long.

The most prominent piece of furniture in the room, which was hung with pastel wallpaper, was an enormous couch able to hold at least twenty people. In front of the couch stretched a coffee table with a top of veined black stone. Silver bowls with peanuts, sweets, cigarettes, and flowers were everywhere.

Three men, who clearly knew all about me and must have helped plan the previous sequence of events, were waiting: The first was Munem Hammed al-Tikriti, director of the Secret Observation Section of the al-Khass intelligence service. Munem Hammed appeared elegant and reserved. He was slim, somewhat taller than me, and gray at the temples. He greeted me amiably, though I'd never met him before.

The name of the second man is familiar to everyone in Iraq: Captain Siad Hassan Hashem al-Nassiri, a friend of Saddam Hussein and the brother-in-law of Rokan, the president's personal bodyguard. Siad Hassan Hashem al-Nassiri was one of Iraq's worst criminals, a mass murderer, a strong, dangerous man with gray eyes, a harsh, striking face, and an extremely hooked nose. Ice-cold, sadistic, a beast. He was rumored to supervise all executions and all the crimes ordered by Saddam Hussein.

He gave no reaction when I shook his hand. His impassive face remained cool.

The third was Captain Saadi Daham Hasaa al-Nassiri, a cousin of Saddam Hussein. This man was small, beefy, unappealing.

Azzam, Uday's bodyguard, introduced the three officers. Munem Hammed al-Tikriti began the conversation genially: "Sit down, relax. Uday has already told us about you and said that you're a brave, determined warrior. I'm happy you've decided to join us of your own volition."

My own volition? What a joke! But there was something soothing in his tone. Munem Hammed spoke to me not as if I were Uday's bondman, but as an acknowledged partner in a complicated mission. The thought suddenly struck me that this was the first Iraqi officer I'd met who wasn't either completely cynical or deranged.

Munem Hammed seemed to notice my liking for him. He spoke softly but in excellent Arabic, clearly and distinctly. His voice was friendly, and not a single word came out in the harsh, contemptuous tone used by others accustomed to issuing orders.

"You have to get used to things, Latif," he said, wrapping an arm around my shoulder. "The best thing now would be to take a look around the house, and then you can freshen up afterward." The other two nodded in agreement.

Munem Hammed left the room like a chief surgeon making his rounds in a hospital, and we followed after. "That, by the way, was Uday's study," he noted, and then asked, "You know each other from school, don't you?"

I nodded. "Yes, that's right."

Motioning toward the swimming pool with the black marble rim, he told me I could use it anytime I liked. "The changing rooms and towels are here," he said, indicating an open door behind the bar, where I could see several changing stalls and baskets full of fresh, thick towels, along with a shower, toilet, sink, and mirror.

I didn't have time to ask whether I could start washing up now, for he had already moved on.

"This is the guest room," said my guide. I could see a double bed in the generously sized room, with a knitted beige coverlet and matching curtains. Next to the bed were a wardrobe, a desk, a small couch, and a Sony television set.

Adjacent to the guest room were the stairs leading to the second floor. But first we checked out Uday's bedroom, which resembled the guest room but was furnished with a larger bed. Instead of a desk, there was a round table with a black top surrounded by several chairs. Directly in front of the bed stood a large-screen television connected to a VCR.

Munem laughed. "This is your room now. Uday wants it that way. You're his brother, and that's why he wants you to live in his room."

A telephone was beside the table. I could see no indication of concealed video cameras at first glance.

Next they showed me the living room, a large, hall-like space containing four different styles of furniture, and then the party room, which was on the second floor of the house and looked like a discotheque. It had an imposing stage with an oversized sound system that surveyed a bunch of cozy seats upholstered in vivid red. This red again, always this red.

Munem Hammed completed the first tour with the quip, "So, Latif, you'll want to rest now and most of all take a shower."

Everybody laughed. Me too.

They dropped me off at Uday's bedroom, which was now my room, leaving open the door to the pool. A cool breeze swayed the white curtains. I sat on the bed, shook my head, laughed, and shook my head again. What was going on?

I got up, went to the door, drew the curtains aside. I couldn't see anyone at the pool, but I could feel their presence. They were probably everywhere, and Uday was probably somewhere observing me through a video camera, as he had done when I was sitting in his office.

The telephone: large, rectangular, an American make. I knew it would be idiotic to pick up the receiver and simply dial my family's number in Baghdad. That would never work, I told myself. That would have been too careless of them. I lifted the receiver from the cradle nonetheless, and heard the busy signal. I pushed several buttons, the nine, the zero, the double zero — it was always busy. Logical.

The mirror was the next thing to catch my eye. I had already tried to catch a glimpse of myself in the car's rearview mirror to see what my beard looked like. I stood up, walked over, and said to myself, *So this is Latif Yahia, officer in the proud Iraqi army.*

I showered hot and long. The bathroom was fitted out with the same black marble, like in a five-star hotel. It had everything I could possibly need: disposable razors, shaving cream, bath oil, shampoo, toothpaste, a toothbrush, hair cream, a hairbrush, a bathrobe, thick, huge towels, body lotion. As I scrubbed away at the dirt of the past week, I began to feel drowsy. That night I slept like a stone.

I woke early the next morning. It was the beginning of October 1987, and Baghdad was still hot and humid. My filthy uniform, which I had thrown over a chair the night before, was gone, as were my shoes and underwear. In their place, fresh clothes lay on the stool in front of the wardrobe, a light suit, a white shirt, slippers. Next to the clothes were clean towels and a new bathrobe. Breakfast was already laid out on the table: tea, sweets, fresh fruit. I drank only a swallow from the thermos, ate only an orange. How could I have failed to notice someone coming into my room to bring these things?

I showered, got dressed, and waited. Just before nine, two of the officers from the day before came by to pick me up. They escorted me to Uday's study, where Munem Hammed was waiting. He handed me a two-page document. "Read this and sign," he said, gesturing for me to take a seat on the yellow couch.

It was a contract between me and the Iraqi Republic, the gist of which went as follows:

I, Latif Yahia, First Lieutenant, swear not to reveal anything about the life of Uday Saddam. Everything that I see, hear, and experience with him during our cooperation remains confidential.

It is forbidden to pass on documents, photographs, video recordings, or any other records to third parties.

Any violation of this contract will be punished by death through hanging.

Latif Yahia, Baghdad, October 2, 1987

I signed. But the next ten days passed without further event.

Munem Hammed had instructed me, "You are now Uday Saddam Hussein, the president's son. Don't speak with any of the servants. Don't try to make contact with them." The servants themselves — a cook, four maids, and a kind of butler — were strictly prohibited from uttering a word to me. They were to treat me as if I were Uday Saddam, and they followed their orders to the letter. Avoiding my glances, they brought clean clothes daily and the best food I've ever eaten: meat every day, prepared European-style, with fresh vegetables and lots of fruit. I could help myself all I wanted at the bar next to the pool. Nobody was around to tell me what to do. I lived as if in paradise, though my paradise was a golden cage. I was conscious of that, of course, but what got to me most was that I couldn't tell anyone, especially my family, where I was and how I was doing.

My parents hadn't heard from me for three weeks. True, that happened relatively often because it was wartime, and as far as they knew I was still at the front. Even before now, there were frequent stretches when I couldn't tell them of my whereabouts.

Strangely, perhaps, I didn't want to confide my worries about this new job. What I daydreamed of was to have them share in my fabulous new lifestyle, to let them know where I lived, how I was living, and what was happening to me.

During the day, I sunbathed next to the pool, then watched the evening news on television and threw back a few gin and tonics to wind down before going to bed. Although anxiety about the future sometimes tormented me, I was beginning to identify with Uday in a vague way. There is something alluring about having submissive servants react to your least gesture. I would be lying next to the pool under the autumn sun, raise my hand — and instantly someone was there to take an order: "A sandwich." I noticed that I increasingly forgot to say "please" or "thank you," and was slowly assuming the same arrogant tone that I used to complain of in others. "Not so much ice!" I shouted irritably at the maid. "I've told you that a hundred times!"

And she would say she was sorry and bring me a new glass with less ice. None of them would dare contradict me. They acted as if I were fragile. No corners, no rough edges, only luxury, although luxury restricted to the grounds of the villa.

I would stride through all the rooms, change towels several times a day, and splash on expensive, thick, sweet cologne, although I had no one to impress. I did it because it was there and I could, and nobody would tell me not to.

On October 12 in the late afternoon, I was lying on my bed when the telephone suddenly rang. "Come to the study," said a male voice. I got dressed and walked the few steps past the pool to Uday's study.

Uday was there, along with Munem Hammed and two other men, who were clearly not Arabs. One of them stood somewhat taller than I, and had brown hair and a pale, round face. The second was smaller and stocky but not fat. Uday greeted me exuberantly, kissed my cheeks as if I were his brother, and introduced me to the men, who shook my hand but remained silent. "These are doctors, specialists who will examine you."

I was surprised because I was in good health, but didn't want to start asking questions. "Fine, where do they want to examine me? Here? Right away?"

Uday answered in the affirmative, the men nodded, and Munem Hammed said, "A purely routine examination, nothing more. You can relax."

One of the doctors then uttered something to Munem Hammed in a language I couldn't understand. It was neither English, French, Italian, nor German, but sounded more like Russian or Polish, some Slavic language. Munem Hammed translated: "Please get undressed."

I had to strip naked. I felt uncomfortable, but there was nothing I could do about it.

I was weighed and measured. They peered into my mouth and ears and shone a light into my eyes, palpated me from head to toe, checked to see if I had a hernia, probed my anus, listened to my breathing and heartbeat, took my blood pressure, drew blood, and asked for a urine sample. Then they read my skin with a special instrument. I was made to do speech exercises, to howl like a dog, enunciate like an orator, laugh hysterically. Everything was recorded on tape, jotted down. The two doctors exchanged comments several times in their language, which sounded almost like code.

Uday seemed bored by it all and left after ten minutes. "I'll review the results, gentlemen," he said, and disappeared.

The examination lasted almost two hours. The specialists' report was several pages long, and when Uday received it the next day, he summoned me again. He was beaming, elated.

Hammed read the report out loud: My pigmentation was 99 percent similar to Uday's. Shape of face, hair, ears, nose, build, all were almost identical. I was only one inch shorter than Uday and about four pounds lighter. Uday weighed 182 pounds; I weighed 178.

"The weight isn't a problem," Hammed commented. "Neither is the height. That can be compensated for with lifts in his shoes."

Our voices were also almost exactly alike, except that Uday had difficulty pronouncing the letter *r* because of his slightly protruding teeth, which caused him to lisp, a defect that Munem Hammed glossed over.

"Are the teeth correctable?" Uday inquired, and Hammed nodded.

Our eyes were also different. Mine were somewhat larger than Uday's, but that could easily be compensated for with makeup, he explained.

"All we have to do is alter your teeth surgically," summed up Munem Hammed almost apologetically. "Do you agree?"

What a question! I thought. *I have no choice.* But I also noticed that my internal opposition had almost disappeared. I was starting to like this game. "Sure, I agree."

Twenty-four hours later I was picked up and brought to the Ibn-Sina hospital on the palace grounds, where we visited the office of Dr. Ahmed al-Samrai. He was the private dentist to Saddam Hussein's family and had studied dentistry in the United States. He knew what to do.

I was asked to lie down in the dentist's chair, which looked more like a hydraulically adjustable bed. Ahmed al-Samrai shone a light into my mouth and examined my jaws, tooth by tooth. He then sent me to have X rays made and instructed my escort to bring me back the following day.

During the next visit, he packed my mouth with a pink substance that slowly swelled up. He left it in for ten minutes, removed it, and blew away the bits of saliva with compressed air, but seemed unhappy with the results and had to repeat the procedure. Plaster casts were made from this second mold and compared with Uday's. On the basis of his comparison, Dr. Ahmed decided in what way my teeth had to be adjusted.

He performed the operation four days later. Under a local anesthetic, my incisors and the two neighboring teeth were ground down to the roots. A new cast was then made. The only unpleasant sensation I felt was the cold air the dentist blew into my mouth.

Two days passed before the crowns were ready. I could

hardly eat during this period, because the temporary crowns fit poorly and it hurt to chew, or to drink something cold.

By contrast, the implantation of the four new teeth took only a few minutes. Dr. Ahmed was observed by his two foreign colleagues, but the men didn't exchange a word.

After examining my jaws once more and asking me to close my mouth so that my teeth fit tightly together, Dr. Ahmed pronounced the operation a success. He ground away a bit further at my incisors, then it was over. I felt my new, peculiarly smooth, projecting teeth with my tongue. They asked me to say something, and it was utterly bizarre: I was lisping. Not a lot, but the tip of my tongue met my teeth differently.

My image in the mirror was also peculiar. My full upper lip somehow seemed even thicker. When I bit down, it wasn't my incisors but my molars that touched. It felt as if the position of all my teeth had been changed, and my jaws still had to adjust to that. I clamped my mouth shut several times, said a few words, and couldn't help but exclaim, "It's strange, but sensational!"

Even though I had had to sacrifice four healthy teeth, I was happy, and Uday, too, was completely satisfied with the results. He seemed delighted. We were now truly like two peas in a pod.

"We must start with the training immediately," he said, and I suddenly perceived how he spoke. "We mussst start wi the training," he pronounced, and I repeated soundlessly, *We mussst start wi the training.*

The next day they brought a hairdresser, who painstakingly cut my hair exactly the way Uday wore his — hair by hair, almost. Then came the beard, which he also shaped to resemble Uday's. The session with the hairdresser lasted almost as long as the doctors' examination.

Then the real training began. They drove me to the headquarters of the al-Khass intelligence service and on the third floor showed me the room where I was to be instructed, a fairly large office with two desks and shelves on the wall. Instead of books or folders full of documents, the shelves contained television sets, large Panasonics about three feet wide and two and a half feet tall. Beside them were VCRs, and dozens of videocassettes, all labeled, lay in piles on a nearby table. Three microphone stands without microphones stood in front of the bank of TVs. Before them were rows of seats, as in a private movie theater. The windows had long, heavy, plasticized curtains, and loudspeakers formed towers in the far corners of the room, with the big "woofers" for bass tones below, and smaller "tweeters" for higher sounds above. Between the stacks of speakers was an elaborate mixing console with hundreds of red, yellow, and white buttons and bars.

A sound studio, clearly, but I couldn't quite figure out what we were doing there. Munem Hammed took me by the arm, pointed to the bank of TV sets, and said "This is where we're going to spend the next few weeks."

Nothing happened for ten minutes. Munem Hammed conversed in undertones with several officers, but I couldn't make out what they were saying. Then they all left. I sat down in a chair, picked up a cassette, and scanned the label: "May 26, 1987, Mr. Uday Saddam Hussein at the main meeting of the Iraqi Sports Federation. Close-ups, hands, face, walk."

Munem Hammed returned with the officers and introduced me to one of them, whose name I can't remember because Munem Hammed spoke quickly and unintelligibly. At the time I didn't care what his name was. I'd gotten to know too many people whose names seemed important in the past few weeks. The officer was tall and had a dark complexion, a thick mustache, and expressive brown eyes, with the left one appearing larger than the right. He seemed friendly and shook my hand, but his handshake was weak. It didn't at all fit his powerful-looking build and broad, straight shoulders.

He asked me to follow him: "We have to go to another room." We took the main stairway to the second floor. Munem Hammed remained behind, which surprised me, for, until now, he'd been like my shadow. He'd become my father, my mother, my protector — everything. The officer and I passed through padded double doors into a room that resembled the one on the third floor, though smaller and equipped with only three television sets, no console, and no rows of movie chairs. He asked me to sit down and explained that what I was about to see was an excerpt from Saddam's Special Treatment Department.

Now I understood. I was in a chamber of horrors, the archives of dread.

The officer inserted a videocassette. It was without sound. Black spots flickered on the screen for a few seconds, then came the first image.

A man about thirty years old, his skull shaven as was his face, his body maltreated, battered, bent. They'd tied him to a massive wooden chair that had been bolted to the floor. He was gasping for breath. His cheeks were sunken, his eyes shut and set deep in his sockets. I noticed after a few moments that they'd even shaved off his eyebrows.

I wanted to ask the officer what was being done to the man, but he only grinned at me and motioned with his head toward the television screen, indicating that I should pay attention to what I was about to see.

The man suddenly gripped the armrests of the chair. The veins on his hands and forearms swelled, seemed about to burst. He strained with his naked upper body, and I could see his ribs, his sternum, his collarbone, which jutted out as if it weren't part of him. He couldn't have weighed more than a hundred pounds or so, though he appeared pretty tall; I couldn't be sure of this because he was bent over in the chair.

Alligator clips were fastened to his nipples, which were as long as a woman's. The clips were made of shiny steel about three-quarters of an inch long, and cut deeply into his dark skin. Other alligator clips were attached to his eyelids, ears, and genitals. The handles were insulated with light blue plastic, and cables led from them to a huge battery — on the left, a red cable and on the right a black one, both about an eighth of an inch thick,

The whole setup was directed from a console next to the chair. A man in uniform sat behind the console, with only his hands visible — big, meaty, hairy hands. I watched those hands push a button. The camera panned to the emaciated man in the chair. His body began to jerk in places, then his whole body trembled, his face distorted into a grimace, his head vibrated, the corners of his mouth cramped downward, the veins on his temples swelled, his lips turned white and squeezed tightly together. The camera zoomed in for a close-up of his face. His deeply set eyes were clamped shut, but it seemed to me they might jump out like glass marbles any second now. The man was trying to master himself, to fight the pain and powerlessness. He refused to give in, wanted to prove he was strong, but he failed. The electric shocks were stronger than his will. Saliva foamed from his tightly closed lips. When he opened them slightly, I saw that his teeth, also clamped together, were yellow and dark brown at the edges, probably from chewing tobacco.

He began to shake his head as if his brain were about to explode, and continued doing this for a second — an eternally long second. Suddenly he opened his mouth and screamed. I couldn't hear the scream, since there was no sound, but I heard it anyway, felt it, experienced the pain as he did.

This torture was repeated several times. I never found out whether the man survived it. His image gave way to the flickering black spots, and my officer looked at me questioningly, as if to ask how I liked this introduction. I controlled myself and concealed my feelings, because it would have been suicide to share my thoughts with him.

The officer explained that most of their methods of torture were adopted from the Soviet intelligence services, the KGB and GRU (Military Intelligence). Other techniques came from East Germany. More than ten thousand Soviet military experts were stationed in Iraq at the time. They manned the computer rooms at missile bases and supervised all the high-tech equipment, of which seventy percent was of Soviet origin. They themselves were supported by experts from the East German state security service, the Stasi, who sold their expertise in Iraq for convertible currency. Nobody knew how many of them were in Baghdad, but it was no secret that the men of the Stasi were the best of their profession in the fields of intelligence gathering, information monitoring, and the recruiting of independent intelligence services.

Other experts supporting Saddam's regime of terror came from Angola and Cuba.

The next video started, and another shaven-headed man appeared. He was younger, his body not emaciated but fit, his muscles smooth and rounded. He stood bare-chested and wore green uniform trousers, which were faded from washing, but not ragged. His hands were tied, his shoulders drooped, he kept his eyes downcast and clearly didn't want to look into the camera. All at once, though, he jerked his head up and stared, eyes wide open, straight ahead. He must have been ordered to do so. The man continued to stare into the camera for several minutes. His eyes were empty, his will manifestly broken.

"That was a policeman who disobeyed orders," my officer explained in a menacing tone of voice. He didn't say what orders the man had disobeyed; he offered no details, and probably didn't even know the man's story. Fates are not interesting in Iraq. There is violence everywhere, the individual is worth nothing, thousands die for Saddam, and because masses are slaughtered, death has become normal, routine.

Slowly the man turned and displayed his broad back to the camera. It looked like a battlefield, trenched and mounded with deep, long wounds: there were dozens of blue weals, and the skin had been broken open by powerful blows. The edges of the wounds were ragged, reddish brown with dried blood and yellow with pus in some places.

The figure of a man emerged from behind the horribly injured policeman. He had his back to the camera and in his hand held a black electric cable about two and a half feet long.

I saw exactly the same kind of cable somewhere, I thought, but couldn't remember where. The man wound up and the cable cracked against the policeman's back. His body jerked, his muscles contracted. I closed my eyes at the thought of the pus flying in the room. But in my mind I could hear the swish of the cable cutting through the air and connecting with the man's skin. Exactly the same kind of cable was on Uday's desk. The man with the cable on the video wasn't Uday, was he? Or did all of them use this black cable as an instrument of torture?

Up to now they hadn't beaten me. Psychological violence was apparently enough. The red room, the red walls, the red blanket, the week of solitary confinement in a closet where many others before me had mutilated themselves, where I found dried blood on the walls. They had actually treated me well. I was valuable. They needed me. My resemblance to Uday was my trump card, my ace. I needed only to cooperate, to do as they bid me, to sublimate my personality, but how would it all end? It could never end. I thrust aside my misgivings, concentrated on the positive. The house, life with Uday, access to the Clan. I was now part of it, on top of the whole structure. I was alive, and I was living better than before, on the front.

The next video started. This time there were two men, both handcuffed and hobbled with thick, heavy chains that were linked to one another, forcing them to take small steps. They were walking in the courtyard of a barrack-like building; I didn't recognize where exactly, but supposed it to be the al-Rashid camp, the largest death camp in Baghdad's city limits. The men were being led to their death. The executioner made them step onto a wooden platform, put the loop of rope around their necks, and tightened the knot.

Suddenly trapdoors opened under the feet of the victims while the bodies remained bolt upright, falling a few inches. The nooses tightened with a jerk, and the heads lolled toward the right — broken necks.

These videos were only the beginning. My mentors showed me a whole series of disgusting examples of how opponents of Saddam's regime were treated. It was a lesson in horror. Saddam Hussein is proud of his torturers. He calls them "the sharp swords of the government."

Video 4. A naked man stands, arms bound, legs spread over a dark green wine bottle with a long neck. The prisoner is forced to sit on the bottle until it disappears up his anus. He screams, pleads for mercy, but his torturers laugh, grin, and make jokes: "Don't you like it?"

The bottle inserted in the man's anus results in serious internal injuries. I see blood; the man faints.

Video 5. A victim is bound naked to a gas heater. The heat is turned up. The blue and orange flames sear the prisoner's skin.

Video 6. The torturers secure a prisoner to a fanlike object fastened to the ceiling. The prisoner's head hangs down toward the ground. The fan is switched on, and the man's body pirouettes through the air, while the torturers swing clubs at his head. He is left hanging and turning for more than an hour. It's incomprehensible to me how anyone can survive this torture.

Video 7. The beard, mustache, eyebrows, and hair of the victim are singed off. This demeaning method of torture is used only for Islamic fundamentalists, such as members of the Dawa party.

Video 8. The victim's hands are tied to an electric heater. The heater is turned on, and the glowing wire elements burn themselves into the skin.

Video 9. A spit is heated to incandescence, then pressed

into the hands, legs, and back of the prisoner — like branding an animal.

Video 10. The victim's hands and feet are drilled through with an electric drill.

Video 11. A heavy black hammer is used to smash the victim's nose.

Video 12. The victim's mouth is pulled apart until the jaws break, a method of torture used on those who revile Saddam Hussein.

Video 13. The prisoner is sat forcibly on a metal chair, strapped down, and his fingernails are ripped off with pliers.

Video 14. A victim's arms and legs are severed with a power saw — sometimes with an ax.

Video 15. A pump hose is inserted in the anus and air is forced in until the tissue rips.

Video 16. A prisoner's arms are tied, with both hands behind him, to a carpenter's bench, which is raised and lowered until his shoulders are broken.

Video 17. The water method: A prisoner is tied down beneath a water faucet, and the tap is left open for hours. The prisoner usually loses control over his body and sphincters in less than half an hour.

Video 18. A victim is forced to remain for days in a well about two feet deep, filled with dirty water.

Video 19. Blows with a stick to the head and between the legs.

Video 20. Psycho-terror: A prisoner, bound and blindfolded, is shoved into an empty room. Shrill sounds blast from a loudspeaker whenever he's about to fall asleep.

Video 21. A prisoner stands with his head wedged between two wooden pegs. His ears are nailed to the wall. The victim tears off his own ears when he can't stand any more, and sinks to the ground.

Video 22. Prisoners are bound and kept for months in a cell without ventilation. Temperatures rise to over 120 degrees Fahrenheit.

Video 23. Holes are drilled through a victim's teeth, or the teeth are yanked out.

Video 24. Needles are shoved under a victim's fingernails.

Video 25. Acid is sprayed on a victim's body.

Video 26. The bodies of murdered victims are thrown into the cells of living ones.

Video 27. Killer dogs are released in cells of prisoners in solitary confinement.

Video 28. The nose of a prisoner is plugged, forcing him to breathe through his mouth for weeks.

Video 29. A victim's tongue is pierced with needles.

Video 30. Feet and hands are immersed in boiling oil.

Video 31. Insect repellent is sprayed into the victim's eyes.

The next videos showed how women and children were tortured:

Video 32. Women are bound hand and foot and suspended by their hair. The husbands and children are forced to watch.

Video 33. Men are forced to rape their wives.

Video 34. A woman is suspended by the legs while she's menstruating and remains that way until her period is over.

Video 35. Children are confined in a room with a beehive. Their parents are forced to watch while the naked children are stung hundreds of times.

The nightmare visions continued. I'd seen more than enough. I knew what they were trying to tell me, but even so I couldn't feel too impressed. These methods of torture were nothing new to me. As an officer in the Iraqi army, I was familiar with the way the system worked. All of us played out such horrors in our heads hundreds of times on the front, though I must admit that until now I never really imagined the people who could carry out such atrocities. But the video images were for real. No faking, no special effects — these people really died. And the cameras recorded them dying.

The intelligence officer gave me a superior grin, but I felt only greater loathing for him; he was a beast, who could find enjoyment even in this madness. What was Uday thinking when he ordered them to show me these videos?

I didn't have time to give it further thought.

He played me the next video. They were using a power saw on a victim, cutting off his genitals. Blood spurted. It was hideous, but I remained cold. They threw two others, arms and legs bound, into a lake; they broke the arms of another with a steel pipe, then crushed his head in a vise. The steel plates of the vise were winched together until his skull broke and the brains spilled out.

My guard brought me back to the video room. Munem Hammed asked if I felt okay. I nodded and lied, "Sure, why not? I feel really good. But the videos don't interest me so much as what's going to happen now."

In his quiet, superior, and elegant manner, Munem Hammed explained what lay ahead. It fascinated me that he never gesticulated when discussing something; he didn't beat around the bush, but got directly to the point. There was nothing exaggerated, complicated, or effusive about him, nothing Oriental. He was more like the British, almost a relic of Iraq's past as a British crown colony.

"Here you have videos of Uday Saddam Hussein," he said, indicating some cassettes piled neatly on a table in front of the bank of VCRs. "Watch each of them carefully, pay attention to every detail, and imitate Uday as if you were an ape."

Munem Hammed inserted the first cassette, dated May 26, 1987, which showed Uday at a meeting of the soccer division of the Sports Federation. He sat at a conference table with half a dozen elegantly dressed gentlemen who were representatives of the Iraqi Soccer Association, of which Uday was president. Why he should be the president was anybody's guess, since actually he was not very athletic. But the office was honorary, bestowed on him because Saddam fills all important positions with family members. The Saddam family needs to be able to present itself to the common folk every so often. Contact has to be maintained between the Clan and the masses. Functions such as the presidency of the Soccer Association are perfect for this purpose. First, the president always sits in the VIP box and is thus far removed from the mob. Second, because soccer games are a regular occurrence, regular and low-key appearances are thus ensured.

Drinks and ashtrays cluttered the longish, rostrumlike table. Uday sat at the center, or rather, slouched casually in his chair. He was by far the youngest of the group. One of the men was discussing the financing of a soccer club. Uday didn't utter a word the whole time. He was wearing a light cotton suit, a white button-down shirt, and a bright tie with a matching tie pin. He held the obligatory cigar between the index and middle finger of his left hand, a Monte Cristo No. 6, imported from Cuba. I couldn't see, but his legs were probably crossed.

Munem Hammed ordered me to slouch exactly like Uday. It was easy. Uday had always sat like that, even when he was a schoolboy, and we used to mimic him frequently. I sat on a chair, hooking my right arm over the back, letting my left shoulder droop noticeably lower than the right. I cocked my arm with a dramatic flourish, and held my fingers as if I had a cigar between them.

Munem Hammed laughed and said, "Latif, the cigar. We idiots forgot the cigar," and then yelled, "Bring us the cigars." A package of Monte Cristo No. 6s was brought in. Munem Hammed handed me one, and I took it but didn't light it.

Then the same thing all over again: Sit in a slouch, right arm draped casually over the back of the chair, left shoulder drooping, left arm slightly cocked, and the fat cigar dangling between the index and middle fingers. I had my fingers too stiff, too straight. "Bend them slightly," instructed Munem Hammed, and showed me how. "Hold the cigar like this." I held it the way he'd demonstrated. I looked first at him and then at the video, and within ten minutes I'd learned how to hold my hand. I laughed, slapped my thigh with my right hand. Munem Hammed also laughed loudly.

In the next sequence, the video showed Uday putting the cigar to his lips and taking a deep, long drag. He didn't inhale, but trapped the smoke in his mouth for a few seconds, tipped his head way back, and canted it to the right as if bored, keeping his lips pressed together.

He looked funny. His protruding teeth, the tightly compressed thick lips — the whole picture reminded me of some kind of animal. People do resemble animals sometimes, and Uday was shoving his lower lip upward exaggeratedly, the way chimpanzees do when they chew on something.

I laughed inwardly, but realized that I was actually laughing at myself. Because of the operation, I too had buckteeth and a pronounced overbite. I'd forgotten about that, because I wasn't in pain anymore, and the four ceramic teeth felt as if they were my own.

I took the cigar, placed it in my mouth, and encountered my false teeth with the butt end. That action reminded me of my operation, which meant that I was still behaving like Latif Yahia and not Uday Saddam Hussein. My movements were still mine, not his. They were still directed by Latif Yahia and not Uday Saddam Hussein. I had to think about how Uday would move, and that was bad. The split second needed by my brain to relay orders to my limbs made my movements artificial.

"You'll be able to coordinate yourself better," explained Munem Hammed, revealing thereby that he'd done this often before, "only if you don't have to concentrate on what you're doing anymore. It's the same thing with a foreign language. You can speak English correctly only if you start thinking in English. You'll never be able to speak without an accent as long as you think in your native language and are constantly concentrating on the vocabulary and intonation."

For four more hours I sat in the video room and watched Uday tapes. I didn't imitate him, just concentrated on what he did, on his movements, his facial expressions, the way he used his hands. He walked erectly, chest thrust out, taking care to hold his shoulders square. He strode, and as he strode, he bounced slightly.

And when he sat in his habitual slouch, it was never with his legs together but always crossed at the knee. He crossed the left leg over the right, remained that way for a few minutes, sometimes jouncing his foot up and down, and then crossed his right leg over his left.

His laugh was not deep and loud. Rather, he giggled in a staccato *hihihihihi*, then stopped briefly, then giggled again: *hihihihihi*. His whole upper body shook and inclined forward slightly as he giggled, and the corners of his mouth turned downward: *hihihihihi*.

I did nothing but study these videos for three days, from nine in the morning to the Muslim evening prayers. Although nobody in Uday's entourage prayed, I tried to adhere to my five prayers a day, and they accepted it, although they poked fun at me. The basic rules of Muslim religious practice are a relic of the past for them. Saddam's people are modern Muslims, and modern Muslims are westerners. They belittle religious belief. Piety renders a person inferior in their eyes, particularly the piety of those who live by the Koran.

Iraq under Saddam Hussein is a far cry from fundamentalist regimes like those of Saudi Arabia, Kuwait, or even Iran. Saddam Hussein's Ba'ath party has nurtured socialist Arabs who think in western ways, and for whom religion is second-class. What counts for them is not the Koran, but socialism as a form of society. Our prophet is not Mohammed but Saddam Hussein, who places his trust in the heroic goals of our party. Our women are equal. They don't have to wear a chador and hide their faces if they don't want to, unless their husbands absolutely insist. The mosques have become purely tourist attractions in the eyes of these Arabs. There is alcohol, public drunkenness, and prostitution, and nightclubs flourish. Baghdad is Babylon of old.

After the third day I felt I knew Uday well enough to intuit the way he felt, thought, and would act. I'd made his movements so much my own that I could stand like him, sit like him, and act the way he acted.

We began speech training, and that was the most difficult of all, because I kept making an effort to speak clearly. I would open my mouth wider and in other ways try to compensate for the impediment that the dental surgery had produced. Munem Hammed criticized me constantly, reminding me like a recording, "Be a parrot, Latif, a parrot."

We rehearsed a hundred times the way Uday would open a conference, how he would act with friends, how he would review a parade. Munem Hammed pounded into my head that Uday, as a general principle, never looked anyone in the eye, never shook anyone's hand, and was always surrounded by bodyguards. He greeted everyone arrogantly, without the trace of a smile and saying little. He was the son of the president, the authority, the power. Everything he did must therefore smack of affairs of state. Relations with bodyguards had to be completely distant, impersonal. They weren't soldiers like me; they were my inferiors, they had to follow my orders without hesitation or contradiction. There was to be no slap on the shoulder, no friendly smile, no hearty contact, no fraternal kiss, only dictatorial distance.

Uday normally wore dark sunglasses, Ray-Bans, always focusing past his partner in order to emphasize the distance between himself and the rest of the world.

We practiced in similar detail how Uday would leave a room and go outside. That was considered one of the most dangerous moments, for it was then that attackers had the greatest chance of success. The passage between a closed room and the waiting column of vehicles was difficult to make entirely secure. At the end of a conference, Uday would stand up and bid farewell to the rest of the partici-pants with a nod of his head. His bodyguards would crowd around him, and he would leave the room at a brisk pace, almost rushing outdoors and dashing to his car, which would be waiting for him with its door open. The way from the building to the car had to be traversed as quickly as possible so as not to give snipers a chance.

Uday never allowed himself to be driven anywhere. He always drove, just like his father, so we also practiced how to drive: sitting casually at the steering wheel, never with both hands on the wheel but with the left arm crooked and resting on the door. He sat casually, leaning back, while he whipped his cars through Baghdad. One hundred miles an hour was a normal speed for him. He applied gas while changing gears, and he loved to floor the gas pedal. Uday maintained con-stant radio contact with his bodyguards, who drove in front of and behind him in identical cars. Most convoys consisted of four cars. They kept close together in a file, and passed each other constantly at Uday's command, such as, "Three passes two, one falls back, takes position three." The idea was to confuse potential attackers with the constant change of positions, so that they could never be sure which car was Uday's. Were the cars to remain in the same order, attackers could concentrate on a single one, but in this way, to be certain of killing Uday the whole convoy would have to be blown up, a pretty difficult operation.

All my training sessions were recorded on video and

played for Uday on a daily basis. However, I saw nothing of him during this period, for he stayed away from Project No. 7.

On October 15, 1987, Munem Hammed called me into Uday's study and told me he was fairly satisfied with my progress. I was disappointed. I considered myself good. Even my speech impediment was under control, and my movements were almost faultless. They should have been really impressed, and I thought to myself, *They're just trying to confuse me.*

Munem Hammed had before him a letter with the Iraqi eagle at the top, a piece of official correspondence. He stated, "We're now going to inform the president. Lieutenant General al-Nassiri wrote this letter and asked me to countersign."

It hit me all at once: They'd never told him. The kidnapping, the psycho-terror in the cell, the entire program of training up to now — they'd done it all without his knowledge.

Uday and his officers had planned and carried out the whole thing on their own. This was an attempt by a domesticated mama's boy to emancipate himself. He probably wanted to impress his father and prove to him that he could provide for his own protection. He had found a fidai who, for the first time, was not part of the family but was nonetheless good and convincing.

Munem Hammed showed me the letter, which they sent to the president later the same day:

> Iraqi Republic
> Head of the Chancellery of the Republic
> Security Service
>
> In the name of God, the Holy
> Lord, honorable president of the Iraqi Republic, may God keep you and protect your rule.
> Mr. President, I wish to inform you that our Secret Service, security branch, commanded by the following officers:
> 1. Maj. Munem Shabib Munem Hammed al-Tikriti
> 2. Capt. Siad Hassan Hashem al-Nassiri

3. Capt. Saadi Daham Hasaa al-Nassiri
has engaged for our service 1st Lt. Latif Yahia Latif al-Salihi,
who bears an extremely close resemblance to Mr. Uday Saddam Hussein.

We arrived at the following, after investigations and in-
quiries about him and his family:

1. His name is Latif Yahia Latif al-Salihi, a Kurd, born June
14, 1964, in Baghdad, Muslim, Sunni.

2. He studied political science and law, graduated in 1986.

3. He began his career and his military duties as lieutenant
with the Special Commando Unit. He was promoted, because
of his dedication and his bravery, to first lieutenant after six
months.

4. He was never cited or punished for political or other
errors.

5. His father owns an import-export firm, "Ahavain
Import-Export," in the Mansur district, on Daudi Street. He
also owns a marble factory in the Bob al-Sham district, on
Diali Street.

6. He has two Mercedes cars. He has an account with the
Iraqi Central Bank.

After learning of these details and because of his resemblance to Mr. Uday Saddam Hussein, we decided, with the
written agreement of Mr. Uday Saddam Hussein, to use him
as bondman and fidai for Mr. Uday Saddam Hussein, for
difficult, important, and dangerous operations and tasks.

We have begun his training and determined that he is a
clever young man and is ready to perform duties for his
fatherland, Iraq.

Everything else is left to you, and you have the last word,
my lord.

May the Iraqi flag wave ever high in our dear Iraq under
your rule.

Signed:

Lt. Gen. Fanar Zibn al-Nassiri
Director of the Security Service
October 15, 1987

I shuddered inwardly as I read this letter, for it dawned on me that up to now I had only been Uday's plaything, a toy for him and his officers. They had tracked me down, commenced my training, and convinced themselves that I was talented and ideologically sound, that I was interested in Uday's life and fascinated by the opulence. But what security had I gained? None. The whole thing was only a prelude. The decision was the president's, and if he said no — what then?

"Munem Hammed, sir, what happens if the lord Saddam Hussein rejects me as fidai for his son? What are you going to do with me?" I asked.

Munem Hammed avoided my gaze, said nothing, stood up, and left.

I knew what that meant. I was a dead man, I would disappear as if I had never existed if the president rejected me. My mind raced to the spots of blood in the torture chamber and the videos of the civilian police officer with the mutilated back and the men in the al-Rashid camp being led to the gallows, their hands bound, their feet chained. The trapdoor opened noiselessly beneath their legs, there was a short yank, the noose tightened, the heads fell to the side, broken neck. Maybe they'd just shoot me.

الجمهورية العراقية
رئاسة ديوان رئاسة الجمهورية
جهاز الأمن الخاص

بسم الله الرحمن الرحيم

السيد رئيس الجمهورية العراقية حفظك الله ورعاك ..
سيادة الرئيس أود أعلام سيادتكم بأن جهازنا الخاص شعبة المتابعة الامنية برئاسة كل من .
١ـ المقدم منعم شبيب حمد التكريتي
٢ـ النقيب زياد حسن هاشم الناصري
٣ـ النقيب سعدي دهام هزع الناصري
قـ قاموا بكسب (الملازم أول لطيف يحيى لطيف الصالحي) شبيه الاستاذ عدي صدام حسين المحترم
وبعد التحري والمتابعة وله ولعائلته من قبل شعبة المتابعة السرية الخاصة بالجهاز اتضح ما يلي .
١ـ اسمه لطيف يحيى لطيف الصالحي من تومية كرد ية تولد ١٤ / ٦ / ١٩٦٤ وسكنه بغداد منذ
اربعين سنة ومن الديانة المسلمة سني .
٢ـ خريج جامعة بغداد للقانون والسياسة عام ١٩٨٦
٣ـ دخل القوات المسلحة العراقية بصنف القوات الخاصة برتبة ملازم وبعد ستة اشهر ونظرا"
لشجاعته واستبساله ترقى الى رتبة ملازم أول قوات خاصة .
٤ ـ لم يحكم عليه بأي جنحة أو تهمة سياسية ..
٥ـ لديه بعض الاملاك الخاصة به مكتب استيراد وتصدير الاخوين في منطقة المنصور شارع الداودي
ولديه معمل للمرمر في منطقة بوب الشام على طريق ديالى ولديه سيارتين نوع مرسيدس
ورصيده في البنك المركزي العراقي .
وبعد حصولنا على هذه المعلومات كلها ولقرب الشبيه بينه وبين الاستاذ عدي صدام حسين المحترم
قررنا وبموافقة الاستاذ عدي صدام حسين المحترم خطيا" قررنا استخدام الملازم أول لطيف يحيى
لطيف الصالحي فدائي خاص للاستاذ عدي صدام حسين في المهمات الخاصة والخطرة وباشرنا
التدريب معه ووجدناه من النوع الذكي جدا" لتفهم واجبة الوطني لخدمة عراقنا الحبيب ودمت
سيادتك لاعلاء كلمة الحق ورفع علم العرق بقيادتك الحكمية في ربوع عراقنا العزيز .

اللواء الركن
فنار زين الناصري
مدير جهاز الأمن الخاص
١٩٨٧/١٠/١٥

Original letter to President Saddam Hussein
(translation on pages 71–72).

5

SADDAM HUSSEIN:

LIKE FATHER, LIKE SON

MUNEM Hammed al-Tikriti was nervous today. I'd never seen him like this. Until now, he had always been restrained, superior, poised, an elegant man whom I admired, despite the growing recognition that he considered me nothing more than a tool.

It was October 23, 1987, shortly after 8:00 A.M., and hot in Baghdad. "Today's the day," he said, and I knew what he meant. The answer had arrived yesterday from the palace: The president had asked to meet me. *He wants to get to know me personally,* I told myself, and felt proud, although there was nothing to be proud of. I was dead if his lordship Saddam Hussein rejected me, if he didn't approve of my selection, or felt slighted by his son and his officers. Hammed probably shared my apprehension, or he wouldn't have been so tense. His fate probably hung by the same thread.

Still I didn't feel nervous, nor was I afraid, as I had been when they brought me back from the front. This time I knew what was happening and realized that success depended to a large extent on me. I could prove myself; I wanted to prove myself. They had discovered me, and I was good. I knew I was good.

"Our appointment is at 4:00 P.M. in the palace. Prepare yourself," Munem Hammed admonished me in a stern tone that I hadn't heard from him previously.

By this time my mouth had healed completely from my dental operation, and my training had been so thorough that not only did I imitate Uday's speech defect, but I did it intuitively, automatically, without thinking. I moved like Uday, held my hand as he did, gave his grin, his wink, his hysterical laugh.

Saddam dispatched one of his cars with the officers Arshad al-Yassien, Abed Hamid al-Tikriti, and Rokan al-Tikriti. He always surrounded himself with a retinue of personal confidants, whom I would get to know as time went on. This inner circle comprised the following persons:

Colonel Arshad al-Yassien, responsible for Saddam Hussein's security, who commanded a whole staff of guards.

Colonel Abed Hamid al-Tikriti, an old friend of the president, who knew Saddam from school.

Major Rokan al-Tikriti, similarly a companion of Saddam for many decades, responsible for the firearms training of all bodyguards and guards in the presidential palace.

Saddam Kamel, Saddam Hussein's oldest friend and brother of Hussein Kamel; he was a high-ranking officer in the al-Khass and husband of Saddam's second daughter, Rina.

Captain Jamal Saad Dahham, another longtime companion, director of the Office of Information in the Presidential Palace.

First Lieutenant Addi Omar, bodyguard.

First Lieutenant Mohammed Fadel, bodyguard, who later went to prison because he murdered two dancers who had rejected his advances at a party for Saddam Hussein.

First Lieutenant Rafed al-Abed, bodyguard and nephew of Colonel Abed Hamid al-Tikriti.

Lieutenant Hakim Kamel, bodyguard, brother of Hussein Kamel, husband of Saddam's youngest daughter, Hala.

Lieutenant Nazem Ahmad al-Tikriti, bodyguard.

Lieutenant Mohammed Kamal Douri, bodyguard.

Lieutenant Saadi Nahi al-Tikriti, bodyguard.

Lieutenant Yassem Sala al-Tikriti, bodyguard.

Lieutenant Rafed al-Tikriti, bodyguard.

Lieutenant Riad Mohammed al-Tikriti, bodyguard.

The three officers picked me up punctually at 3:00 P.M. We hurried outside through the foyer and ran to the Mercedes. A man opened the door, I jumped into the back, and the convoy sped off with the doors still open, two Mercedes in front of us, two behind. The average speed on the short strip between Project No. 7 and the Family Gate exceeded fifty-five miles per hour. High speeds were just another security measure, like the passing of one car by another.

At the gate we slowed, the guards waved us through, we passed the antitank obstacles, the hospital, and the ministerial dwellings, and stopped twenty minutes later in front of the Information Building, the eastern wing of Saddam's palace.

My guards sprang from the car and secured it, and only once they were in position did I emerge. Everything had to look real, just as during training: no mistakes now. I jumped out of the car and, with Saddam's people beside me, moved double-time to the broad, sweeping steps of the building. Three officers waited for us there.

We hurried into the hallway, and Rokan disappeared into a side room. Everything seemed prepared for my visit. Then nothing happened for ten minutes. We cooled our heels in the hallway. Nobody spoke. Nobody smoked.

A high-ranking officer entered. He was an athletic man with broad shoulders, a thick neck, and strong hands. His green uniform jacket fit tightly over his chest. Everything about him seemed too big, too massive, too powerful. The officer knew who I was, although he'd never seen me before. "So you're Latif. You know the rules?"

"I know them."

I knew about Saddam's poison phobia, his obsession. During training they had told me a story about Interior Minister Izzat Ibrahim. Ibrahim, for whom nothing was holy and who had used every means possible to kill during his career, was summoned by the president. Before Saddam received him, his guards undressed Ibrahim, threw him into the pool, and then smeared his body with Detol, a harsh disinfectant. Saddam suspected him of being a carrier of mysterious microbes or of some transferable poison that could be passed on by a handshake. Everyone, not only I, had to submit to painstaking examination before being allowed to see the president.

The officer began with a thorough body search. He checked everything: my pockets, the folds of my uniform jacket, my underarms. He patted down my rear, my crotch, my legs, and ordered me to remove my shoes and socks. Saddam hated having his subjects stand before him in worn socks. He despised worn socks. So the officer gave me a new pair of socks, white cotton, in my size. I put them on, and he called the doctor.

Like the two doctors who had examined me weeks earlier, this man seemed to be non-Arab. He entered without saying a word, set his brown leather doctor's bag on the table, and opened it. He had red hair. His sharp-featured face was covered with freckles, and his eyes were close-set. He looked mysterious, crafty. The doctor embarked on an examination that struck me as ludicrous, considering I had had no chance to hide anything on my person. I was under constant supervision, a prisoner. Uday's physicians had examined me several times.

Or does Saddam Hussein not even trust his own son? I asked myself, amused at the thought.

The doctor palpated my skin, dipped a cotton swab in some kind of fluid, and wiped it over my face, my ears, my throat. He replaced the swab several times, dunking the used ones in a blue solution, which showed no effect. Presumably it would have changed color, had I had some kind of special poison on my skin.

He examined my eyes, pulled down the lids, checked the mucous membrane. My eyes watered, but that seemed to have been normal because the doctor didn't react. The officer ordered me to open my mouth wide, and the doctor took a smear from my tongue, shone a special chrome lamp into my throat, checked my teeth, and slid his finger over my gums, top and bottom, inside and outside.

A ridiculous ceremony, a ritual, a schizoid-paranoiac piece of theater—I doubted this examination could have prevented anything.

Though I'm no physician, the last part seemed the most sensible to me. The doctor handed me a small plastic bottle containing Detol, and signaled for me to cleanse my hands with it. I sprayed the solution on both hands and rubbed them together until they were dry again.

With that, the examination was complete. The doctor put away his things and disappeared. The officer told me in a fatherly tone, "Latif, remember, don't kiss Saddam."

Now I too was ready for the final stretch, ready like a Muslim at the holy hajj in Mecca, before kissing the Kaaba. The crucial difference: The hajj is the highest fulfillment, the highest duty of a Muslim. Each Muslim has to go to Mecca at least once, the Koran prescribes. But my walk to President Saddam Hussein was to decide my life or death. If he rejected me, my fate was sealed.

I marveled at my calmness, my composure. Saddam was the Prophet, the incarnation of power, the judge of good and evil. Millions of people in Iraq would sacrifice anything for this moment, including their lives. But I was no more nervous than if I were driving to the Tigris with my father in his white Volvo, to go fishing. I wasn't afraid to die.

The door opened. The officer entered and asked me to follow. I was standing in the president's office.

The room looked like a copy of Uday's study in Project No. 7, and I was instantly certain that Uday had furnished his office using his father's as a model. The same pastel-colored wallpaper, the dominant light yellow couch, the massive English desk, the bookshelves with Arab literature.

Saddam sat behind his desk. He was talking on the telephone and studiously ignored me, again a parallel with Uday. Uday would never welcome someone immediately, for making a person wait means exercising power over him. Uday had clearly learned that from his father.

Saddam was wearing a dark double-breasted suit and a tie in a bright floral pattern, without a tie pin. He held the receiver of the Siemens telephone in his left hand, while his right hand rested on the desk. He tapped rhythmically on the desktop with his middle finger. At brief intervals he laughed, and his voice sounded soft and warm, almost whiny. There was no power in it, no force, no tone of command. He spoke without punctuation, without emphasis, without any special intonation. Nothing stood out, not a single word struck the listener. Saddam was discussing with an aide a speech he planned to give soon. The vestiges of an old tattoo were visible on the back of his right hand. At first I thought they were liver spots, but the tattoo had simply been poorly removed.

Saddam's fingernails were carefully manicured and polished. His haircut was faultless, as was his mustache. When he laughed, you could see his perfect teeth. His eyes were brown and brimmed with expression, and the only signs that this man was already fifty were the traces of bags under his eyes and the deep lines above his mouth. He looked like a combination of the young Jean Gabin and the Sultan Saladin. Saddam was a good-looking, trim, well-groomed, and imposing man.

He hung up, rose to his feet lightly, moved away from the desk, and laughed resoundingly and full-throatedly as he looked at me.

This laugh wasn't artificial, but real and powerful. Saddam moved two steps toward me and started making small talk. He asked about my time on the front, my parents, my siblings. He gave me no time to answer, but answered for me, and I always nodded in the affirmative. Saddam inspected me from top to bottom, scrutinizing my hands, my lips, my eyes, my facial expressions, my gestures. He said nothing, but I thought I could read his appreciation in his face: *He really looks like my son. Excellent work was done with him.*

Suddenly, and without warning, he spread his arms and exclaimed, "Yes, it's you. Allah gave me two sons, and you're the third!"

I was confused. The whole ceremonial up till now, the examinations, the evident mistrust, the physical and psychological pressure brought to bear on me, the mixture of cold-blooded force and calculated recognition of what I'd accomplished, seemed far away. I was alive. I had survived and passed the first and most important test. Saddam's comment made me happy and left me concerned at the same time. He'd accepted me as fidai, as his son's double. So now I was a member of the Clan, a part of it—and yet not a part of it. I was still nothing more than an instrument, a useful object or toy, to be thrown away when no longer needed. When would I stop being Uday's fidai? Would it ever end, and could it end positively?

Saddam's character preoccupied me even more than my nagging doubts about my fate, however. I had imagined him completely different—more overbearing, colder, more arrogant, brutal.

He must be different than he appears, I told myself. *He has hundreds of thousands of lives on his conscience. Or does he have a conscience at all? Probably not. Cruelty probably becomes something impersonal if it occurs in the name of the public interest. To murder one person is a crime. But if one kills thousands, then it's a matter of state. Saddam cannot think or feel any other way.*

Nothing about Saddam in person appeared cruel, cold, repulsive. He was a man with strong charisma, and an allure that people found captivating.

So this was the man who had the whole country in a chokehold, whom millions of people exalted regularly, who could transform Iraqis into a fanatical and euphoric mass, ready to sacrifice itself for him unconditionally. Saddam Hussein is the creation of a culture that is as far removed from western understanding as are the humanitarian values of Islam.

He was born on April 28, 1937, in the sleepy little village of al-Ouja, about fifty miles north of Baghdad, near Tikrit, birthplace of the legendary Sultan Saladin. His peasant parents named him Hussein Saddam al-Tikriti. His mother, Subha Talfah, was unmarried when she became pregnant with him, and she tried to abort him through hard physical labor. His surname Saddam, "Steadfast One," was given to him because his mother was unable to "lose" him.

The natural father of the child died before Saddam was born. Subha Talfah then married Ibrahim al-Hassam, but the new husband wanted nothing to do with a child that wasn't his. Saddam was sent to live with his uncle, Khairallah Talfah, an officer in the Iraqi army unit that participated in the 1941 rebellion against the Hashemite king, Feisal II. Khairallah spent several years in prison as a result of his involvement.

Between 1936 and 1941, there were six attempted insurrections in Iraq. Saddam's childhood thus began in unstable, turbulent times. After the head of the family was released from prison, the uncle's clan survived through trade, robbery, and fraud.

The village knew about Saddam's birth out of wedlock and excluded him from community life. The boy became tough, skipping school to the despair of his teachers in Tikrit. By the time he was only ten, he displayed signs of the violent nature that would catapult him to the head of a totalitarian system. He was in the habit of carrying an iron bar to keep stray dogs and his fellow students at bay. While at school he hid it under his djellaba. Afterward, he sometimes heated it in a fire until it glowed, and shoved the tip into the eyes and anuses of captured dogs and cats while other children looked on. This iron bar was his fetish, his father, his power, his only friend and protection against a cold society that excluded him because his father was dead and his mother was married to someone else and nobody knew where she lived. He probably hated society because society hated him, and the only thing he could cling to was the glowing iron bar, with which he could torture to death the only creatures he was superior to: animals.

His uncle moved to Baghdad in 1955, and Saddam started attending the al-Karkh school. He grew to maturity in the Tekarte district. Numerous members of the Tikrit clan earned their living through robbery and quickly made their presence felt in Baghdad society with their Mafia-like methods. Gradually the Tikrit clan achieved more and more influence. Blood flowed whenever family feuds were settled.

Saddam committed his first murder about this time. He shot dead his distant uncle Saadi, a rival robber, on orders from his uncle Khairallah, underscoring by this act his close ties to the Tikrit clan. This was his first step in securing his existence by means of violence without scruple.

Despite his propensity for violence, Saddam also developed an unbelievable thirst for knowledge. He finished high school in Baghdad with good marks.

He was still a high school student when he started to cultivate an interest in politics. He quickly became an enthusiastic believer in the nationalistic and revolutionary goals of the Iraqi Ba'ath party, the Party of Arab Renewal, which was banned and operating clandestinely at the time. He joined the party in 1957 and became an active opponent of the Iraqi dictator, General Abdul Karim Kassem. Saddam was selected to participate in an assassination attempt on the dictator on October 17, 1959. The Ba'ath party had adopted European ideologies like nationalism and socialism and sought to realize them according to the rules of the region, through violence. Though General Kassem paid lip service to the proper slogans, his basic problem was that he belonged neither to the Tikrit clan nor to the Ba'ath party. As an outsider to the clan, he was an enemy who had to be eliminated. Kassem was also hated by the people, whom he brutally oppressed and exploited.

The assassination attempt failed, and Saddam was slightly wounded in the leg. He had to flee the country. He cut out the bullet and managed to escape to Syria, where he stayed for six months. The lawyer Michel Aflaq, founder of the Ba'ath party, became his mentor. In 1962 Saddam went to Egypt and began to study law. He became a leading member of the Ba'ath party in Cairo. Although he had played a minor role in the assassination attempt on General Kassem, his participation would later turn into one of the cornerstones of the heroic myths surrounding him.

While Saddam was studying at the university in Cairo, Kassem was deposed by the Ba'ath party under the leadership of Ahmad Hasan al-Bakr, and publicly executed. Saddam promptly returned home and asked his uncle for the hand of his cousin, Sajida.

Their marriage was an arranged union, already decided when the two were children. It conformed to the rules of the Tikriti clan, by which one never married outside of the extended family.

The young couple had little time to enjoy their marriage. Hasan al-Bakr was deposed a few months later by Marshal Abdul al-Rahman Arif and his supporters, bitter opponents of the Ba'ath party. As a member of the party leadership, Saddam was once again persecuted and arrested. While in prison, he was chosen deputy leader of the party by its eighth national congress. He managed to escape shortly afterward.

The Ba'ath party succeeded in deposing Marshal Arif and returning to power only in 1968, after several years of civil strife. Once again Hasan al-Bakr, the secretary-general of the party, became president. His deputy, and the strongman of the regime, was Saddam Hussein al-Tikriti.

Saddam took control of the Committee of Investigation, located in the infamous Qasr al-Nihayah prison, whose name means "The Palace Where It Ends." Hundreds of political opponents were tortured and murdered within several weeks. In addition, Saddam had more than a hundred men hanged before a fanatical crowd in Baghdad's Republic Square for being "Israeli and American agents."

As deputy secretary-general, Saddam was responsible for the daily workings of the party, and revealed himself to be a capable planner and organizer. In 1972 he turned the western-dominated oil industry into a state-run concern and signed a friendship treaty with the Soviet Union—a treaty that resulted in the massive rearmament of Iraq. President al-Bakr, a longtime opponent of the friendship treaty, changed his mind only after Saddam shot him in the arm with a pistol while he was in his office.

Despite this friendship treaty with the Soviet Union, Saddam had numerous communists executed, as well as opposition supporters of all stripes. Increasingly, President al-Bakr turned into a pure figurehead. He died of heart failure on May 16, 1979, according to the official version. It was common knowledge that in reality he was poisoned. Saddam Hussein was only forty-three when he assumed power.

He was now Iraq's head man, and exploited his position mercilessly. He had high-ranking officials executed, including Baghdad's mayor. The new president made criticism of his person punishable by death and nurtured a personality cult comparable only with the one that surrounded Romania's notorious and durable dictator Nicolae Ceausescu.

Like Ceausescu, Saddam appointed relatives to the most important and influential positions. The whole al-Tikriti clan took power along with him. In effect, Iraq became their private property, as stipulated by the unwritten rules of Oriental clan society. Iraq was turned into a Tikriti Iraq, just as earlier in the century Arabia became Saudi Arabia, even if in Iraq's case the process was intended to be less visible. Officially the country is governed by a fifteen-man-strong Revolutionary Command Council, which is headed by Saddam Hussein. But parallel to that council exists a Special Bureau, which is nothing other than a family council that controls the whole country. Another point of comparison between Ceausescu and Saddam Hussein is the misfit sons of both rulers. Nicu Ceausescu, whom Uday Saddam Hussein knew personally, would make headlines with his wild booze parties and rapes. He once hit two pedestrians while driving completely drunk, and the two died of their injuries. The Romanian security service covered up the incident, just as the Iraqi security service covered up Uday's crimes.

So now I, Latif Yahia, was part of all this, not as a full member of the Clan but as Udai's fidai. I felt the pulse of power, and would become familiar with command structures and the details of rule that remained hidden to millions of others. I would participate in their lives. I was Uday and "Saddam Hussein's third son," just as the president had said.

I felt nervous for the first time, but didn't let it show. The president continued, "What I demand from you is that you carry out your duties well."

"Yes, my lord," I interjected, and Saddam went on, "If you perform well, I'll be satisfied with you. If you fulfill your duties one hundred percent, I'll always be available to you to deal with all your problems . . ."

He paused, inhaled deeply through his nose, and added, ". . . including problems with Uday. Make sure I have no reason to be angry with you."

I waited for a moment, then answered formally, "I hope I will do everything well and properly, my lord."

Saddam Hussein didn't say another word. He turned without shaking my hand and went to his desk, picked up the phone, and pushed a red button. Officers appeared within a few seconds to take me away. In the hallway they clapped me on the shoulders, and one of them asked how I felt. I nodded and said, almost casually, "I'm okay."

6

THE FIRST PERFORMANCE

I LAY stretched out on my broad bed in Uday's bedroom in Project No. 7 and inhaled big gulps of the clean fall air. It was the end of October, and the weather in Baghdad was no longer so hot. They'd stepped up my training since my visit with the president. Again and again they would escort me to the video room and make me watch films of Uday, until I knew almost all of them by heart. The routine changed little: two days of studying videos, then two of parroting, talking like him, acting like him, practicing dialogues. Munem Hammed usually served as my dialogue partner. He played his roles perfectly, even when he was irritated by the presence of Siad Hassan Hashem al-Nassiri — the Bulldog, the mass murderer, Saddam's master executioner — who was always shadowing our efforts. The Bulldog urged us on, and even Uday manifested some respect for him, particularly because he seemed to have a direct line to Saddam Hussein.

One day we practiced the role of Uday as president of a sports club, and the next day he was again the son of the president, about to inspect a special military unit. Munem Hammed drummed into my head Uday's sloppy way of saluting, his obsession with perfect dress, and his mannerism of playing with his sunglasses — slowly removing the dark green, gold-framed Ray-Bans from the case, slipping them on, and arrogantly looking down his nose and past the people around him.

My eyes slowly got used to the glasses, and I started wearing them all the time like Uday, even indoors in windowless rooms. They saved me from having to have my eyes made up daily to make them look smaller, like Uday's.

Not one day during all my weeks of training was there time off for me to be Latif Yahia. I had to play Uday even in my golden cage in Project No. 7, and without exception the servants had to treat me as though I were the president's son. A violation of this rule would result in "special treatment" by the Bulldog's men, and everyone in this house knew what that meant. So they followed the absurd rules of the game.

My life changed only in one major respect after the visit with the president. Before, Uday rarely stayed in Project No. 7. Now he was here all the time, and even slept here. He was no longer satisfied with studying the videos they made of me, but began to supervise my training in person. He sought out my company, though initially he avoided any expression of friendship.

In fact, it was more the other way around. The longer my training took, the more extreme became his bursts of rage. I tried hard, committing myself to his cause, but he shunned me sometimes as if I were his greatest enemy.

By now it was early November, and Uday was appointed by his father to chair the Iraqi Olympic Committee. I had no idea whether an Iraqi athlete had ever won a medal in any discipline, or even come close. As usual, the job of committee chairman was only a PR position for Saddam's son. However, my duties had now expanded, inasmuch as I was now the fidai not only of the head of the national sports associations but also of the chairman of the national Olympic committee, which meant that I must also receive international guests as Uday Saddam Hussein.

Uday's appointment took place on a Tuesday and was announced the same day in the main news program on Iraqi television. The Iraqi newspapers also devoted major articles to it, especially the *Baghdad Observer*, Iraq's only English-language newspaper. The next day we were back in our video theater, where Munem Hammed and I played out the scene, "The Chair of the Iraqi Olympic Committee Receives an Olympic Delegation at the Airport."

This was the first time Uday was present during a session in the video room. He sat in a chair in the back, observing everything closely. I stood before a podium with microphones, and next to me were my guards, all wearing dark sunglasses. For props we also had a red carpet and floral arrangements. The video room had been decorated as much as possible like the reception room of Saddam Hussein's private airport.

We had visited the airport in the morning so that I could visualize the scene exactly. It's located about five or six miles from the palace, and consists of two landing strips long enough for jumbo jets to touch down. The palace and the airport are connected by a broad stretch of road under constant surveillance by members of the security service, who wear civilian police uniforms only as camouflage and are relieved every four hours. These quasi-cops, who stand on the edge of the streets like trees, are called *Ba Murur* in Baghdad.

Their main job, however, is not to observe the airport part of the road, since Saddam Hussein doesn't leave Iraq often. Rather, he uses the same street daily to drive to another private domicile, his palace in al-Ameriya, which he calls Mujamaa al-Riasi, or headquarters. The palace lies to the west of the airport road, and halfway to the airport there is a turnoff. Even as schoolchildren, all of us knew that mere mortals were prohibited from using the road. Anyone mistakenly passing through in his car would be detained and imprisoned, maybe even executed.

The airport building wasn't very large, and reminded me more of the administrative section of some midsize company. In front spread a generous parking lot, ample enough for the presidential convoys to approach the building in style. The main room, a large reception lounge with rows of chairs separated by plants in hydroculture boxes, was dominated by a huge portrait of Saddam Hussein. A resplendent Iraqi eagle was affixed to the wall beneath the portrait and beside it stood the red, white, and black Iraqi flag with its three green stars.

Under Saddam's gaze, a podium with microphones was set up on a kind of stage. There were plush carpets everywhere. It was here that the first flowery speeches were given, the first polite phrases exchanged during state visits.

Two Boeing long-range aircraft, five helicopters, and two MiG fighter-bombers were kept at the airport in hangars with hydraulically operated doors. These aircraft were always fully fueled and ready to take off. Their crews had to be on standby day and night for the president's call.

One of the chopper pilots was my friend, Captain Mazhar al-Tikriti, who had flown the most missions for the president. Saddam Hussein affectionately calls his aircrews "The Eagles of Iraqi Airspace."

I didn't memorize each physical detail of the airport, since that was secondary. Instead, I concentrated on how Uday would act while welcoming the foreign delegation. Back in the video room, they had me stand on the red carpet in front of the pedestal. My training officer directed me: "The delegation has just landed, and you cordially welcome the delegation leader before inspecting the honor guard."

I tried to remain focused, approached the imaginary delegation leader, and shook his hand. Suddenly it all seemed extremely funny. I couldn't walk past the imaginary honor guard without the urge to burst out laughing, which I did, loudly and clearly. I immediately apologized — but it was already too late. Uday jumped from his seat and rushed toward me. He had his electric cable in his right hand. His face was like stone. I couldn't see his eyes, since he was wearing his Ray-Bans.

He screamed at me to turn around. I obeyed, knowing

what was coming next. He lashed me with his electric cable, following the first blow with another and another as if he were crazy, and the cable struck my back again and again. As in a trance, Uday groaned and exhaled loudly through his nose with each blow. None of the officers dared to intervene. I felt the burning pain, but endured it without a word. Worse than the sting was the humiliation. He had lit into me almost without provocation. What had I done? I had laughed during training. That was enough for him to lose control.

I counted each blow. He stopped at thirty-three. He was breathing heavily, his forehead bathed in sweat, and suddenly he began to laugh hysterically. That staccato *hihihihi*. He seemed satisfied, released, as if this spontaneous outbreak of violence had given him sexual satisfaction. Was Uday a sadist, a person who could overcome his sexual and psychological inhibitions only through the crudest violence? Immature, unfinished personalities hate without reason, tend to work off aggression against helpless objects. Sadists are psychologically immature people.

In his youth, Saddam Hussein had vented aggression with a red-hot iron bar, impaling hapless animals. What had Uday inherited from his father? Was he even worse than Saddam? This senseless explosion of violence seemed to me nothing more than an excuse to assert his identity. Uday probably hated himself.

"Continue," he commanded after a few moments, and left the room, still breathing heavily. We resumed as if nothing had happened, all of us extremely precise, applying the finishing touches.

We practiced various scenarios in front of the bank of video recorders every day until December 27. In the evenings we reviewed the tapes, analyzing the mistakes in order to correct them the next day.

I got to know Uday better during these weeks. I observed him, listened to his every word, tried to remember each detail of his behavior. I wanted to take notes but didn't dare at first, because I feared the consequences that their discovery might entail. Besides, my apprenticeship wasn't over yet.

We spent the next weeks on close combat and target practice — interesting, but for me nothing new. I'd learned most of it in the army, and this part of my instruction was almost identical to the officers' courses.

They taught me how Uday, who had carried a Magnum even as a child, would pull out his weapon and use it. How he brought his submachine gun into position and started to fire into the air in an expression of childish joy.

I learned how to play with my revolver the way Uday did, like a hero in a Western. During an ordinary conversation, he would sometimes draw his weapon from its holster for no obvious reason, play with it, aim it at the person he was talking to, place his finger on the trigger, laugh, switch hands, and twirl the pistol on his finger like a cowboy after a gunfight. An unusual exercise, but I had to practice it anyway.

I stopped worrying about whether what I was doing was useful or not. The longer I served the dictator, the more removed from reality I became. The system in which Uday lived his daily life was so absurd that even his excesses weren't exceptional, but instead represented normality. In this unreal context, questions of usefulness or meaning had little sense.

My training as fidai was finally complete on February 29, 1988. The next day, March 1, Munem Hammed al-Tikriti dictated a brief letter to the director of the state security service:

Iraqi Republic
Chancellery of the Republic
Security Service
Secret Observation Section

In the name of God the Merciful
Secret and Strictly Confidential
To the Honorable Director of the Security Service

My Lord, I wish to inform your lordship that I and my group of officers responsible for the special training of 1st Lt. Latif Yahia Latif al-Salihi have completed said training. First Lt. Latif Yahia Latif al-Salihi learned the use of all categories of weapons in order to serve as representative of Lord Uday Saddam Hussein. He completed the training successfully.

Everything else is left up to you, my Lord.

Maj. Munem Shabib Hammed al-Tikriti
Director of the Secret Observation Section, March 1, 1988

It was no more than a form letter. My training was finished. Uday accepted me. Presumably his father did, too — at least, there had been no reaction from the palace up to now, which suggested that everything was fine.

After Munem Hammed's letter, I received dozens of uniforms: a bodyguard's uniform, a pilot's uniform, a black uniform bearing the name tag Uday Saddam Hussein. I was also issued new papers with false names. Sometimes I was Captain Ahib al-Hadisi, sometimes Mohammed Sami Ahmed of the Social Ministry, sometimes Muteb al-Kamali, an employee of the Economics Ministry. Thus, should something go wrong and I be assassinated, there could be no mistake: It wasn't Uday Saddam Hussein who was shot, nor was it Latif Yahia, who didn't officially exist anymore, but rather Captain Ahib al-Hadisi, an officer in the al-Khass security service.

Everyone congratulated me that day, and even Uday acted friendly, sharing a Hennessy cognac with me, served without ice in a crystal snifter.

For the next four days nothing happened. Uday ordered me to take it easy. There were no more training videos, no speech sessions, just time to switch off my mind. I hung around the swimming pool, lay under the spring sun, and had the servants spoil me. I combed through Uday's wardrobes

الجمهورية العراقية
رئاسة ديوان رئاسة الجمهورية
جهاز الامن الخاص
شعبة المتابعة السرية

بسم الله الرحمن الرحيم

سري وشخصي للغايه

الى / السيد مدير جهاز الامن الخاص المحترم

سيدي اود اعلام سيادتكم باني ومجموعتي من الضباط المشرفين على الدورة السرية الخاصة
(بالملازم أول لطيف يحيي لطيف الصالحي) والخاصة بتدريبه على السلاح بانواعه وتهيأته
ليكون ممثل الاستاذ عدي صدام حسين المحترم وبذلك قد انتهت الدورة وبنجاح الملازم الاول
لطيف يحيي لطيف الصالحي في تأدية الواجبات كلها على اتم وجه وبدقة متناهية فأود
اعلام سيادتك بهذا الخصوص .

ولكم الامر سيدي .

المقدم
منعم شبيب التكريتي
مدير شعبة المتابعة السرية

١٩٨٨ / ٣ / ١

Original letter to the director of the Security Service
(translation on pages 92–93).

with the hundreds of suits, the silk underwear, the socks from Paris, and the shoes from Rome. I indulged in my unreal world, feeling special.

While the siesta lasted, I thought as much as possible about nothing at all. I preferred not to torture myself with self-doubt, and instead accepted my fate. My inner distance from everything was soothing. Anyway, it made no sense to worry all the time, when there was no way to change my situation.

On the evening of March 4, 1988, Uday and the Bulldog came into my room. At first I didn't notice them, because the door was open and I was absorbed in a video of martial arts — samurais wielding swords, kung-fu fighters shadow-boxing. Uday loved these videos, and I liked them too. They had no real plot, but something was always happening, more or less a reflection of my present life.

While the Bulldog remained standing, Uday sat in a chair and blurted in his hectic, hysterical manner, "Latif, the opportunity is perfect. We're going to test you."

"When?"

"The day after tomorrow, late afternoon, in the People's Stadium."

The occasion was a soccer game between two Iraqi teams, and attendance was expected to exceed fifty thousand. Since the president's family had its own box, far removed from the common folk, the normal spectators would glimpse me only from a considerable distance. Any mistakes I made wouldn't mean a lot.

"Latif, this is your first major appearance. Concentrate. Everything that happens that day will decide the future."

Should I fail, I was likely a dead man; and if everything came off without hitch, then my existence as a fidai could actually begin.

After Uday left, I didn't see him again until March 6. But that afternoon I was ready. I was completely calm, just as

calm as I was when they brought me to his lordship Saddam
Hussein.

Yassem al-Helou, Uday's personal adviser on the proper
way to dress, was dispatched to assist me. Yassem had been
part of the Clan for years. He came from a poor family in
Baghdad, was trained as a tailor, and most likely was a homo-
sexual. His movements were feminine, his intonation soft
and deliberate, and he always smelled of heavy, cloying cologne.

Uday never had any taste as far as clothing was concerned. "He ran around like a simple peasant boy," sniped
Yassem, his voice betraying outrage. "He always chose colors
that didn't match." Yassem amused me, particularly the way
he gesticulated with his hands. When he complained of
Uday's inadequacies with clothes, he threw open the wardrobe, stared with dismay at the dozens of suits, and asked
breathlessly, with a sweeping motion of his hand, "What am I
supposed to dress the young gentleman in this time?"

Yassem decided, and Uday obeyed. Everything stylish
and tasteful in Uday's wardrobe had been purchased by
Yassem, who accompanied him whenever Uday flew to London, Paris, Rome, or Milan for a weekend of pleasure. Always
present, Yassem took care of all of Uday's wants or needs in
the way of clothing: shoes, underwear, shirts, or suits. Uday
normally changed suits four times a day. For conferences or
conversations in the club, he would even take Yassem to his
office to be his personal dresser.

Yassem tendered a light-colored suit, a striped shirt, and
a burgundy tie, asking me excitedly why Ismail wasn't with
us. Ismail al-Azami was Uday's private hairdresser. He was
part of the inventory, like Yassem, and cut Uday's hair every
ten days. Uday had rewarded him with three salons, and he
was considered *the* hairdresser in the Iraqi capital. It was
Ismail who had cut my hair and beard before I went to meet
the president.

I dressed carefully, and Yassem straightened my tie. I

tried on my glasses. They were dirty; I wiped them with a towel lying on the bed. I felt like an actor who has learned his role until he can study no more. I felt no stage fright. The tension rose only when Azzam and the other bodyguards came to get me.

Our convoy consisted of more than ten cars. This time I drove my Mercedes myself. We rushed clean through Baghdad on the Street of the Palestinians, one of the most impressive boulevards in the capital, straight as an arrow, with two lanes in both directions and grandstands on either side. This was where parades and ceremonies in honor of the party took place.

Traffic rules meant nothing to us. Ordinary vehicles had to move over and wait humbly at the side of the road, for a convoy from the president's palace always took priority. Munem Hammed sat beside me. He asked several times how I felt, and the closer we got to the stadium the stronger the tingle of anticipation in my stomach became. "So you *are* nervous, Latif," he pronounced as we drove to the stadium entrance.

"Nothing can go wrong," he said to calm me. I opened the door. He reminded me, "Uday, the cigars," and grinned. I grinned back, took the silver box with the Monte Cristo No. 6s, put it in my jacket pocket, and climbed out. While the bodyguards secured the way, I straightened my jacket and tie and put on my Ray-Bans. Few people were in the parking lot, since the game was about to start in a few minutes, but my heart began to race nonetheless. I felt it pump, felt it in each fiber of my body. My pulse rate had to be higher than 130, but I tried not to let my excitement show.

My bodyguards hustled me up to the presidential box. It was located in section A on the long side of the stadium, and furnished with upholstered chairs, Astroturf on the floor, Iraqi flags, and the obligatory, larger-than-life portrait of the president. I took a seat in the front row; next to me sat my bodyguards. The fifty thousand spectators greeted my appearance with applause. This wasn't a euphoric outbreak of affection. They applauded because they had to; it was their duty when a member of the president's family took his place in the box of honor.

The game began. I lit my first Monte Cristo and smoked just as I had learned in training. I took care in every detail, moved my hand the way Uday moved his, even cut the tip of the cigar with a silver cigar cutter as he did, which was a senseless piece of acting since my audience was much too far away to appreciate such trivia. For the people in the stadium, I *was* Uday Saddam Hussein, the president's son.

I concentrated so much on my job that I missed the game completely. By the end of the first half the score was tied at zero. The camera of Iraqi state television, which was broadcasting the game, panned several times over the box of honor. I was never filmed close up from the front, or in profile. Uday's media experts had instructed the cameramen accordingly, and Uday had assured me several times that I wouldn't have to worry about the camera giving me away.

The goals came in the second half, but I'd be lying if I claimed to know who shot them. After the game, Munem Hammed deposited eleven burgundy velvet cases in my hand. "Do your best, Latif, and believe that God is with you," he said, encouragingly. I was supposed to award the medal cases to the members of the winning team. I got up self-importantly, waved twice to the public, and my bodyguards escorted me down to the playing field. They kept so close to each other that I could hardly see what was around me.

Besides, I was too excited to pay attention to stray details. I was focusing only on what I had to do: pass out the cases, shake hands, nod approvingly. Not a word, not a syllable, just as I'd been told. A bodyguard handed me one of the cases, I took it, gave it to a player. A firm handshake, then the next one. None of the players dared to ask me a question, and I was careful to avoid direct eye contact with all of them, even though it couldn't matter since I was wearing my sunglasses and they couldn't see my eyes anyway.

It took an eternity to finish walking past the line of players. Then I swung around briefly and waved to the remnants of the crowd still left in the stadium. We hurried back to the cars, then raced madly back to Project No. 7.

Munem Hammed told me I was good, very good, which put me at ease. I had no idea whether I was really convincing. I felt unsure of myself, unable to judge the quality of my performance. It was like meeting a woman. You look at her, she looks back, and you don't know whether her glance was only friendly or meant something more.

I have to conquer this insecurity, I told myself. It didn't matter whether my bodyguards considered me good or not. What I had to acquire was the overbearing, dictatorial arrogance that Uday evinced so well. I must be convincingly arrogant, then I would be for real. Everything else was secondary. The main thing was to remain focused as I worked toward my goal of becoming Uday Saddam Hussein.

Uday was waiting for me at the swimming pool. He held two cognac snifters in his hands, rushed toward me, and kissed me on the mouth.

"I watched you on television," he gushed. "You carried out your tasks one hundred percent. It was perfect. Nobody noticed a thing, the people thought you were me. All of them. The players too."

He took me by the arm, shoved a cognac snifter into my hand, and said, "Drink something. We'll go through the videos tomorrow."

They woke me at eight the next morning. I drank a quick coffee without milk, then Munem Hammed called me into Uday's study. For the first time we didn't repair to the video room to review the tapes made the day before, but came here instead. And truly, everything looked faultless. Me in the box of honor, waving to the crowd, distributing the gifts. Uday repeated "perfect" at least thirty times. He was proud of me, and I felt elated, relieved. The months of training, the self-doubt accompanied by Uday's frequent fits of rage, all that was suddenly erased, and only one thought remained: Latif Yahia didn't exist anymore.

I couldn't help but think of my parents. They hadn't heard from me for more than six months and didn't know where I was, what I was doing, or how I was doing. They didn't even know whether I was still alive. I could have fallen on the battlefield or been taken prisoner by the Iranians. They didn't know. At least, on the front, I used to write them a brief letter every week or so, or called from headquarters when I had the chance. But now, no letter, no call, nothing.

I was concerned about my mother. Worries about her health gnawed at me. I was twenty-four years old and an officer in the Iraqi army, but my parents remained holy for me, and my mother was a goddess. She loved me and I loved her, and she had the right to know what her oldest child was up to, how he was faring.

I intended to discuss this with Uday, but not now. It was still too soon. On the other hand, I thought now would be as good a time as any, given his euphoria about my stadium performance. I finally decided not to make demands for the moment. I wanted to enjoy my first victory, and it wouldn't help to alienate him.

Uday is a man of pleasure. He normally slept until 10:30 A.M. His bodyguards had to stay awake all night and watch over him. They mostly lounged around the pool next to the bar, cleaning their weapons and discussing trivial things. Eventually I got to know them all.

Their leader was Azzam al-Tikriti. Azzam was only two years older than Uday. I knew him from school, where he had always been a poor student. Once — it was after my performance at the People's Stadium — when we were sitting together next to the pool and drinking, he confided after a few glasses that he had faked his school records. The principal had found out and reported him to the Teachers' Commission. Though he was sixteen at the time, the commission showed no mercy and threw him in jail for six months. He left school without finishing.

He found his way to Uday through Dabi al-Masihi, a socialite. Dabi was always the life of the party whenever he showed up in the al-Alvia Club. He had a persuasive, appealing way about him, was educated, sensitive, handsome, and funny. Graced with a fascinatingly perfect face and the clearest and lightest complexion I'd ever seen in a man, Dabi was Uday's friend and knew Azzam too. When he introduced them to each other, Uday spontaneously declared Azzam his best friend and companion.

Dabi disappeared a few months later, after he approached one of Uday's women at a party. For that transgression, Uday made sure he was thrown out of the al-Alvia Club and ostracized by Baghdad's finest from then on.

As we sat beside the pool, I asked Azzam what had happened to Dabi. He hung his head, avoided my gaze, and said only, "I saw him not long ago, and he looked terrible. I don't know what they did to him."

Uday's second close confidant among his bodyguards was Ahmad Suleiman. Sinewy and of average height, Ahmad was college-educated and a trained karate teacher. A natural charmer, he could get along easily with anyone and was particularly smooth approaching girls. If Uday wanted to get to know a woman, he would send Ahmad. Consequently, Ahmad was not only Uday's bodyguard but his chief procurer. He exploited this position shamelessly and was in fact a brutal rapist and murderer, something I was to discover only later.

Salam al-Aoussi was Uday's stool pigeon, a walking notebook. He spied on Uday's friends and informed him of their activities. A wrong word, an indiscreet comment, and you'd end up in Salam's notebook, which was as good as an indictment. Salam was a slimy creature whose athletic build concealed a basic vileness.

Muajed Fadel was called the Animal. He had a university degree but no scruples, and enjoyed carrying out rapes on Uday's orders.

Saadoum al-Tikriti was a torture specialist. He too boasted a university degree. The unanswered question was, from which university? Saadoum was completely devoid of feelings and didn't hesitate to commit any crime.

Namir al-Tikriti was responsible for organizing parties. A direct relation of Uday's, he was an expert master of ceremonies with a talent for decorations and music, who made a feast of every party.

Maksud al-Tikriti was the social secretary who administered Uday's calendar, scheduled his appointments, and decided which girls got his private telephone number and which ones didn't.

The list of Uday's intimates was much longer than this, and read like a directory of Baghdad's underworld. Uday loved dark, impenetrable types and was attracted to deviants of all sorts — the worse, the more extreme, the more perverse, the better. After spending a few months at his side, I began to understand that even if he weren't in danger of being assassinated, he would never be able to live a halfway normal life. And this danger was constant, for the number of his enemies was legion.

Yet slowly I came to realize why they had chosen to recruit me at this particular time, why they were so eager to find and train a double as quickly as possible before the spring of 1988.

The Clan knew months in advance that a crime of historic proportions would be committed then, an act of genocide akin to the mass murder of the Jews in World War II. Saddam was planning something similar: the use of mustard gas against his own people.

7

THE FEAR

OF ASSASSINATION

ALI Hassan al-Majid looked like a near copy of Saddam
Hussein. He was about the same height and build, with only a
slightly more prominent belly, and wore the same mustache
and haircut. The only major difference was that he always
appeared in uniform. Like Saddam, who was a cousin of his,
al-Majid came from the Tikrit region. In the 1970s he served
as a noncommissioned officer in the army of President
Ahmad Hasan al-Bakr. His particular characteristic as a soldier was that he was a butcher of almost indescribable brutality. He showed no scruples, particularly against Kurds.

The Kurds' fight for independence isn't confined to
Iraq. The Kurdish people are scattered across several
countries — Turkey, Iran, Syria, and parts of the former Soviet republics, as well as Iraq — and have struggled over
decades and across international borders to establish their
own state.

Since the regime of President Ahmad Hasan al-Bakr, the
Kurdish freedom fighters, the Pesh Mergas, had been waging
a bitter war against the Iraqi government. They were excellent
fighters. *Pesh Merga* means "to look death directly into the
eyes." Their battalions were hidden in the caves of the Makok
Mountains in northern Iraq and supplied mostly by Iran.
Their weapons came almost exclusively from the arsenals of

the Iranian army. From their strongholds they launched attacks on the oilfields of Iraqi Kurdistan, in the border region of Turkey, Iran, and Syria.

Though the Baghdad government tried every conceivable means to subdue the rebels, deploying MiG fighterbombers, combat helicopters, and several infantry divisions, they hardly made a dent.

In the 1970s, when Ali Hassan al-Majid was participating in the war against the Kurds, he was taken prisoner during an attack by Iraqi infantry. He should have been executed immediately, but the Kurdish leadership waited too long. He bribed a prison guard, promising him a dream career in Baghdad and bragging about his close relationship with Saddam Hussein, who was at that time still Iraq's vice president. The corrupt guard freed him and escorted him to Baghdad. Instead of rewarding the guard, al-Majid killed him.

The escape and murder made headlines. Ali Hassan al-Majid was commissioned as an officer and ascended rapidly in the party hierarchy. Saddam Hussein supported his cousin's quick rise, prizing the man's utter lack of scruples.

That was in 1972, at the time when the struggle for power between President al-Bakr and Saddam Hussein, the ambitious people's hero, first became evident. When al-Bakr had become only a figurehead, Saddam Hussein made treaties. In 1975 he signed a treaty with the Persian shah, Reza Pahlavi, temporarily resolving the contentious matter of navigation rights on the Shatt al-Arab. Baghdad renounced its claims to the left bank of the waterway. In exchange, Tehran's ruler pledged no longer to support the Kurdish separatists.

With that deal, Saddam had a free hand to strike at the Kurds, who represented about twenty percent of Iraq's population. This was al-Majid's great moment. His troops killed thousands, and hundreds of thousands were resettled. Yet, despite the carnage, Saddam Hussein failed to bring peace to Kurdistan, and the conflict continued.

After this first wave of killings, Saddam sicced his blood-

hound, al-Majid, on the south of the country, a region inhab-
ited by Iraqi Shi'ites and members of the Iranian opposition
who had taken asylum among their coreligionists. The
Shi'ites vigorously opposed the godless society of the Ba'ath-
ists in Baghdad and formed a protest movement, headed by
the ayatollah Baqir al-Sadr.

One of Ayatollah al-Sadr's guests was the ayatollah
Ruholla Khomeini, who had been expelled from Iran under
Shah Reza Pahlavi and granted asylum by Iraq. Khomeini
lived in the holy city of Najaf for fourteen years, under constant surveillance by the security service and prohibited from
spreading his fundamentalist teachings within the country.

In 1978, amid growing Shi'ite unrest, Saddam Hussein
concluded a second treaty with the shah, in which he agreed
to stop granting asylum to Iranian dissidents. From one day
to the next, he had all Iranians, including Ayatollah Khomeini, expelled from Iraq. The ayatollah was literally beaten
out of the country. This humiliation became the basis for the
burning hatred that Khomeini bore Saddam Hussein until
the day of his death.

Khomeini went to Paris to prepare for the fall of the
shah's regime from there. He came to power in February
1979 as the supreme leader of the Iranian revolution, and
turned Iran into an Islamic dictatorship.

On Saddam's orders (Saddam is a Sunni), al-Majid ran
amok in Najaf. He threw Baqir al-Sadr, now leader of the
Iranian-influenced Dawa party, and the ayatollah's two sisters
into prison. Al-Majid strangled the ayatollah to death; the
women were hanged. The official charge against Baqir al-
Sadr was insurrection and the attempted assassination of
Saddam Hussein. The Dawa party was banned, its supporters
threatened with the death penalty. Al-Majid had Shi'ites by
the hundreds executed. Twenty thousand fled to Iran.

As all this was happening, Saddam Hussein loosed a
political and psychological offensive with the goal of stirring
up the whole Arab world against Iran. At each summit

conference, he warned that the complacent Sunnis risked being swept away by fanatical Shi'ites. "Iran and the Ayatollah Khomeini are a scourge of mankind," Saddam repeated over and over, and western leaders believed him and lent him support.

Saddam unleashed war on his mortal enemy, Khomeini, when he invaded Iran on September 22, 1980. Six Iraqi divisions, with 400,000 men, crossed the border on an eight-hundred-mile front. It was supposed to be a Blitzkrieg, but turned out to have been fatally ill-conceived.

The war was now in its eighth year, and although Saddam Hussein assured us incessantly that we were going to win, nobody believed him anymore — particularly since battles were breaking out in the north once more. Iraqi Kurds, who had gone to ground in Iran, were launching attack after attack from their safe haven.

On March 16, 1988, not quite two weeks after my first public appearance as his son's double, Saddam Hussein dispatched al-Majid to Kurdistan with a fiendish plan. By this time, al-Majid was Iraq's interior minister and a powerful, influential man. He had suggested to Saddam that poison gas be used to end the Kurd's rebellion with one blow. He now produced a masterpiece of inhumanity, in which he had mustard gas sprayed on Kurdish civilians from helicopters flying little more than thirty feet above the ground.

Five thousand people died in the attack on the town of Halabja alone. Women, children, old people — nobody had a chance. They died in agony. Everything perished within a radius of a couple of miles: trees, plants, animals, humans. Ten thousand people were wounded. To this brutal campaign, al-Majid owed his macabre nickname. Henceforth, he became known as the Chemist.

No one in Project No. 7 talked about the poison gas attack on Halabja, although everyone knew about it, because images of its horrible effects were broadcast several times in the main news program. I, too, remained silent, for my grandparents came from northern Iraq. Uday was aware of this. He hated the Pesh Mergas, denouncing them as a wild, murderous mountain people, stirred up by Israel and Iran. "They're all misguided murderers," he said, invoking his standard argument. "They should be exterminated."

Yet, despite my grandparents, I was accepted by Uday. I had been born in Baghdad, like hundreds of thousands of other Kurds. We Baghdad Kurds were viewed as fully integrated Iraqis, loyal to Saddam Hussein's regime. Several Kurds were even members of the government.

The whole world expressed outrage over Iraq's use of poison gas. Voices were raised even in Saddam's inner circle, with some branding him a criminal. Police chief Feisal Barat was the most outspoken critic. He publicly protested the atrocity to Interior Minister al-Majid. The police chief was liquidated, along with twenty-eight of his associates.

Saddam Hussein personally executed another critic, Health Minister Rijad Ibrahim, who condemned the use of poison gas both against the Kurds and in the Iran-Iraq war. In parliament, Ibrahim demanded Saddam's resignation. Saddam reacted characteristically: he pulled out his pistol, grabbed Ibrahim by the hair, and killed him with a shot through the mouth. Thus ended the cabinet discussion — along with criticism of Saddam.

A national opposition movement was formed nonetheless. The Kurds in the north, and the underground fighters of the Shi'ite Dawa party in the south, jointly declared war on the regime. Dozens of assassination attempts followed, but Saddam survived them all. None of this ever reached the public.

Only one thing was noticeable. Saddam used to seek out the people. He'd drive to the smallest village, visit ordinary family homes, encourage his subjects. He was always accompanied by hundreds of bodyguards, who took over whole sections of a city hours before his arrival and slowed traffic to a crawl. But he showed himself to the people. Such "spontaneous meetings" became increasingly rare and finally stopped altogether.

In the final years before they ended, Saddam always sent his doubles rather than go himself, a policy that proved well founded. Dawa terrorists assassinated his first fidai in an attack shortly before I was engaged to serve as Uday's.

The use of fidais was plainly much more than Uday's way of having fun or proving himself to his father. It was a matter of survival for the president's son, because an attack could come anytime, anywhere. Uday knew this, and I became increasingly conscious of it following the poison gas attack on Halabja. Until then, I was seduced by the life of a playboy, but the events of the last few days threw an urgent and darker light on everything.

I didn't have a lot of time to reflect. The Saddam family needed public appearances. Saddam Hussein's second double, Faoaz al-Emari, completed one appearance after the other. I would see him performing as Saddam on television, and Munem Hammed always smiled when he spotted him. Faoaz bore an uncanny resemblance to the president, but those in the know recognized him.

My next appearance had already been planned. It was supposed to take place on April 28, 1988, and promised to be a much more difficult assignment than the visit to the soccer game. Munem Hammed and Uday were sending me to the front. To the south. To the Fourth Division.

April 28 is Saddam's birthday, an event that's celebrated nationwide. The Fourth Division was deployed south of Basra, the center of the Shi'ite Dawa movement. The plan was to have me flown in by helicopter with my bodyguards, land at headquarters, get out, shake hands with the commander and his officers, and briefly discuss the situation.

Yassem, the personal tailor, brought me Uday's black officer's uniform, a pistol, and a belt. Our departure was scheduled for 10:00 A.M., and everything went smoothly. The flight from Saddam's private airport to the headquarters of the Fourth Division lasted two hours. We landed on the drill square, where several companies were waiting in formation. In front of them stood the commander and several of his officers. First to climb out of the helicopter were Munem Hammed, Captain Siad Hassan Hashem al-Nassiri, and Captain Saadi Daham Hasaa al-Nassiri, then came my bodyguards, then I.

I hurried toward the commander, Munem Hammed introduced me, and we inspected the honor guard with appropriate gravity. Then came the photographers. The cameraman filming the scene for television was one of Munem Hammed's crew. We were photographed for more than ten minutes, and the conversation between me and the commander during that time was completely meaningless. I inquired about the situation on the front; the commander recited the situation in his best military voice, and assured me how happy he was at my presence, which gave him the opportunity to congratulate the great leader Saddam Hussein on his birthday. I'm sure the commander had never seen either Saddam Hussein or Uday in person.

For my part, I concentrated on not making any mistakes while speaking. Saadi Daham Hasaa al-Nassiri answered all political and strategic questions.

We stayed at the military base for two hours, toasting the health of our leader, and then the helicopter took off again at 2:30 P.M. When we got back to Baghdad, Uday's reaction was just as euphoric as after the first time: "Magnificent." He inundated me with expressions of gratitude after watching the video of my performance.

"One hundred percent again," he lauded.

One event followed another after this appearance. Delegations representing athletic associations from various Arab states were due to arrive in Baghdad for a conference beginning May 7. They were scheduled to remain for several days, but Uday was planning a trip to Europe just at that time, and he didn't want to postpone it for any reason.

He devised a risky plan, in which I was to meet the delegations at the airport, welcome them, then bring them to the hotel where the meeting would take place. Uday himself would open the conference and participate in the discussions for two days. I was to bid the delegates good-bye on the final day.

May 7, 1988, late morning. I waited with my bodyguards in the airport reception lounge until the aircraft with the delegations landed. Directors of athletic associations from Saudi Arabia, Kuwait, and Bahrain flowed in. As we greeted one another, none of the delegates seemed to notice anything unusual, although the Kuwaiti representative confused me momentarily. After I shook his hand and bid him welcome, he said he brought me greetings from my friend Fahd, and asked if he should transmit my greetings to him.

I had no idea who Fahd was, and didn't even know that Uday had a Kuwaiti friend. Munem Hammed was able to explain only when we were back in the car. "Uday has known him for a long time," Munem said. "Fahd al-Ahmed al-Sabah is the brother of the Kuwaiti emir. Fahd is also vice president of the FIFA, the international soccer association, and chairman of the Kuwaiti Olympic Committee and thus a colleague of Uday, as well as president of the Kuwaiti Soccer Association."

I led the group to the Olympic Club quarters, then disappeared through a back door, and Uday took over. None of the delegates noticed a thing. Uday took his leave again after lunch. I met him in a side room for a moment, where he complained how much these people bored him. After that, I escorted the delegates to the conference venue in Baghdad, the Ashtar Sheraton Hotel.

Uday tended to the group again that evening, but by the next day, May 8, he wanted to fly to Europe earlier than planned. The mood was gloomy. Munem Hammed tried to convince him this was crazy, but Uday remained adamant, and his instructions were clear: "Let Latif do it, and if something goes wrong, throw him to the dogs."

Another major event was also supposed to take place at that time, in addition to the conference in which Uday was allegedly participating. The Iraqi national soccer team was to play an exhibition game against a European team on May 9. The Europeans were to arrive in Baghdad in the afternoon of May 8. The result was pure chaos. The only ones who didn't lose their cool were my officers.

Uday was excused from the conference for reasons I wasn't privy to. I had to return to the airport to greet the Europeans — an easy job for me, because of course the athletes had no idea what Uday Saddam Hussein looked like. They too were lodged at the Sheraton. There was a lot of stress and running about, but all went according to plan.

Nobody seemed to notice anything out of the ordinary. Journalists wrote enthusiastic articles about Uday and his appearances, with the most detailed stories being published in the *Al-Baas-al-Riyadi* and the *Babel.* These were Uday's newspapers, given to him by his father, and they were the only media not directly subordinate to the Minister of Information.

The international exhibition game was played the following day at 4:00 P.M. in the People's Stadium. The conference participants shared my box. The spectators cheered our team on frenetically, but the Iraqis lost. A great shame! How could that happen? Iraqi teams were not supposed to lose!

I again distributed gifts to the players nonetheless, and invited the athletes of both teams to a formal dinner at the Sheraton. I was at the dinner only briefly with my hangers-on. Nothing untoward happened, no incidents my companions would have to report. The foreign players and the delegations stayed until the next day, and when I bid them good-bye at the airport, I actually felt pretty good. I told myself, "Uday's going to be pleased with me when he gets back from his holidays."

Uday was in Geneva, Switzerland. Geneva was his favorite place. He flew there regularly, as did the rest of the dictator's family. Only Saddam Hussein avoided such social excursions, which in his case would have entailed all sorts of complications. In addition, he was well known in Europe, whereas the average European wouldn't recognize members of his family.

When in Geneva, Uday always stayed with his uncle, Barzan al-Tikriti. Barzan al-Tikriti was one of Saddam Hussein's half-brothers, and had an enviable career behind him. He had started off as an army officer and eventually became head of the secret service, the Mukhabarat, inviting PLO terrorist Abu Nidal to Iraq several times and appearing with him publicly. Yet his true duties consisted of administering the unbelievable wealth of the Saddam clan. He was thus known in Iraq as "the secret finance minister."

After being replaced as the head of the Mukhabarat, Barzan al-Tikriti was sent to Geneva as the permanent Iraqi representative to the United Nations. But once again his real task lay elsewhere: the transfer of Saddam's funds from Iraq to Switzerland, as well as the purchase of all weapons systems for Iraq. Barzan was the key figure in the procurement of nuclear equipment. "International businesses are pounding on his door" was the mantra Uday repeated before his departure.

Uday returned on May 18 in a bad mood, and came directly to Project No. 7, accompanied by Milad, a flight attendant. It didn't take me long to find out from his bodyguards why Uday was so angry. He had lost a lot of money at a casino.

There are no casinos in Switzerland, so he went to a neighboring country. With him were his bodyguards and friends, Muajed Aani, Said Kammuneh, Ahmad Kola, and Dureid Ghannaoui, as well as the pilot, the copilot, the technician in charge of his private jet, and the stewardesses, including Milad. Uday had slept with Milad several times, and now he took her with him as the chief cabin attendant on all his trips to Europe. She was tall and had long brown hair, a generous mouth with large lips, and a complexion so light and delicate that you could see the tracing of blood vessels.

Uncle Barzan al-Tikriti went along too.

Uday's pockets were stuffed with dollars — over one million, according to the bodyguards — because he loved games of chance: "You can win a lot only with high stakes," he always said. He won, too, sometimes — but not this time.

Other numbers came up, no matter which combination he chose. Uday had the croupiers replaced, and even reserved a whole table for himself. The highest stake rule was waived for him, meaning he could bet more than other players. The higher the stakes, the more Uday sank into a trancelike state.

I've seen him in this state. He gets hectic-looking red blotches all over his face, his gaze turns into a dull stare, minor things make him furious. He just can't deal with something going against his will. He can't have anyone opposing him, or refusing to recognize his will as supreme law.

Roulette balls aren't impressed, however. Neither are the croupiers, with their automatic smiles. They gathered his chips elegantly from the table, and Uday finally began writing checks.

Barzan al-Tikriti tried to stop him, but Uday wouldn't listen, because he was convinced that he'd win back the money he lost. He seemed intoxicated with gambling, drank one cognac after the other, and finally ended up losing more than four million dollars. I didn't want to believe it, but all who were there swore to it.

Uncle Barzan stopped endorsing checks and left the casino, which enraged Uday even more. Another player, also from Iraq, then made him the following offer: The man had a stake in the casino, and his suggestion was, "I'll lend you another million, but then Milad belongs to me for the night."

Uday glanced briefly at Milad, nodded, and Milad knew what was expected of her. That was the first time Uday acted as a pimp. The son of the president, and the president of the Iraqi Olympic Committee, had sold a woman in exchange for a betting stake from a friend. A scandal.

He also lost this million.

He literally dragged Milad back from the airport after the return flight and brought her to his study. The door remained open, allowing everybody to hear him screaming hysterically at her, "What did my friend do with you? Say something!"

Milad said nothing. Uday beat her. We heard the slapping sounds all the way to the pool.

"What? Tell me, what?"

Milad started crying. Uday beat her again, and she screamed at him, "He told me you're conceited and arrogant. He bought me to teach you a lesson. Yes, that's what he said. I'm supposed to tell you that!"

Uday had her taken away, and we all knew we'd never see her again.

Then it was my turn. When he learned that the Iraqi team had lost, he beat me, ignoring my bland comment that there would always be winners and losers, and ordered Azzam to take me away. They brought me to a cell at headquarters, where I was kept for almost two weeks. It was bigger than the horror chamber they had thrown me in before I agreed to become a fidai. The food was okay, and the guards treated me well.

On the fifteenth day, they came to collect me, but instead of taking me to Project No. 7, they brought me to the al-Hayat, a ten-story modern building within the palace grounds. It was administered by the security services, and I was assigned a kind of office apartment there: a living room with a desk, a side room with a toilet, a bathroom. My bed was in the living room.

Eventually, Uday visited me in my apartment. He was

outwardly friendly, calm, and acted superior as always. Then he came so close I could feel his hot breath. He took off his glasses, drilled me with a stare, and hissed, "Don't ever involve yourself in my affairs again. Your task is to obey me, not to have discussions with me."

8

THE EXCESSES

JUNE 18, a Monday. Uday called to let me know he was going to have me picked up that evening. I should shave my beard, leaving only the mustache, and put on a standard bodyguard's uniform. Then he hung up. Although he was fairly brusque, his voice sounded friendly.

Our differences were forgotten. He had even secured a new apartment for me. This one was on the palace grounds too, in the Mujamaa al-Qadisiya, a house used by the security services. The apartment was designed to impress, with a large living room, an office, a room for receiving visitors, and various other rooms. I also had servants.

My birthday had come and gone four days earlier, on June 14, but I didn't celebrate it. What was there to celebrate? I stayed alone in the apartment (the servants had the night off) and paced around with long strides, thinking of my parents, who had always considered this day special.

My birthday could have been a great party, I lamented to myself. *We could have rented a banquet hall in a hotel, with music and singers and dancers. It would have been perfect. All my friends would have been there.*

This year, June 14 fell on a Thursday, which by itself is a special day in Iraq. Most hotels and nightclubs stay open all night because Friday is a holiday, the Islamic Sunday.

Yet, as I dreamed on, the nagging doubts, the senseless questions about my present situation returned: Would they really have come? They hadn't heard a thing from me for months. Were they still thinking of me at all? By now every one of them had to know I was missing. I drowned this growing self-pity in whiskey, which at least cleared my head of despair.

So I was grateful when Uday asked me over. I could easily imagine what was in store for the evening in Project No. 7, although Uday hadn't said. Not only could I imagine, I knew. I'd gotten to know Uday and his eccentricities well enough by now. Besides, the preparations of the past few days had been impossible to ignore.

Namir al-Tikriti had thoroughly redecorated Project No. 7. He had champagne delivered by the case and forced the cook to work overtime, while Hilal al-Aki, a relative who always collaborated with Namir al-Tikriti when something major was afoot, shuttled back and forth between the palace and Project No. 7, bringing whatever was needed.

Unlike me, Uday had every means to celebrate his twenty-fourth birthday. For years he had turned June 18 into a holiday, and his parties were always a hot source for gossip in Baghdad. The excesses they gave rise to couldn't be kept quiet, since the celebrations usually took place in one of the big downtown hotels.

But not only his birthday parties had gotten more and more out of hand. Uday's life was actually one big excess, a constant aberration in the search for his true self, made possible by his enormous financial resources. Uday had everything: money, power, influence. His world consisted of decadence, heedlessness, and sin. For him there were no sexual morals, but only the pursuit of pleasure.

His cohorts would always cover for Uday whenever he went too far. And when his mistakes could no longer be covered up, he was shielded by the powerful hand of his father or mother.

I'd thought a lot over the past few days about why he had turned into the misfit son, why he seemed bent on absorbing life like a drug, not realizing he was being overwhelmed by his own opportunities.

He had been a zero in school, and he knew it. He knew that the teachers thought little of him and that he got good marks only because he was the son of Saddam Hussein. He probably didn't understand the implications of his behavior at the time. He was a child, and children tend to glorify their parents. Uday glorified his father by acting like him and ordering his subjects, the teachers, around. He did no homework, came and went as he wished. He brought his girlfriend to class, his bodyguards wrote his dictations, private tutors prepared his homework. He wanted to prove that he was in a position to dominate the teachers.

At age fourteen he sped around the schoolyard in his Porsche. At fifteen he acquired the first of his "colleagues" who procured girls for him. At sixteen he fired salvos with his Kalashnikov wildly into the air at the al-Alvia Club and everybody applauded, most likely his father among them.

I carefully shaved off my neatly trimmed beard and observed myself at length in the mirror. I opened my mouth wide and inspected my new teeth. I'd adapted well to them by now, and they didn't bother me. They were mine; my jaws had adjusted to the overbite. While I went on shaving, my thoughts lingered on Uday's brutish drive to excess, on his thirst for pleasure.

His lifestyle had changed little over the past few years. Every day at around 2:00 P.M., after lunching at either Project No. 7 or one of the Baghdad clubs, he and his bodyguards would set off on what they called "the grand tour." The convoy rolled from one coffeehouse to the other, checking them out. Then the group continued on to the university and the girls' schools. Once there, Uday would swing back and forth, like a policeman on patrol. He honked the horn and stopped the car when he saw a girl he liked, drove behind her on the sidewalk, and pursued her until she responded. If she refused his advances, it was the turn of one of his teams, specially hired for pickups. If they failed, he simply had her abducted.

He needed sex almost every afternoon. Sometimes they brought him three or four girls at once. He would either pick one and go to bed with her, kicking the others out, or else keep them all and coerce them into group sex.

Uday would start drinking during the early evening, normally beer, cognac, and whiskey. He wasn't the type to guzzle alcohol; he drank for pleasure. Still, there were few nights when he went to bed sober.

He would call dozens of girls on the phone before getting ready to go out. Then he'd spend an eternity thinking about what he should wear. In the end, he normally accepted whatever Yassem had chosen for him, but only after lively discussions between the two of them.

Putting on accessories also took a long time. Uday had hundreds of watches and countless rings and gold chains. His jewelry cases were opulent beyond belief.

Although he possessed almost every material thing one could want, Uday remained envious of others. He would have his bodyguards eject anyone better or more extravagantly dressed than he was. If someone sported a more exclusive Rolex, he would covet it. He would lose self-control at the sight of someone driving a fancier car.

As a consequence, everyone in the Taliyat al-Daravic, al-Said, al-Savarek, and al-Alvia clubs took extreme care not to come into conflict with him. All who could avoided him. It was the same at the Baghdad hotels. There was not one porter, barman, or nightclub manager who didn't know him. All rules were suspended when he and his horde invaded an establishment like a ravenous swarm of locusts.

He usually showed up with eight to ten women, all of whom had to walk behind him when he entered a hotel. His favorites were the Babel Obri, the al-Rashid, and the al-Meridian. Everyone present was required to stand and greet him when he came in. The same was true in halls, restaurants, bars, and ballrooms.

Uday considered it an affront for any man to dare to dance in his presence. He had the dancer removed by his bodyguards, beaten, and, in the worst cases, imprisoned for insulting the president. He wanted the floor for himself and his girls. He would start by having the girls dance alone, observing them licentiously and occasionally screaming vulgarities at them. If he was in a really good mood, he would grab his revolver and fire at the ceiling, the chandelier, or the paneling on the walls.

Sometimes he even fired at the personnel, especially if they were Egyptian guest workers, of whom there were thousands in Baghdad. Uday hated them; he considered them worse than the plague.

These binges obviously made him feel strong and powerful. He acted as if he had something to prove. Whom did he want to impress so much with his self-destructive lifestyle? Who else but his omnipotent father, who had others honor him as if he were a god, and whose wealth and power had erected eighty-three palaces across the land?

It must have driven Uday absolutely crazy to go speeding around the country in his Ferrari and encounter a mural, a statue, or some other heroic representation of his father on every street corner. Or to turn on the television and hear the newscaster gush, "Saddam, the president, the supreme commander, the head of the National Command Council, the Hero of al-Qadisiya, the Knight of the Arab Nation, Alfari al-Mighvar — the fierce and courageous knight. Saddam, direct descendant of the Prophet. Saddam, the noble warrior, from the family that gave issue to Imam al-Hussein, the Ancestor, the son of Imam Ali Ibn Abi Talib."

As the president's first son, Uday was born into a world so unreal, so absurd, that a child couldn't hope to understand what was going on around him and in him, or to develop in any normal way. School was a joke, his study of architecture likewise. He slipped quickly through phases that form other children. He didn't endure them long enough for them to leave their mark. He finished his studies in record time with excellent marks, although he never took one exam, and in his architecture courses in college never designed one house. He probably doesn't even know that a house needs a foundation.

I remember the day when all the important professors of Baghdad's universities were invited to a closed ceremony in the main auditorium. We students weren't invited, out of fear of a possible scandal. For, at age twenty-three, Uday was being named honorary director of the university. The president's son had financed the construction of the Saddam Technical University — not from his own pocket, of course. The Iraqi people paid for the construction. But officially it was "Mr. Uday Saddam Hussein" who had donated the needed millions.

Not only was he appointed honorary director of Saddam Technical University, but one of the professors, Mazen Abd al-Hamid, suggested also making Uday Saddam the university's president. The suggestion was approved unanimously. A student who couldn't even speak properly thus became the head of the university. This was an affront to all of us ordinary students and no doubt to the professors as well, but none of us had the courage to protest. A wrong word and we would have been expelled, perhaps even killed.

Uday's selection as president of the Olympic Committee was no less ludicrous. He doesn't know to this day how many players are on a soccer squad, the disciplines in the decathlon, or how frequently the Olympic games are held.

I went to the living room to make myself a drink while I dried off. It was just after noon, but I wasn't hungry. I sat on the comfortable couch and for the first time started writing rudimentary notes, using only key words, about Uday. I tried to recall conversations and details, people I knew from university and those I'd met since my training.

Munem Hammed, I thought, *he can be trusted. He's fair, the only officer who sees through all the shit and acts at least halfway normal. He's part of this deal, but at least he suffers from it and that makes him appealing.*

But I started my list with Abbas al-Janabi, not Munem Hammed. Beside his name, I wrote, "Director of Uday's papers."

He made me laugh. Al-Janabi was a weakling, whom I'd met once in the Olympic Club. He had been given the job of director of the papers the *Babel* and *Al-Baas-al-Riyadi* as compensation because Uday had raped his niece the year before.

The *Babel* and *Al-Baas-al-Riyadi* had been placed under Uday's care because his father wanted control of the media, and suddenly Uday developed delusions of being a great writer. He arranged for an actual ceremony to have himself appointed president. In one of the first editorials bearing his name, but surely written by someone else, he even compared himself with the well-known Iraqi author al-Javahiri.

Uday immediately had the "significant" work of his grandfather, Khairallah Talfah, printed in order to raise the "intellectual level" of the country. The title of this work, a Ba'ath party pamphlet? "Three Things that God Should Not Have Created: Persians, Jews, and Bluebottle Flies."

Khairallah Talfah was a shining light in the lives of the Husseins, the power behind the throne, at the center of everything. He had shaped them all, as much Uday as Saddam Hussein.

I marked down the name Khairallah Talfah. Then I asked myself, *Who is this man who hates Persians, Jews, and bluebottle flies like the plague?* This was the founder, originally from Tikrit, who was an officer in the 1941 rebellion against the Hashemite king, Feisal II, and after decommissioning and prison, had fed his family through robbery and shady deals. He started his climb to power as a common street thief.

I wrote after Khairallah: "First officer, then thief."

The next step in the familiar story: Saddam Hussein's father died before he was born. After his birth, his mother married Ibrahim al-Hassan, who wanted nothing to do with the child. Saddam was packed off to his uncle, Khairallah Talfah, at age nine.

I wrote: "Saddam sent to live with Khairallah Talfah."

This reminded me of some things Uday had recounted when we were in school, but I pushed them away, so as not to lose my thread: Khairallah had a son, Adnan Khairallah. He was the only friend Saddam had in Tikrit. When Khairallah Talfah left Tikrit for Baghdad in 1955, he took Saddam, Adnan, and his daughters with him. Sajida was the oldest. Sajida and Saddam had been chosen for each other when they were still children, as is the Muslim custom.

I wrote on my slip of paper: "Saddam's future wife, Sajida, daughter of Uncle Khairallah."

The Talfah family amassed wealth and power in Baghdad. Saddam Hussein married his cousin Sajida Talfah in 1963, after the Ba'ath party came to power. The first son, Uday, was born in 1964. Saddam had no time to spend on him. Politics came first. His second son saw the light of day in 1966. His name was Qusay.

I leaned back and remembered the relationship between Uday and Qusay. Uday used to make disparaging comments about his younger brother at school. Qusay was the favorite child; he was spoiled, overprotected. And it's a fact that Qusay was never cause for scandal during his school years. He was always considered the calmer, the more balanced, the one who had received more of his father's attention.

By contrast, Uday had virtually grown up with his grandfather. Just like his father in Tikrit, he too was bundled off to Uncle Khairallah Talfah. And Uday often stressed his close ties to his grandfather. For example, one day he stamped his foot in front of us and thundered, "My grandfather taught my father to kill every enemy!" Then he added, threateningly, "Just wait until I become president. I'll be crueler than my father ever was. You mark my words. You'll yearn for the time of Saddam Hussein."

This memory stirred my anxiety about being Uday's fidai, his bondman. I jumped up, took a few steps, and stared in the mirror beside the couch. I saw Latif Yahia, who hadn't been Latif Yahia but Uday Saddam Hussein for the past ten months. The double. My days were numbered if Uday should ever take over. The people of Iraq hated him already. How much more would they hate him if he became Number One?

After Saddam Hussein assumed power in 1979, Adnan Khairallah was named defense minister and Uncle Talfah governor of Baghdad. In other words, Saddam immediately gathered his family around him on the pinnacle of power. From the start, the Clan dominated everything.

I wrote: "Saddam president, Adnan defense minister, Uncle Khairallah, governor of Baghdad."

I was perspiring. Had the fan stopped working? Or was it just fear? Thinking made me tired. I took another sip, put down the piece of paper, looked for some diversion. Went to the bathroom, turned on the cold water, and splashed it on my face twice, three times. That felt good. *Keeping cool is important in your situation, Latif,* I told myself.

What were the origins of this madness? Why was Uday the way he was? He always needed to oppress others to prove himself. No wonder, when you think what his grandfather was like. Saddam got his violent side from Khairallah, and he lived out this violence in his politics. In turn, Uday let off steam in Baghdad's high society.

At thirteen, Uday would tell us how ruthlessly his grandfather had acted against the English, how he had created the Mafia-like clan of the Tikritis in Baghdad. He gloried in the methods that this little thief from the streets of Baghdad used to tighten his net of violence and power.

The thief of Baghdad — for Uday he became a mythical figure, someone to emulate, a spiritual father, just as he had been the mentor in violence for Saddam Hussein. He taught them both the law of murder. Exercise of this law had brought Saddam Hussein to the pinnacle of power, and Uday knew it. This truth was literally pounded into him.

But Uday could never put his knowledge into practice. How could he ever become better than his father, the president, the god, the direct descendant of the Prophet? As a child, Uday was beaten with an iron bar when he did something wrong. If he seemed timid, Saddam forced him to watch videos of executions and tortures. Saddam loved these videos, and Uday didn't dare oppose him. As far as Saddam Hussein was concerned, cruelty was not reprehensible, but something positive.

Whenever things got to be too much for Uday, he would flee to Grandfather Khairallah. "He understands me, he listens to me, he's interested in me," Uday would tell us in school.

It was a bit past 3:00 P.M. now. In a little less than two hours, they would come to pick me up and drive me to Project No. 7. As I reflected on my notes, something else came to mind.

While in school and later at the university, Uday spoke frequently and adoringly of his mother. He referred to her as if she were a goddess, a mythical being, an ivory statue. Sajida never appeared in public with Saddam Hussein. Her task was to remain in the background and perform her duties as wife and mother. By contrast, Saddam's affairs were an open secret in Baghdad. The women were always smuggled into the palace by Kamel Hannah, his foretaster and most loyal servant. For a long time Saddam was able to keep things quiet, but it all came to light during a relationship with Majida, the wife of Culture and Information Minister Hamed Youssef Hammadi. Reportedly, Saddam had been ready to leave his wife and repudiate his family because of her.

Uday deeply hated Kamel Hannah. "He brings my father women and destroys my mother," he would bellow at three in the morning, lying drunk next to the pool in Project No. 7. He also claimed that his grandfather Khairallah wanted nothing better than to kill the foretaster.

Who would come to Uday's party? Not his father and mother. Not his brother, either, I was certain of that. First, it would be far too dangerous for the whole family to appear, for Project No. 7 couldn't be made as secure as the palace. Second, I was sure a birthday dinner had been given several days earlier with just the close family in attendance.

Not many politicians would show, either. Because Uday's reputation was so bad, the cream of Baghdad society would avoid the president's son, as they had taken pains to do for years. Knowing his unpredictability, they did everything, absolutely everything, to make sure they weren't drawn into an embarrassing situation with grave consequences. Besides, if they had been expected, Uday surely wouldn't have invited me, his double. Or was he so confident of himself that he didn't care if people learned he had a fidai?

On the other hand, it was no secret in Iraq that everybody in the president's family had one. The ordinary folk, who were supposed to be fooled by the fidais, simply never had the chance to approach any of us closely enough to notice the small differences. Anyway, public appearances were always such a show that their attention was drawn more to the spectacle than to the actors in it.

As for Uday's close personal friends, almost all of them had gotten to know me in Project No. 7 over the past few months. They were bound by the same conditions of secrecy as I was. The rules of the game applied equally: Anyone revealing anything about the president's family to the outside world was a dead man.

At about 5:00 P.M., they came to fetch me, and we drove to Uday's house. The masters of ceremonies had done their work well. Lush flower arrangements bloomed everywhere. A small stage with a sound and light system had been set up next to the pool. The party room on the second floor was dazzling. The servants all wore luminous, starched white uniforms with golden buttons and the obligatory white gloves.

Uday greeted me curtly, tossing a "Have fun" my way. His distant manner meant I was to remain in the background and not get into conversations.

The guests began to arrive after a while. Dafer Aref, the director of the Olympic Club, was Uday's lackey, and was married to the actress Hanan Abdul-Latif. At the university, Uday had had Hanan Abdul-Latif picked up repeatedly by his bodyguards and brought to one of his farms outside Baghdad. She couldn't stand Uday, but succumbed because she had no other choice. At the time everyone knew what Uday had done to Nahle Sabet, the architecture student who had turned him down and whom he had raped and thrown to his famished attack dogs.

Hanan Abdul-Latif greeted Uday in a friendly way, but he didn't even deign to look in her direction. She ignored the slight, turning to Adel Akle instead. A small, strangely built man with sloping shoulders and a weak handshake, Adel Akle was nonetheless a star in Iraq. He was Uday's favorite singer, had made lots of records, and was always on the radio, on television, and at Uday's parties.

Adel hadn't started performing yet. His band was playing pleasant background music, so he and Hanan Abdul-Latif sat at a table with her husband. I couldn't tell what they were saying, but they were obviously having fun and broke out in happy laughter several times.

Next to arrive was Mohammed al-Baghdadi, a friend of Uday known in Baghdad as an insatiable womanizer. He had bought Uday's friendship by giving him his sister as a present. He was accompanied by Dureid Ghannaoui, the dealer whom Uday had made rich with his mania for expensive cars.

I never counted them, but I'm sure Uday owned more

than a hundred: Maseratis, Ferraris, Porsches, Jaguars, Mercedes, in all models and colors. Cars were like weapons for him. They were sacred objects, fetishes, mobile charms used to enhance his self-confidence and make him special. He even had a law enacted prohibiting Ferrari imports, so that he would be the only person in Iraq to own one.

His cars were parked in two garages next to the al-Hayat high-rise on the palace grounds. I went there several times during my training as fidai — yet I still hardly credit what I saw! Dozens of mechanics were employed to service and care for them. The chief mechanic was Tamal al-Tikriti. The cars were parked in blocks. Block No. 1 comprised the fleet of Mercedes, arrayed one next to the other, in all colors, and with the latest options, including ABS and speaker configurations that made you think you were in a rolling Walkman, not to mention television, telephones, and built-in bars of the finest woods.

None of the Mercedes was inferior to a 300 model. Most were race-tuned 500s. Six were the 500 SEL, the stretch model, and ten the 500 SE, the most powerful Mercedes had to offer. There were SL convertibles in black, dark blue, and fire-engine red, sixteen of them. Not one of these cars cost less than $100,000.

Next to them sat the fleet of Ferraris: several fire-engine-red Testarossas, an old Dino, four 348s. The cars sparkled and shone — you couldn't find a speck of dust anywhere. Everything had to be clinically clean, as sterile as a postoperative ward, but I doubt any hospital ward was as well equipped. The garage walls were laid out with tile, and the floor had a special coating.

The Lamborghini Countachs were kept behind the Ferrari fleet. These were sports cars that looked like aircraft, with top speeds of more than 160 miles an hour. Uday loved racing through Baghdad in them, thundering down the Street of the Palestinians at 140 miles an hour. Luxury vehicles like these made him a star even in high school, though personally I always disliked his mania for flaunting his wealth. It was fascinating nonetheless.

Uday's obsession with cars probably came from his father. Saddam Hussein also had an almost uncountable fleet, which was stored in different garages around Baghdad. Like his father, Uday always drove his cars himself; he never allowed himself to be driven by a chauffeur. And, like his father, he always felt the need to lay rubber every time he sped off. "Driving," Munem Hammed repeated during our training sessions, "is something holy, valuable, special. Don't ever forget that."

Next to the sporty Lamborghinis were the silver-gray Maseratis, the bi-turbos. Cars as quick as an arrow, whose appearance belied their speed. These were classic sports cars, not your turbo-monsters.

The Jaguar and Porsche sections were the most impressive, however. Uday owned every version of the Porsche 911, in all models and colors. He had convertibles, Targas, turbos. He had them all.

Ditto the Jaguars. He owned four model Es, the cigar-shaped classic that looks like a phallus. Two of them were convertibles. The burgundy pigskin seats were as soft and smooth as a woman's inner thigh. The wire wheels were gold-plated. The mountings were of the finest chrome, and the engine sounded like a Scud missile taking off. A few yards farther on were twenty-eight twelve-cylinder models, both the newest models and the understated Jaguar old-timers — worth a fortune. Car fanatics should never be admitted to a fantasy world like this.

All of these luxury cars had to be meticulously cleaned to Uday's satisfaction. He even checked under the hood. Though clueless about the technical details of the engines, he would go berserk at the least smudge left by a mechanic on the chrome cylinder heads.

A car would be junked, not repaired, after an accident.

Uday always personally tested new arrivals for speed and

comfort. Before the test, he would order sections of the well-built and -maintained al-Qadisiya freeway blocked off. The event itself was absurd. The day before, he would instruct his chief mechanic, Tamal al-Tikriti, to put on new tires, sticky Goodyear slicks like those used by Formula One race cars. In addition, "all unnecessary ballast," such as the passenger seats, had to be removed. Master Uday would then appear at the garage with his bodyguards on the day of the road test and assign them to other cars. They were to be his rivals, his imaginary opponents. The "test team" would speed off in a convoy to the blockaded freeway.

Two cars at a time went head-to-head. Uday might sit in a Lamborghini Countach, strapped down in the bucket seat. Next to him might be a Ferrari Testarossa, with a serious-looking bodyguard at the wheel. A referee counted down: "Five . . . four . . . three . . . two . . . one!" The projectiles peeled off, laying rubber, thundering down the freeway, and who won? Uday, of course! Always. Pity whoever was rash enough to best him. For the car's performance was always secondary; the only important thing in this matchup was "the profound driving expertise and the boundless courage of the president's son."

Endless discussions about the car's roadability, acceleration, and technical advantages followed. Uday loved to bandy about the technical lingo, although he usually had no idea what he was talking about. He would revel in oversteering, understeering, aerodynamics, and downward air pressure.

A paint and body shop was built behind the garage, and one of Uday's favorite pastimes was to have his car match the color of his suit or tie. If he was wearing a gray suit, the car, too, must be gray. If none of his Mercedes happened to be gray at the time, he had one spray-painted.

He also possessed four helicopters, and even these might be repainted in the shop whenever he yielded to one of his extravagant whims. Uday hated drab military colors; his helicopters had to look like those of the Saudi and

Kuwaiti princes, with interiors like living rooms and exteriors like elegant and sporty aircraft. He usually preferred them emblazoned with blue and white rally stripes.

The supreme toy, the absolute incarnation of decadence, however, was a special creation, a unique piece of machinery found only in the tiled garage of the Iraqi president's son: a 500 Mercedes with an unbelievably powerful Rolls-Royce engine. An Italian automaker had been flown to Baghdad just to create this wondrous object and to supervise its assembly. It took two months for Uday's mechanics to get everything right, but in the end the motor sounded like those rocket-powered speedsters used to set world records on the salt flats of Utah.

He purchased most of his luxury cars directly from the European dealers, and all Dureid did was to arrange the transport. Yet Dureid made a hefty profit on every transaction. Money had no meaning for Uday. None of his employees received a regular salary, including me. I asked Munem Hammed about my pay at the end of training. I used to get twenty-two dinars a month as a soldier, a paltry wage: twenty-two dinars equaled a little less than twenty U.S. dollars. Munem Hammed gave me this tip: "Go directly to Uday if you need money. He'll tell his paymaster to give you as much as you require." I hadn't yet followed through on his suggestion, since I didn't need money. My servants attended to food and drink. Clothing was always provided and was freshly washed and ironed daily. Toiletries like toothpaste, aftershave lotion, and shampoos were replenished automatically, as in a five-star hotel.

Uday greeted the car dealer exuberantly, hugging and kissing him, and Dureid grinned sheepishly.

Within minutes, Dureid was followed by Ali Asuad, Said Kammuneh, Muajed Aani, and Amer Aasami. These men played a special role in Uday's life, for they were directly or indirectly occupied with supplying him with women and girls.

Ali Asuad was actually employed by Uday to procure fresh young girls from the universities and schools whenever his own "grand tour" raids were unsuccessful. Uday had him marry one of the girls he had raped.

Said Kammuneh was one of Baghdad's chief pimps and a generally unsavory character. He controlled various bars and nightclubs, directed prostitution in Baghdad, was the godfather of sex. Officially, he owned an import-export business. But the firm was only a cover, his main import being girls from Asia. Asian prostitutes worked most Baghdad bars. Said controlled these women, and Uday had a piece of the trade. Said's profits were plowed into hotels and bars, his private pastimes. He was rumored to own half of Baghdad. Muajed Aani also dealt in women.

A whole flock of young women accompanied these men. All wore gorgeous, tight-fitting dresses, and some had on very short miniskirts such as you'd never see in other Arab nations.

But Uday didn't care about religion. He never prayed, and his motto was, "What did Allah ever do for me? Nothing. Has Allah ever given me a single dollar? No. Turn to Uday instead. He has dinars and is thus greater than Allah." The only time I'd seen him pray since September 1987 was when, for PR purposes, he visited the holy site of al-Takija al-Sufia. The event was of course filmed by cameramen and newspaper photographers and became the next day's lead story.

Meanwhile, Adel Akle, the singer, had climbed onstage. He wouldn't step down for the next several hours. Uday wouldn't have anyone else, and Adel Akle was capable of performing six to eight hours at a stretch.

He started with Uday's favorite, "Saddam, Oh, Saddam, You Great and Powerful One," to get the mood going. This was a saccharine, disingenuous hymn of praise to Hussein that could be heard playing constantly in public life in Iraq, but Uday remained moved by its soft rhythm and seemingly endless verses declaring Saddam's greatness over and over.

Everyone joined in, and Uday waved his cognac snifter in time with the music.

He was sitting next to the stage with three women, who were unknown to me. He started to bawl, drank, bawled again. He was already slightly drunk. As Adel started the next song, Uday jumped up, pulling with him a girl in a tight, dark blue silk dress. With her black, stiletto-heeled patent-leather shoes, she stood taller than he. She had dyed her hair blond and wore lots of makeup, just the way Uday liked. Her lips were dark red and shiny. A bluish rouge highlighted her cheeks. She'd applied it subtly, not in a circle like the others, whose rouge made them look as if they'd been beaten, but more softly, unevenly. She had big breasts, which almost bounced out of her dress as she moved rhythmically to the music. The neckline of her dress was cut low and pressed the smooth, white breasts vulgarly together.

"Dancing is like fucking," Uday said with a laugh.

He took the blonde in his arms. She closed her eyes and yielded passionately to the rhythm. She writhed like a snake, swung her hips in a circular motion; her belly shook and her hips pressed forward as if she already felt Uday inside her. Rhythm and sweat.

Uday danced twice with her, left her standing there, and took another who was also a fabulous dancer.

Uday's movements lacked elegance and grace. He was no sleek jaguar on the black marble next to the pool, but more like a clumsy caterpillar bumping into the others. Nobody complained, though, because Uday seemed to be having fun and that was the idea.

He grabbed the woman, pressed his mouth against hers, his body against hers. He licked her face. His tongue was everywhere, and she didn't really like it, but she giggled, and everybody watched, laughing. She then rubbed up against his body, twisting sensuously. Uday sighed theatrically and bellowed, "I love your mouth, I love your hair, I love your nose — I must have you!" And he grabbed her by the hips, dug into her firm buttocks, pulled her toward him, and jerked his hindquarters like an aroused dog. He laughed uproariously and shouted, "Nobody has an ass like yours."

The buffet was declared open.

The guests were asked to proceed to the party room upstairs. The masters of ceremonies had also outdone themselves there, creating a buffet with the help of Jakob al-Masihi and Said al-Masihi that the Rashid Hotel couldn't improve on. Jakob al-Masihi was Uday's private cook and foretaster, and Said al-Masihi always accompanied Uday on his trips abroad.

More than a hundred different foods were elegantly displayed on a table at least twenty yards long. In the middle was an Iraqi eagle made of butter, surrounded by melons, peaches, nectarines, apples, oranges, grapefruit, strawberries, and pineapples. Among them were exotic fruits I couldn't identify because I'd never seen them before. They were most likely imported from Kuwait especially for this evening.

The cooks, lined up like toy soldiers, stood to one side of the table. In front of them were shiny chafing dishes with gold handles and engraved Iraqi eagles. All kinds of entrees were available, Arab, Far Eastern, and European, including sautéed pink breast of duck on a bed of red peppers, rolled breast of turkey with a poultry liver sauce, and saddle of rabbit in pepper sauce. The cooks offered their delicacies politely, asking whether they should put together a menu or if the guest would care to choose his own.

The cold buffet was also served creatively: salmon on silver trays, three different kinds of caviar in silver bowls, including translucent red salmon caviar and silver-gray beluga, arranged tastefully on splintered ice. Lobster tails, oysters on the half shell, French pâté de foie gras, Italian Parma ham, fillet of beef alla Carpaccio, pink roast beef with various sauces, Barbary duck with plums and kiwis, deboned chicken and blinis with caviar, salmon tartar, a smoked salmon mousse, asparagus salad with plucked herbs and shrimp. Cleverly arranged vegetables and carrots shaped like rose-buds, lemon, and radish twists were placed between the different foods, along with the whole range of Arab delicacies.

I did as I was told and stayed in the background, avoiding every opening for a conversation, trying to look uninterested, and staring past anyone seeking to catch my eye. I made my way through the crowd, walked around aimlessly. Every time a waiter proffered his tray full of champagne flutes, I took a glass. I drank deliberately, not quickly. I wanted to keep a clear head.

Adel Akle sang without pause. I wasn't counting, but I'm sure he performed the hymn of praise to Saddam ten times. By now, Uday was completely drunk, staggering through the crowd and probably seeing everything through a purple haze. The girls literally clung to him.

As I strolled around, I noticed Ahmad Fadel, a first lieutenant in Uday's troop of bodyguards and a dangerous man. He had a habit of grabbing his weapon and shooting if someone rubbed him the wrong way, whether man or woman didn't matter. He treated prostitutes like dirt. "They're scum" was his justification.

Ahmad was deep in conversation with Hassan Sabti. Hassan was a goldsmith and gold designer. Nobody knew if he was good or not, but he was Uday's friend, so everybody bought from him. The tall, sleek-looking woman at his side was wearing a pink formal pullover embroidered with pearls and a pink silk skirt. She was beautiful.

It was already long after midnight, and the party had spun out of control. Uday was literally sprawled on top of his women. Next to him sat Amer Aasami, a transvestite who was the son of a pimp. Amer had breasts like a woman, moved like a woman, and dressed like a woman. He was lascivious, loud, and vulgar, shrill like a many-colored tropical bird, and

Uday was fascinated by him. There was something animallike about him. His whole appearance reeked of open, uncompromising sex, and Uday loved to have him near, to touch him. Amer was obscenity personified. Uday even had him exempted from military duty, so that he could never be taken from his side.

Amer wasn't the only bird of paradise close to Uday. The transvestite Issam al-Mullah also belonged to the circle of his closest friends. Issam was the only person who dared to snub Uday. Everyone knew that he had a relationship not only with Uday but also with Shaabani, an athletically built secret service professional. Issam al-Mullah loved the secret service man but didn't want to give up Uday, because Uday was his life insurance.

"Rip the whores' clothes off!" Uday screamed suddenly. That was the order his friends were waiting for. They chased the giggling, screeching women, most of them drunk, through the house, and ripped off their garments and threw them into the pool. Uday grabbed two of the women and disappeared into his room, the one where I had lived for months. He left the door and curtains open, so that everyone clustered by the pool could see him tying the women and beating them with his cable as he looked at the television screen. He had shoved a porno cassette into the VCR, which was spooling out sadistic scenes of men being pleasured by European women in patent leather outfits, women crawling in front of their master and enjoying the tortures he meted out. Uday had hundreds of these videotapes.

The birthday party turned into a wild orgy while Uday amused himself on the black silk sheets in his room. The only ones not naked were the waiters, with their white uniforms and starched collars. The guests copulated everywhere, even in the bathrooms, standing as they did it and observing themselves in the baroque mirrors.

Saddam Hussein and his eldest son, Uday, in an Iraqi news agency photograph distributed in 1990. (AP/WIDE WORLD PHOTOS)

*Saddam Hussein and his family. Seated beside Saddam on the couch is his wife, Sajida.
In the back row, from the left, are his sons-in-law Hussein Kamel and Saddam Kamel; Saddam's
daughter Rina, the wife of Saddam Kamel; Uday; Saddam's eldest daughter, Raghd, the wife
of Hussein Kamel, shown holding their son Ali, Saddam's first grandson; an unidentified woman,
possibly the wife of Saddam's son Qusay; and Qusay Hussein. The other children in the photograph
are unidentified. 1991.* (AP/WIDE WORLD PHOTOS)

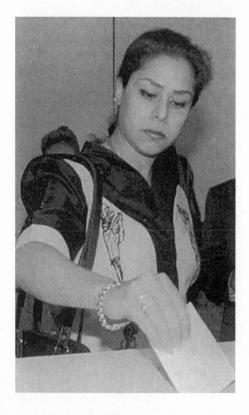

*Hala Hussein, Saddam's youngest daughter and the
wife of Hakim Kamel, brother of Hussein and
Saddam Kamel. 1995.* (AP/WIDE WORLD PHOTOS)

Latif Yahia, Uday's double or fidai.
(AP/WIDE WORLD PHOTOS)

Uday Saddam Hussein and Latif Yahia.
When Saddam was introduced to Uday's double for the first time,
he remarked, "Yes, it's you. Allah gave me two sons, and you're the third!"

Latif Yahia, in the black military uniform bearing Uday's name tag that he sometimes wore when doubling for Uday. (NEWS/HERRGOTT)

Ahmad Hasan al-Bakr, Saddam's predecessor as president of Iraq. Saddam served as his vice president and for years was the power behind al-Bakr. He is rumored to have had him poisoned to death in order to succeed him in office. 1971. (AP/WIDE WORLD PHOTOS)

Barzan al-Tikriti, Saddam's half-brother. Barzan was the head of the Mukhabarat intelligence agency and later served as Iraq's representative to the UN in Geneva, where he administered Saddam's and Uday's fortunes abroad, and was in charge of procuring armaments. 1991. (AP/WIDE WORLD PHOTOS)

Adnan Khairallah, Saddam's cousin and brother-in-law, was one of his closest friends from childhood. He was a general and defense minister and a hero of the Iran-Iraq War, but when he became a threat, Saddam had him killed. 1988. (AP/WIDE WORLD PHOTOS)

Hussein Kamel, the eldest of the three brothers in the al-Majid clan who married Saddam's daughters. Hussein Kamel defected to Jordan in August 1995 with his brother Saddam and their wives. They were subsequently lured back with full pardons, and the brothers were assassinated. (AP/WIDE WORLD PHOTOS)

Iraqi TV images of Latif Yahia (above and left) confessing to having taken advantage of his resemblance to Uday in order to plunder Kuwait for his own profit. The confession was a sham, devised as a means to clear Uday of responsibility for having looted Kuwait to the tune of $120 million. 1990. (KARL WENDL)

A beaming father and son on the day of Uday's wedding to his cousin, the eldest daughter of Saddam's half-brother, Barzan al-Tikriti. July 17, 1993. (REUTERS/FALEH KHEIBER/ARCHIVE PHOTOS)

Saddam Hussein during the Gulf War. As the Allies began their air assault, he declared on Baghdad radio, "The great showdown has begun. The mother of all battles is under way." January 1991. (AP/WIDE WORLD PHOTOS)

Saddam Hussein waving to supporters on October 18, 1995, after having been sworn in as president for a new seven-year term. He had won a national referendum in which he was the only candidate.
(AP/WIDE WORLD PHOTOS)

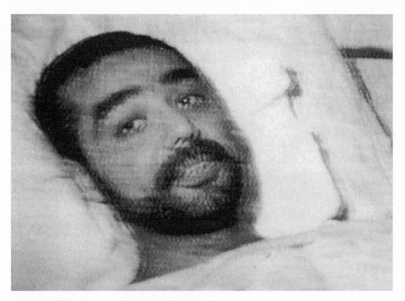

Uday in his hospital bed, recovering from wounds suffered during the assassination attempt against him on December 12, 1996.
(REUTERS/FALEH KHEIBER/ARCHIVE PHOTOS)

9

THE KILLING BEGINS

FOR days after this party, I heard nothing from Uday. There was no mission, no training, nothing, just waiting. I didn't even know whether he was still in Iraq or had flown to Europe to recover. Only Munem Hammed called occasionally.

To kill time, I played poker with the officers from the security service. The stakes were low. It didn't register why, but I won most of the time. Through my conversations with them, I got to know the organization of Saddam Hussein's presidential guard.

Saddam divided his guard into three units. Each had its own tasks and missions, with, in addition, the first troop supervising the second, and the second the third. The whole system was supposed to be self-monitoring and self-regulating. The idea was that, because nobody trusted the others and all changes were to be reported immediately, infiltration by potential assassins would be impossible.

The first troop comprised officers known by Saddam Hussein for years and was supervised either by him personally or by his closest aides. They accompanied Saddam everywhere, were always at his side, even stood guard outside the door when he went to the toilet. They were either members of the Tikriti family or came from the vicinity of the village of Tikrit. This group numbered one thousand to twelve hundred men. Each was an expert in close combat; each had to have completed special training. Their weaponry was also excellent. The lower-ranking officers were equipped with a large-caliber revolver, a submachine gun with two magazines, and two or three grenades suspended on their belts. They had access to all intelligence facilities, carried sophisticated hand radios with their own designated frequencies, and wore bulletproof vests under their uniforms, not heavy ceramic ones but light vests made of carbon, which protect much better than the conventional ones. The higher-ranking officers carried only a revolver or an automatic pistol during normal duty hours.

The guards of the first troop were considered privileged, and they had it made so long as Saddam Hussein remained in power and they served him loyally and selflessly. Their salaries were astronomical. They received a new car every six months. If they didn't want the car, they got either additional cash bonuses or property and houses. A separate administrative department busied itself with handing out gifts and bonuses to these men and their families.

Anybody wishing to join this group had to have an immaculate intelligence service career behind him. The president himself was their commander.

The second guard troop was set up basically the same way. Most of the men were from Tikrit, the inferior officers had to carry submachine guns and hand grenades, and the superior officers small arms. This was a kind of standby troop. Members of the second contingent automatically replaced any men from the first who were killed or wounded. There was no other way into the first group. One could rise to the loftier, more prestigious guard only to fill a vacancy — an extremely tough system, which led men in the second group to wait like vultures for their chance. They informed on the others, scrutinized their every move, reported any mistakes they made. Infractions of the rules led to expulsions from the first group, of course. This predatory dynamic meant that almost everyone had a secret archive of his comrades'

activities. Each alcoholic excess, each visit to the bordello —
everything was observed and noted down and used to out-
maneuver rivals.

Saddam Hussein imposed this system of falsehood and
denunciation in whatever situation he could. He always tried
to play one subordinate against the other. He would over-
whelm his enemies with praise. The more famous the victim,
the greater the honors bestowed on him.

Such was the case, for instance, of General Salah al-
Kadi, who ordered his troops to withdraw from Basra in
1982. Saddam, who considered the position defensible, had
him discreetly executed a few days later, and then bestowed
the title of martyr on him. His family, to whom Saddam
personally offered his condolences, received all the bonuses
associated with this title: a car, a piece of property, and a
long-term, interest-free loan.

Once, my poker partners told me, the president had 21
high party functionaries and 180 officers executed; they were
allegedly guilty of conspiracy. The cameraman Chaker
Yassine filmed the massacre. His films are used for "educa-
tional purposes" during psychological training of the guard
troops. They contain the following scenes:

Hundreds of party cadres are sitting in the great Khulde
Assembly Room (the Assembly Room of Infinity). All of the
seats are filled. Saddam enters the room, elegant as always, a
fat cigar in his right hand. He orders the secretary-general of
the Revolutionary Command Council, Abdul Hussein
Mashhadi, to approach the microphone. The secretary-
general looks terrible, as if he has just been tortured. Saddam screams at him, "Speak, reveal the foul deed!" Abdul
Hussein Mashhadi recites a bunch of names, and Saddam
yells after each, "Out! Go!" You can see his bodyguard escort
the men outside.

The men are taken into the garden of the presidential
palace and lined up against the wall, eyes bound. Barzan

al-Tikriti, Saddam's brother and the head of Mukhabarat (later UN ambassador in Geneva), is in charge of the execution in front of the rolling camera. The condemned are first shirted in red soccer jerseys, Barzan al-Tikriti's "brilliant idea," following an old Ottoman tradition of dressing victims in red. The condemned are shot not by the bodyguards but by their relatives.

The video shows two children standing next to Barzan al-Tikriti: Barzan's eight-year-old son, Mohammed, and Uday, not yet fifteen at the time. Barzan tells his young son, "Take this gun and find the one you want to kill." And the little boy shoots. The video doesn't show whether Uday fired too.

My fellow cardplayers described these video scenes to the last detail, as if to imply: "There's no fooling around with the Issaba, the Gang. They make short work of you. All members of the guard are potential killers."

The third guard troop was by far the largest: the Republican Guards. The Republican Guards were recruited from the Tikrit, Baghdad, and Nineveh districts. Only recruits recommended by the intelligence services or the Ba'ath party were accepted. They had to come from good, loyal families. No member of the family could have a criminal record, or the candidate was disqualified.

The Republican Guards comprised more than ten battalions. Each unit had mastered all the weaponry used by the regular Iraqi army. They were the spearhead of the Saddam regime. Their main task consisted of securing the areas visited by Saddam. Forty-eight hours in advance, the commander (after Saddam Hussein) of the first guard troop would be told of three areas Saddam planned to visit. He passed this information on to the head of the Republican Guards, who immediately dispatched the so-called control troops. Complete city districts were cordoned off and combed through. A guardsman took up position on every corner.

Saddam wouldn't decide until the last minute which of

the destinations to set off for. He'd go by car if it was close to Baghdad, in which case his convoy would consist of more than thirty Mercedes limousines, ten of which were identical. The president determined at the last minute which one he'd drive personally. Following close behind were ambulances equipped with mobile operating facilities and a supply of blood plasma.

He would take a helicopter or a Boeing for visits to the front. Which aircraft he'd fly in was likewise a last-minute decision.

Saddam always invented ingenious new tricks to test his pilots and traveling companions. Once, just before a business trip, he ordered his colleagues to show up at the airport in heavy winter clothing. All of them came in thick shoes, fur coats, and fur hats. Only Saddam wore a light summer outfit.

"Why?" he was asked. "Are we going to Moscow?"

Saddam replied, "No, we're heading south."

During each of his rare visits to the front, the Republican Guards made sure that all soldiers and officers in the vicinity had divested themselves of their ammunition prior to the president's arrival.

The Republican Guards received pay six times that of a normal soldier. In addition, they were showered with presents at every possible opportunity, for example on the president's birthday.

While the Republican Guards had their own barracks, the first two groups of guards lived and trained on the palace grounds. They had their own gyms and shooting galleries, where I practiced too, their own canteens and recreation facilities with pool halls, bowling alleys, cinemas, and Ping-Pong rooms.

All of these facilities were available to me so long as I kept Uday's bodyguards informed of my whereabouts. This way my isolation was easier to bear, and I was always able to pick up the latest news. Thus I eventually learned through a bodyguard that Uday had flown to Geneva after his birthday party to visit his uncle, and that he had come back yesterday with sensational news: Barzan al-Tikriti had brought truce negotiations with Iran to a decisive phase at the United Nations in Geneva.

While the official news organs continued to vaunt our army's glorious achievements at the front, we all knew the truth: Saddam had failed to accomplish his war goals despite the use of poison gas. Although our troops had managed to penetrate deep into Iran at the war's beginning, they couldn't hold their positions. Now they were happy if the Iranians didn't push into our territory.

Very early on July 18, 1988, I was summoned to Project No. 7. The hour was unprecedented. I had never been asked to appear this early before. I hurried to dress, and my driver sped me there. Waiting for me was Bakr al-Nassiri, the house administrator. He was excited, and everyone else was too, most of all Uday. "We've won the war," he triumphed. "They've signed."

We heard later on the news what Uday meant. After long and tough negotiations, Barzan al-Tikriti had consented to UN Resolution 598 and signed the cease-fire with Iran. That meant an end to the longest war ever fought by two sovereign nations in the twentieth century.

Uday was almost beside himself with joy. He had the cassette with Adel Akel's song about his father inserted in the tape player and the volume cranked up. He hugged, embraced, and kissed all of us. He declared himself, his father, and Iraq victors, and we agreed with him. "Iraq has dealt a mortal blow to the fundamentalists in Tehran."

In reality, the war ended in a stalemate. Our armed forces held practically the same positions as in 1980, when they began. Saddam had launched the war because he wanted control over the Shatt al-Arab waterway, and to prove, in his boundless megalomania, that he was the greatest Arab leader of all time. He had seen the fall of Shah Reza Pahlavi and the ascent to power of his mortal enemy, the Ayatollah Khomeini, in 1979, as a unique opportunity to make Iraq the principal Persian Gulf power and to ensure his own immortality.

My doubts, of course, were not a topic for discussion in Project No. 7, and I was very careful not even to hint at anything that could cloud the glory of our "victory." Uday ordered cold, sparkling champagne. We toasted each other, embraced, drank, toasted again.

Many of Uday's friends began to appear one by one, including Dr. Mahmoud Samarai, the man responsible for preparing Uday's interviews with the media as well as all meetings and conferences chaired by him. Uday sequestered himself with Dr. Samarai for some time, then the two left Project No. 7 for three hours, probably to meet with reporters.

The following days and weeks merged into a single bout of celebrations, drinking, and more celebrations. All of Baghdad was electric. Millions crowded the streets. Nobody felt like staying home. It was like the time when Saddam assumed power. Strangers hugged each other, kissed, rejoiced.

The climax came on August 8. The end of the war was officially announced at midnight. All factories were to stop production — a meaningless decree, since nobody was about to show up for work on this day anyway.

Saddam's court portraitists and propaganda specialists had used the preceding days to polish the tarnished image of the great commander-in-chief. Whole armies of workers had rushed to complete new pictures of Saddam and distribute them nationwide.

At the start of the war, Saddam had suddenly presented himself as a military leader. He had ordered hundreds of uniforms made for himself, and contrived to appoint himself field marshal of the army. Oversized images of Saddam sprang up everywhere, as a fighter in the trenches, as a pilot, or as a Saladin at war. He had the myth of the victorious commander-in-chief propagated to the point where he became the personification of the war for everyone. But as the number of war victims grew and Iraqi troops were forced to relinquish the captured Iranian bases, the military portraits were gradually replaced by civilian ones: Saddam wearing a suit, Saddam with children, Saddam as a religious Muslim with the traditional headcloth of the southern Arabs, Saddam in Kurdish costume.

The strategy was being switched once more now that hostilities had ended, and the media specialists were again presenting the president as a military genius. Posters popped up everywhere depicting Saddam as a warrior beaming in victory. The new portraits appeared by the hundreds, and they graced all the newspapers. Some editions carried his picture on almost every page. It was the same thing on television, Saddam here, Saddam there. The cult of personality knew no bounds, and occasionally one got the impression that the president had started believing his own propaganda.

Uday ordered me to fly south to Basra on the day of the announcement of peace. I was to visit the Third and Seventh Units to congratulate the soldiers on their glorious victory. We again traveled by helicopter. Instead of civilian clothing, I wore the black uniform bearing the golden name of Uday Saddam Hussein. Some of my bodyguard had already left for Basra on the previous day in a convoy of several trucks loaded with toys and presents. When our helicopter landed, the companies were already in formation. We inspected the guard of honor with the commander. I gave no speech, but instead conveyed greetings from the president and transmitted the decrees given to me by Munem Hammed.

The official visit with the soldiers was followed by the supposedly unofficial one. I was to leave the barracks and make contact with the "ordinary people" who had been assembled before my arrival in a crowd of three to four thousand strong, comprising children, women, and old folks, but hardly any young men. They screamed, "Long live Saddam Hussein, long live Saddam Hussein!"

The women sang, screeched, and broke out again and

again in cries of "Long live Saddam Hussein!" My body-guards surrounded me, and we marched in formation to-ward the children, who were holding Iraqi flags and standing in front. The trucks with the toys had already been parked in position. My bodyguards handed me three packages, which I distributed to the little children with the huge, dark eyes and the dirty hands. I asked them inanely how they were. Mean-while the soldiers had begun to pass out the rest of presents from the trucks. They simply threw the gifts into the crowd.

I was startled by the loud crack of a shot.

I had no idea where it came from, who fired it, or for whom it was intended. My bodyguards flew at me, shielded me with their bodies, shoved me toward the car, and bundled me inside. We raced back to the Seventh Unit, clambered into the helicopter, and sped to Baghdad as quickly as pos-sible.

I didn't know for sure what had happened until I lis-tened in on the radio traffic during the flight. It had been an assassination attempt. I breathed deeply several times, broke out in a sweat, realized all at once the danger I had run. The bullet could have hit me, wounded me, killed me. I leaned back, stared at the back of the pilot before me, and listened to the sound of the rotor blades. Then came the second radio message. The copilot jotted it down and yelled over to me. "Abdullah al-Dalimi is badly hurt. A chest wound." Abdullah al-Dalimi was one of the youngest bodyguards, no more than nineteen or twenty years old. He had been standing right next to me, and had intercepted the bullet.

"Is he going to make it?" I shouted back. The copilot shrugged, yelled, "I don't know!" We learned from a third radio message that they'd overpowered the culprit and de-tained him. He was a deserter, aged twenty-three, who had lost two of his brothers in the senseless war.

Back in Baghdad, I wrote a detailed report about the attack, and submitted the sequence of events to Uday. But Uday wasn't interested, so I gave it to Munem Hammed, who reacted coolly. After consulting briefly with his superiors, he ordered the immediate execution by firing squad of the would-be assassin. There was no trial, no interrogation of the man. The execution was carried out the next day. That was the end of it, and Munem Hammed asked me not to mention the assassination attempt again or to make a big deal out of it. I did as he said.

For his part, Uday ignored the whole thing as if it had never happened. He was interested only in the celebrations in Baghdad and the triumphal marches in honor of "The Great Victor, Saddam Hussein." Despite the obvious security concerns, he wanted to immerse himself totally in the ecstasy of the celebrations.

Our convoy drove to the al-Mansur district, where thousands of people were crowding the Street of the Palestinians. Everyone was pushing and shoving, but all were joyous. All of Baghdad seemed finally relaxed, liberated, and happy. Uday was ensconced in an armored Mercedes with a sun roof, and for once he had himself driven. In his left hand he held a Kalashnikov, in his right his pistol. As we turned into the Street of the Palestinians, teeming with people of all sorts, Uday stood up, eased his torso through the sun roof, pointed both weapons at the sky, and fired off salvo after salvo. His bodyguards followed suit, shoving their Kalashnikovs through the open windows and firing until their magazines were empty.

Uday's act was pure madness as far as security was concerned. Hundreds, thousands of people on the street had weapons, and Uday was a perfect target as he stood up in his car and fired. Besides, his shooting was lost in the racket of all the others firing into the air for joy.

Europeans sometimes shoot off fireworks to express ecstasy and high spirits, but an Arab prefers his weapon. It's normal for us to shoot into the air for joy. I, too, stuck my weapon out the car window and fired until I had to reload. We drove through Baghdad for three or four hours, firing from our cars in celebration. Even Saddam Hussein didn't pass up the chance to convoy through Baghdad and take part in the orgy of shooting.

The rejoicing continued for days. Convoys of cars sped through the city, and the drivers and passengers stuck their weapons out of the windows and let loose. Sometimes the shooting orgies spun completely out of control, and the television warned repeatedly of the need for increased caution after several people were killed or wounded by stray bullets. Yet the people ignored such warnings. Shooting in the air was like a drug for them, an expression of boundless joy. Why should they act differently from their leaders? I'm sure Uday alone shot off more than ten thousand rounds in his triumphal tours through the city.

Our convoy drove past my street and house several times. I spied the entrances, my father's white Volvo, my brothers' cars. I was no more than a few yards away from the loved ones I hadn't seen since September of last year.

I had this irrational hope of catching a glimpse of one of my brothers, my mother, or my father. *They might just be leaving the house or coming back,* I told myself. At least then I would see them, although making contact was out of the question. Leaving the convoy or stopping was strictly forbidden unless ordered by Uday. The only thing I could do was wave and hope that someone would recognize me. But the street was always empty whenever we drove by.

I decided nonetheless to ask Uday for permission to visit my parents. On August 14, I broached the subject early in the afternoon. He reacted completely differently than I expected. "Latif," he said, "you've been with me for eleven months now, and you've performed your tasks one hundred percent. You're a good man." He then revealed that he had had me under round-the-clock observation for the entire eleven months, although I'd never caught on. "You haven't made one mistake," Uday pronounced solicitously, "and therefore you may see your parents."

"When?"

"Tonight if you wish," he answered, "but first talk to Munem Hammed."

Munem Hammed issued detailed instructions about my visit: "Not a word about your job, not a word about Uday, no clues, no subtle hints, nothing. Is that clear, Latif?"

I nodded.

The visit was scheduled for 11:00 P.M. They wouldn't allow me to call my parents beforehand, but the intelligence service personnel assured me that my parents, my sisters Galalha and Juan, and my brothers Jotie, Robie, and Omeed were all home. I realized with a jolt that my home was under constant surveillance too.

We arrived at my house in al-Azamiya at exactly eleven. I rang, and my mother, Bahar, opened the door.

The outside light was so weak that she didn't recognize me at first. Besides, I was wearing a dark djellaba, a kind of clothing I hadn't worn before because I preferred the western style of dress.

"It's me, your Latif," I said, and embraced my mother.

I could feel a spasm going through her body. She took my head in her hands, almost tearing at my hair. She wanted to say something, but her voice broke; she wept, kissed me, and I felt her tears. I was having a hard time keeping my composure, and nudged her into the house. My father and my siblings rushed from the living room toward me, alerted by my mother's sobs.

Having my family around me again was an almost indescribable joy. We hugged for a long time. I kissed them all.

The first minutes were silent, taken up with kissing and staring at each other, and tears filled my eyes for the first time in months. I could weep freely.

It took us twenty minutes to regain enough composure to be able to sit down in the living room. My mother reproached me bitterly. She recounted how she had spent desperate weeks on the phone, trying to find out whether I had fallen in battle or been taken prisoner by the Iranians. "They never told us anything other than that you were picked up and taken away almost one year ago. Latif, my son, we prayed for you. We were sure you were no longer alive."

And with that, my mother started crying again. My sisters hugged her, tried to console her, but she remained disconsolate.

My father broke his silence for the first time. He had noticed the change in my teeth. "What did they do to you, son?" he wanted to know. But I shook my head and replied, "Don't ask. I can't tell you. I can only tell you that I'm well and have an interesting job."

"What kind of job, Latif?" interjected my little brother, Robie. "Are you a spy?"

I had to laugh. We all laughed, and I repeated my little speech. "I can't tell you, so please don't ask again. Don't discuss any of this with my friends. Just tell them I'm well."

I was allowed two hours with my family, and left at 1:00 A.M. sharp, as arranged. My family accompanied me to the door. They saw my bodyguards pick me up, escort me to the Mercedes, and drive me off into the night. I felt good and replayed every detail, every word, every laugh from my sisters and brothers, my father, my mother, in my mind. It had been a lovely visit. I hadn't lost control once, or said one wrong word, or dropped any hints. Nobody knew for certain what I was doing. Maybe my father suspected something, since he'd asked about my overbite, but he'd never mentioned the name of Uday. He, too, knew the rules.

Four days later we departed with Uday for al-Habbaniya, a resort about forty miles west of Baghdad. al-Habbaniya is a favorite holiday spot for the cream of Iraqi society as well as for tourists and newlyweds. It has discreet hotels, two lakes with all kinds of water sports, and lots of restaurants.

Uday owned a villa and six houses there, and knew the area like his back pocket. His father is a passionate hunter, and Uday used to accompany him there regularly to hunt deer. Saddam taught Uday how to shoot and how to gut the dead animal. "Some days," Uday recalled during the ride, "we shot up to twenty deer. My father loves to kill."

In the days preceding this brief holiday, Uday seemed to spin almost completely out of control. He dedicated nearly every waking hour to pursuing hedonistic pleasures. Then he'd sleep till noon to recover, more or less, from the alcoholic excesses of the day before. Following breakfast came the meeting with Yassem to discuss what to wear and which of the hundreds of Rolex, Breitling, Patek Philippe, or Cartier watches would be the best accessory. The most expensive watch in Uday's collection was an IWC Grande Complication from Schaffhausen, Switzerland, made of platinum and packing a complicated system of 659 parts and nine hands. This timepiece was a classic worth more than a Ferrari Testarossa. After getting dressed, Uday would drive straight to the Olympic Club high-rise, near the People's Stadium.

He never worked on any athletic events when he went there. Instead, the club had been turned into a combination of private office, bar, and temple of amusements. His pimp friends would come and go, and some of them also had offices in the building. The secretaries looked like women from the nightclubs, which most of them probably were.

Uday usually remained at the club until about 2:00 P.M., then drove home to eat something grilled and very spicy for lunch. He began drinking at that time: cognac, whiskey, beer. After lunch he would order his girlfriends to one of the houses he owned, either his dream villa next to the Olympic Club, or the house in al-Habbaniya, or one of his palaces in Mansur or in al-Azamiya on the Tigris. Sometimes he would retire with them to his farm in al-Rashdiya. The evenings would end in a club or a bar at one of the various hotels in Baghdad. It almost seemed as if Uday wanted to drink or love himself to death since the end of the war.

Instead of moving into his villa in al-Habbaniya, we took several suites in the al-Medina Hotel, a favorite of newlyweds.

The hotel boasted a magnificent swimming pool and exqui-sitely designed, expertly maintained gardens with lush, green plants. Uday's bodyguards trucked in his "playthings," as they did whenever he traveled to al-Habbaniya. They brought a black Honda 750 with an impressively chromed frame and motor, several BMW motorcycles (Uday didn't like BMW cars, but was fascinated by the 1000 motorcycle), and two Harley-Davidson choppers.

Though Uday loved to talk about how much he wanted to go hunting, what he called hunting was usually limited to roaring through the beautiful landscape on his motorcycle, stopping short as soon as he saw pedestrians, and firing off rounds at their feet. He found it immensely gratifying when they ran off in panic and he could shoot after them.

"Fishing" was a similar pastime. Uday owned several Yamaha and Kawasaki water scooters, which were quick as arrows and produced a hellish racket. We would scoot across the surface of the lake for hours. Uday would give us the "halt" sign in the middle of the lake, and the whole horde would stop, turn off the motors, and bob quietly until the surface of the water had become relatively transparent while Uday tried to locate fish with his naked eye. Of course, the noise of the motors had already scared them all off, but he didn't care. He'd suddenly start firing his pistol into the water as if he'd lost his mind, shouting, "I'll get you. I'll get you, you beasts."

Once, furious that he hadn't hit any, he ordered us to jump in and swim back to the shore. None of us dared to contradict him. We plunged into the cool water in our body-guard uniforms and swam back, and the water scooters were collected later.

"I must educate you," Uday explained when we reached the shore, every one of us exhausted.

We continued with this sort of mad leisure-time pursuit for two or three days, and went duck hunting in between. All of us had to shoot at least one duck. Those we brought down were fed to Uday's hunting dogs. Not surprisingly, Saddam Hussein also loved duck hunting. He was an impressive marksman, who trained frequently at his own private shooting gallery. "Once," related one of our bodyguards, "Saddam was duck hunting with his political adviser. He handed his gun to his secretary and said, "See that bird in the tree over there? Shoot him." When the secretary refused, Saddam screamed at him, "What? Twenty years in the party and you still can't kill?"

On the way back from duck hunting one day, Uday spotted a young couple, who were clearly newlyweds, walking hand in hand in the garden. Uday found the woman attractive, so he stopped his motorcycle and shouted something in their direction. The two walked on as if they hadn't heard a thing. This was an affront to the president's son. Uday dismounted, nodded to his bodyguards, and went for the couple.

I knew what was next. Uday wanted the woman at any cost. It didn't matter whether she was pretty or ugly, he wanted her. He coveted her, probably more because they hadn't responded to his call than for any other reason. He hated when someone tried to resist him.

The two saw us, started to hurry, and Uday began to run. His escort sprinted to catch up. Uday overtook the lovers, grabbed the girl by the arm, and blurted, "You're much too good for this simple person." The man was in uniform, an officer with the rank of captain.

"Come, leave him. I'm more suited to you. Come with me to my suite."

The officer had been standing next to his wife as if turned to stone. All at once he screamed at Uday and started to attack him. The bodyguards restrained him, beat him brutally, and yanked him away. He cried out and defended himself desperately, but didn't stand a chance against the six bodyguards.

They dragged both of them into the foyer of the al-

Medina Hotel. The man bellowed and struggled in a rage, but was pummeled mercilessly every time he tried to break free — in the face, in the belly, in the kidneys. They didn't care that the entire hotel staff and the guests were witnesses to the scene. Everyone realized what was happening. I felt ashamed and sorry for the man, but what could I do?

Uday had the young woman brought to his suite, and we followed him. He tried to soothe her in the living room, but in her fear and shock she barely managed to utter a word, beyond stammering that they had been married only yesterday. He offered her a whiskey, which she declined, and he asked her whether she'd prefer champagne. She shook her head again, fought back tears, huddled on the couch.

Uday's voice immediately changed. Now it had the hysterical screech to it that was just as characteristic as his staccato laugh. He screamed at the woman, commanding her to undress. She pleaded desperately, "No, lord, no," but this enraged Uday even more. Before our eyes, he removed his belt, wrapped the part with the buckle around his hand and smacked the leather end into her face. The woman screamed, tried to run away, but Uday went after her, grabbed her, wrapped the belt around her throat, and pulled tight until she gagged. Only then did he loosen it again. She fell to the floor, pleading to be left alone and not to be dragged into dishonor. But he took her by the hair, hauled her into the bedroom, and threw her on the bed as if she were a sack.

Uday continued to beat her until she was bloody. He was breathing heavily, having worked himself into a state of ecstasy. The blood, the welts, the pain suffered by his victim — all that excited him, drove him into a frenzy. He threw himself on the woman, tried to kiss her, to shove his tongue into her mouth. She struggled to defend herself, but had no more strength to do so. Her cries had turned into a soft, desperate yammer. He forced her thighs apart. She managed to turn away twice, three more times. Uday slapped her face with the backs of his hands. Blood poured from her nose. He penetrated her. We heard no more screaming, but only his heated, gasping groans. It was the most degrading thing that I've ever experienced.

Uday emerged from the bedroom grinning after having satisfied himself, poured a cognac, spoke in a conversational tone of voice, as if nothing unusual had happened, as if he had just finished a dinner with a good friend.

Suddenly we heard a long, piercing scream that seemed to last forever. Then complete silence. I rushed into the bedroom, saw the open door to the balcony, rushed out, looked down. She was lying motionless, half naked, on the concrete, directly in front of the hotel entrance.

Uday joined me on the balcony. I stared at him, but he avoided my gaze, asking only, "Is she dead?"

She was dead. She had jumped from the seventh floor because she couldn't bear the humiliation.

I hurried to the foyer with the other bodyguards. Everyone already knew about the woman's suicide leap. The people stared at us, their eyes brimming with pure horror. They said nothing, but I saw in their expressions how much they must hate us, Uday, the bodyguards, me, whom they couldn't quite place. Was I Uday's brother?

The husband of the victim was screaming, "You murderers, you animals."

We called Uday, and he ordered us to have the man taken to Baghdad: to prison in Qasr al-Nihayah, "The Palace Where It Ends."

The officer — his name was Saad Abd al-Razzek — was sentenced a short while later by a military court. His crime was "insulting the president," for which paragraph 225 of the penal code specifies the death sentence. Saad Abd al-Razzek was therefore executed. A captain who had served in the Iraqi army for ten years and defended his country on the Iranian front was killed by a firing squad.

10

THE DEATH

OF THE FORETASTER

I HATED myself for being too weak to prevent the woman's rape. But what could I have done? I wouldn't have stood a chance against Uday's bodyguards, who enjoy his cruelty almost more than he does. They would have killed me. They would have executed me on the spot.

The young woman's act of desperation was taboo as a topic of conversation in the palace, as was the officer's execution. Nobody mentioned them, except that the bodyguards sometimes made crude jokes: "Why did he go so far as to insult the president? The woman wasn't worth it."

Such callousness stunned me and brought home how this kind of thing could happen anytime. What was the value of a human life among such people? Zero. What would happen if I ever met a woman Uday found appealing? Would I be ready to die for her, like the young captain?

In the weeks after returning from al-Habbaniya, Uday kept an extremely low profile. His tours of Baghdad shrank to two or three a week, as if he instinctively sought to avoid the limelight. Too many people had witnessed the events in the al-Medina Hotel. No matter how intimidated, they were bound to talk at home among themselves and to their friends. Such stories are like dominoes. Line them up, and the slightest breeze is enough to start them falling.

It seemed, however, that Saddam Hussein still hadn't gotten wind of what had transpired. The newspapers carried only a small announcement about the young captain being executed for insulting the president.

Uday concentrated increasingly on his newspapers and business ventures in Baghdad. He had several meetings with al-Haj Khaled al-Kabisi, a close friend who directed all imports from Jordan and had an office near the al-Saa Restaurant.

As a practice, Uday avoided conducting meetings or negotiations in the offices of fellow businessmen. He feared bugs and hidden cameras. His motto was "Never negotiate in a place suggested by your business partners. Mistrust everything. Question everything. Even friends can be cheaters and blackmailers." Consequently, he transacted most business in his office in the Olympic Club, where he could take advantage of his own secret microphones and subject his partners to *his* conditions.

Uday had a share in almost all of Baghdad's international hotels, and controlled all imports into Iraq. The biggest portion of his business, however, was food production. He had farms in all of Iraq's fertile regions. Agro-commercial factories, they were equipped with the latest technology and were planned along American lines. Only the best products were used, such as special seed grains that gave three times the yield of those available to the ordinary Iraqi peasant.

Uday's farms were administered by Afif and Jaudant, two specialists who had studied agriculture and agribusiness in the United States. Another man, Bahar al-Abdullah, was responsible for the gigantic cattle and sheep herds. The farms were set up as a kind of cooperative. The peasants were obliged to deliver their products to Uday, in return for which they received ridiculously low prices. In turn, they had to buy all their seed, fertilizer, and farm machinery from him.

Uday's agricultural Mafia thus controlled production and supply.

The goods were then sold in Baghdad for ten times what Uday had paid for them. And the merchants in Baghdad were forced to buy predetermined amounts from his farms, because he was the president's son. In this way, Uday profited several times on each piece of meat, each egg, and each grain of wheat that came to market via his farms. It was the perfect money machine.

Income from these ventures was administered by Uday's financial advisers, Medhat and Salhan al-Shahbander, who transferred all his profits to Switzerland. The Swiss bank accounts were accessible only to Uday and his uncle, Barzan al-Tikriti, who also administered Saddam Hussein's fortune abroad. In the tightly knit net of this corrupt system, everyone had a role to play.

Salhan al-Shahbander, who directed this empire's financial affairs, was married to an ophthalmologist named Samira. A beautiful, successful, westward-looking young woman, Samira caused a scandal and created a family crisis whose effects continue to be felt in the palace. When she was first introduced to the president, rumor had it that he fell head over heels in love with her. For weeks he showered the young doctor with favors, sending her jewelry, cars, clothes, and expensive perfumes. He was crazy about her.

Women consider Saddam a handsome, attractive, fascinating man. He is strong, powerful, and dangerous, but also brutal and without scruples — normally repulsive attributes, which, in Saddam's case, make him nearly irresistible. Baghdad's finest women fight for a private audience with him. There are unbelievably long lists of men and women seeking the chance to meet him one-on-one. A photograph showing you together with Saddam Hussein is priceless. During the war with Iran, Saddam put this allure to peculiar good use, when he initiated a campaign aimed at persuading the population to donate their valuables in order to boost Iraq's sagging financial reserves. Evening after evening, the television would display elegantly dressed women from the cream of society coming to the palace to donate rings, necklaces, gems, and family heirlooms. Of course, this footage was also a way of intimidating the wealthy families, giving them cause to worry about the disgrace of refusing the president's appeal.

But the success of the appeal sprang mostly from the narcissistic desire of the women, who were eager to meet the Leader, to appear with him on TV, and to pay homage to Iraq and praise his policies. Saddam Hussein would kiss their hands in front of the running cameras, turn on his charisma full strength, and melt them with his impressive charm.

Dr. Samira reacted differently. She was reticent, refusing to encourage him. Initially, she turned Saddam down, and he dispatched Kamel Hannah, his closest bodyguard, as well as his friend and foretaster, to her practice laden with gifts. Saddam besieged her, flattered her — the murderous despot revealed his charms as a subtle seducer. She couldn't resist. After weeks of courtship, Samira accepted his tryst. They met in one of his eighty-three palaces. The president managed to keep the affair a secret for more than half a year.

Kamel Hannah was perfect. He kept everything hidden from Saddam's wife, Sajida, as he did when Saddam had the affair with Majida, the tennis-player wife of Culture and Information Minister Hamed Youssef Hammadi. In that incident, Saddam had been ready to leave his wife for Majida, but ultimately decided to end the affair for reasons of state.

This time though, Saddam chose a different course. He married Samira clandestinely, taking her as his second wife. Only Kamel Hannah and Samira's husband, who had to be told, knew about it.

The rumors didn't start circulating until Samira became pregnant and gave birth to a son. Sajida caught wind of the rumors.

Sajida had been the one generating tranquillity in the family up to that point, although she, too, was given to some eccentricities. Her passion for shopping rivaled that of Imelda Marcos, the wife of the deposed Philippine dictator. Her hunger for acquisitions was like an addiction, causing her to jet to Europe every month with her fashion advisers. She was a regular at Dior, Yves Saint Laurent, and Chanel, though she never set foot in their salons. Instead she had their collections and models flown to Geneva.

In clothes fetishism, Sajida even outdid Uday and Saddam Hussein — she was known to change outfits almost hourly. Whenever she was bored, she had her ladies in waiting bedeck her with jewels, and then she walked through the palace, regarding herself in front of the long, baroque rows of mirrors.

Only one thing obsessed this woman more than clothing: how to acquire more and more exclusive jewelry. Jewels were her only topic of conversation during her rare appearances at parties; she'd go on enthusiastically about where she got which ring, and in which city a particular earring was purchased.

She, too, had her own special police bodyguards, and like Uday, she treated them like bondmen. Once she planted tomatoes in her garden in a time of scorching sun. She was playing at being an ordinary housewife. Of course, the tomatoes couldn't stand the heat, and withered after a few days. She was so irate, she had six of her bodyguards, who had been ordered to water the plants, whipped and thrown into jail for ten days.

When Sajida got wind of her husband's secret marriage, she turned to her father, Khairallah Talfah, whom Saddam had made governor of Baghdad. That started a sequence of events that rocked even the tightly knit Saddam clan. Khairallah publicly censured the behavior of his stepson and son-in-law. He advised his daughter to leave the palace, and she consequently moved into a grand villa on the palace grounds, next to the villas of her daughters Rina, Raghd, and Hala.

Uday was consumed with rage when he heard about her moving out, and learned what his father had done to his beloved and revered mother. He had always been her favorite child. She covered up his scandals, protected him from his father's rages, forgave him everything. And now this.

But Uday hated not so much his father as his father's bodyguard and foretaster, Kamel Hannah: "He's the one who's always providing my father with women and girls. If only he hadn't brought that whore. If only he had killed her like all the others," he complained at every opportunity.

Until Samira, Saddam Hussein had had most of his lovers disposed of by Kamel Hannah and his men after he'd tired of them. They were run over, encased in concrete, and their bodies dropped into the Tigris, east of the palace.

By pure coincidence, I once witnessed a couple of such murders. Our convoy with Uday was on its way to Project No. 7, when we came upon Kamel Hannah's men chasing two women with black Mercedes limousines. They hit them, drove over them, and backed up and drove over the lifeless bodies several times more. Then they dragged the corpses to one of the feeder roads connecting Saddam's palace with the steamboats plying the Tigris. Uday had us stop the convoy, got out, and spoke with Kamel Hannah. "Whores of my father," he told me then.

After the melodramatic separation from Sajida, Saddam moved Samira and her child into a wing of the palace. Saddam referred to his principal palace as Project 2,000. It had been designed by Austrian architects and constructed by French firms at a cost of more than $500 million.

His decision to have Samira move in was felt as a disgrace and a humiliation by the whole family, especially Uday. I knew Uday well by now. I had to dress exactly like him every day, change clothes when he changed, have my hair cut when his was. I conversed with him and imitated him. I got to know his soul through my forced external resemblance to him. I noticed when he was feeling well and when he was suffering. Besides, he wasn't exactly one to hide his thoughts and feelings in normal circumstances. He bragged about his women, recited the stories of his shooting orgies at the clubs over and over, and had himself heaped with praise after yet another hotel guest was beaten senseless by his bodyguards.

Uday had become like an open book for me, even when he tried hard to be as discreet as possible — like now. In fact, all of us noticed that the family council was meeting exceptionally often. These meetings, usually convened in different palaces and arranged by telephone just beforehand for security reasons, normally occurred no more than once a week. Now they were taking place almost daily. Every time he returned from one, Uday seemed frustrated and full of anger. He spoke contemptuously of Kamel Hannah, calling him "the spineless lackey who destroyed my mother." His fury also found a target in Farouk Abu-Omar, who was considered Saddam Hussein's private pimp. Farouk procured the women who were passed on to Kamel Hannah.

Uday never spoke disparagingly of his father. But I noticed that he had stopped wearing one of his favorite watches, a special concoction in gold that bore Saddam Hussein's image on its face. He also ceased the gushing praise that used to culminate in his father's literal idolization. I remember one scene from his birthday. After the party had turned into an orgy, Uday took a twenty-five-dinar note, lit it, held it up, and screamed at the naked men and women seeking their pleasure beside the pool, "Do what you want, but remember one thing always: Any one of you speaks ill of my father, and you'll burn like this banknote."

And Uday knew no limits. Why should he? His father and grandfather had taught him as a little boy that rivals had to be eliminated. Uday considered Samira his mother's rival. He couldn't eliminate Samira, but Kamel Hannah was another matter.

It had been weeks since he had given me something to do. My job was often monotonous. It offered little variety and sometimes bored me to tears. Yet, even when Uday had no public appearances, I received daily instructions, if only to inform me which suit to wear the following day. These clothing decisions applied, by the way, to all the bodyguards. Uday had suits not only in each color, but also in every shade of each color, and he loved it when all of us dressed the same. Getting dressed and undressed became a daily ritual, an absurd routine that helped to allay the sense of tension within the Saddam clan. For a while everything seemed okay again — until the day we were told that Kamel Hannah had been ordered by Saddam Hussein to organize a party on the occasion of the Ministers' Meeting.

This was in early November 1988.

Invitations went out to all the ministers, the leading party members, and the elite of Baghdad society. Suzanne Mubarak, wife of Egyptian president Hosni Mubarak, was expected to attend. Kamel Hannah also sent an invitation to Qusay, Uday's younger brother, but not to Uday. Uday was furious, considering his omission a provocation and a sign of total lack of respect. He spent days thinking of ways to rid himself of this disgrace. Together with Namir al-Tikriti, his master of ceremonies, he came up with a ludicrously childish solution: He would throw a competing party at the same time, in a part of the garden adjoining Kamel Hannah's gala.

He had loudspeakers set up and ordered his cooks to create a huge buffet that would be more lavish and exquisite than Kamel Hannah's. Invitations were sent to all of his friends, including members of the underworld. "We need Baghdad's most beautiful, attractive, and clever women," he told Ali Asuad, his procurer. Even I was invited.

It was a warm evening. The liveried servants circulated trays of chilled champagne and hors d'oeuvres. Although the two parties were separated only by a low hedge, the music from Kamel Hannah's party was almost impossible to hear.

Consequently, Uday ordered Adel Akle and his musicians to play only unobtrusive background music. He was clearly looking to make a scene — all of us could feel it — but he maintained enough self-control not to appear to take the first step. We ate, made small talk. The mood was tense, self-conscious, and constrained, far removed from the usual relaxed and vulgar atmosphere that was the rule for his parties. One danger sign was that Uday started in on the hard drinks early. Even before getting something to eat, he threw back several whiskeys, without ice or water. Instead of wine, which we all drank with our food, he had cognac. He drank not for enjoyment but for the high proof.

Kamel Hannah's party was very different. Almost all the ranking politicians had come, but the atmosphere was informal and easy, the mood was right, and the guests were enjoying themselves. Even Suzanne Mubarak had turned up, as well as Qusay Hussein with his wife, Zainab, the daughter of a general. Occasionally, Qusay's laughter could be heard over the hedge, not a *hihihihi* like his brother's, but hearty and loud.

Born in 1966, Qusay was two years younger than Uday and me. Unlike Uday's, his time at the Baghdad School for Boys hadn't been marked by scandal. While his daily appearances differed little from Uday's, in that he too came with bodyguards who would sit at the front of the class and next to him, Qusay's manner was always reserved at recess. He hated the loud, screeching, offensive displays of his older brother. If Qusay, too, shuttled to school in a convoy that brought him right to the main entrance, he didn't then thunder through the schoolyard in an open convertible, with music pounding. Qusay seemed introverted, intellectual, sensitive, a tranquil young gentleman at first glance. In his made-to-measure British suits, he appeared the opposite of his brother. Uday was always the wild one. When we wore our hair short, he had an explosion of hair like Jimi Hendrix. When our attire consisted of dark trousers and a white, short-sleeved shirt,

Uday wore jeans and a T-shirt, printed with American slogans. He wanted to be different.

Qusay finished school with top marks in 1984 and registered at the University of Baghdad, where he majored in law and political science. Like Uday, he was a poor student, attending no more than fifteen to twenty lectures a semester and sometimes leaving them after a half hour. But, though extravagant, his behavior was not as provocative as Uday's. He'd just stand up and go — calmly, head high, back straight. Qusay always had an aura.

He knew he was special, but didn't have to prove it. Everyone felt it from the way he moved and acted, the way he spoke. Not a single loud word, no screeching, no pretensions born of late puberty. He was someone special, but not necessarily someone you'd want to, or could, get too close to.

Because he didn't like sitting next to his "sweaty" fellow students in the lecture halls, he'd sit in the office of the dean, Dr. Mohammed al-Douri. Al-Douri was a slimy, base careerist. He'd bow obsequiously every time he encountered Qusay on his way to class. Qusay would nod curtly and continue on his way, his eyes focused straight ahead and his step quick, followed by his horde of bodyguards, normally consisting of twenty to twenty-five people. Al-Douri would try to keep pace like a loyal lapdog. The dean would personally open the door to his office whenever Qusay decided to study there. The fact that Qusay would always sit at al-Douri's desk, leaving the dean standing in front of the president's son, was a constant source of amusement at the university. Qusay wrote his final exams in the dean's office, instead of with the other students.

He had his own clique, just like Uday. It was made up exclusively of sons and daughters of ministers and the highest party members. Young people of "lower" social standing had no chance of being accepted, or even of approaching its members.

Qusay's closest friends were: Bassem Latif Nassif Jasim, son of the then media and culture minister; Sael Souheil, a general's son; Marvan Adnan Sharif, a minister's son; Aiad Saadam Ghaidan, another minister's son; and Ali Ghateb, son of a ranking party member.

None of his friends attained the eighty-fifth percentile in high school needed to qualify for study at an Iraqi university, but Qusay fixed that problem for them. He completed his university degree in 1988 with excellent grades, which were so good they were published: "Qusay Saddam Hussein, the top graduate of the year 1988, achieved 99.9 percent out of a possible 100."

Saddam Hussein spent noticeably more time with Qusay than with Uday. He started to mold and prepare him for higher duties during his time at the university. The idea was to use every means possible to prevent Qusay from slipping into the underworld as Uday had done. Saddam had Qusay marry Zainab, the daughter of the renowned general Maher Abd al-Rashid, who had been responsible for numerous victories during the Iran-Iraq war, among them the battle of Tahrir Alfan. After the war, the general was hailed as a glorious hero.

Saddam Hussein valued the general, appreciated his capabilities, needed him. Through the marriage of Qusay and Zainab, he secured the general's loyalty and gained as allies the respected al-Rashid family, which was untouched by scandal, something more valuable for Qusay than any education.

Nine months after the marriage, their daughter Zaina was born. Qusay was appointed president of the Iraqi riding club after graduation. At the same time, Saddam appointed him to the top echelons of the intelligence services. Qusay became deputy director of the al-Khass.

I'd seen Qusay only once since my training as fidai. He too had a fidai, but, unlike me, his was a direct relative, a distant cousin who looked just like him. I have no idea whether this cousin had to undergo the same training as I.

Qusay and his wife left Kamel Hannah's party a little before midnight. Uday's bodyguards observed them going.

Uday had become completely drunk in the meantime. He no longer cared whether or not he was interfering with the foretaster's party, and directed Adel Akle to play louder. He strode from table to table like a tiger. He spoke with no one. In his right hand he clenched his Magic Wand, a battery-powered electric knife with a blade as sharp as a scalpel. Uday used the device to cut his roses, but all evening he had been holding it in his hands. He would turn it on, then off, then on again. He cut the linen napkins in half, and sliced fruits from the buffet and even his cigars.

Right before midnight, we suddenly heard shots from next door. Several salvos, one after the other. Then loud laughter and more salvos from a Kalashnikov. Uday immediately sent several bodyguards to Kamel Hannah's party, among them Saddam al-Tikriti. Smiling, Saddam al-Tikriti returned with his men a few seconds later. "What happened?" Uday snarled. Saddam al-Tikriti grinned, his arms spread wide. "Kamel Hannah is standing on a table and firing in the air for joy." We heard the gunfire again as he spoke. It was nothing unusual to fire into the air at such parties. Uday did it almost every time he cruised through Baghdad.

But this was different. It wasn't Uday letting off steam, but Kamel Hannah, the foretaster, Saddam Hussein's loyal dog. Uday screamed at Saddam al-Tikriti, "Go back and order the son of a whore to stop! Tell him the president's son doesn't like it!" Al-Tikriti returned not two minutes later. His face was like stone. You could tell his report was going to lead to something bad. Uday screamed, "What did he say?"

We heard the firing again.

Al-Tikriti replied, "Kamel Hannah says he obeys only the president's orders." All at once, Uday broke for the hedge separating the two parties as if he'd gone mad. He forced his way through the bushes and ran to Kamel Hannah's table, his rage and defiance obvious to all. Kamel

Hannah was standing with legs spread, right hand grasping a Kalashnikov, in the left a spare magazine. He fired yet another salvo when he saw Uday. He held the weapon casually with one hand, the recoil shaking his body. He laughed, clearly and loudly.

Uday screamed at him, "I order you to stop!" The babble of voices suddenly ceased, and the musicians stopped playing. Uday bellowed again, "Get down!"

Kamel Hannah slowly climbed down from the table. Everyone watched him. His expression was serious. He planted himself in front of Uday, very close to him.

"I obey only the commands of the president," said Hannah, clearly also drunk. Rage shook Uday. It was the first time in his life that anyone had publicly defied him. A foretaster, a protégé of his father, a slimy creature dared to provoke him, the first son of the Prophet's direct descendant. Openly. In front of Baghdad's finest. In front of Suzanne Mubarak. Uday found no words to express his fury. Nobody can say what was going through his mind during those seconds — the humiliation had to have extinguished the last spark of rational thinking. Rules and morality had never meant anything to him anyway. His father used to take him to executions when he was five. He used to watch tortures when he was ten. All of that, all the violence and hatred and lack of self-control, suddenly overwhelmed him.

He raised his electric knife and hit Kamel Hannah on the head with all his might, once, twice. Kamel Hannah hadn't expected the attack. He staggered back two steps, and Uday went after him like a wildcat. Like a fencer, he drove at him and slit his throat with one powerful and well-aimed thrust.

Kamel Hannah gasped. The blood welled from his gaping wound. His eyes opened wide, he fell on his side onto the table, the plates and cutlery crashed to the floor, women screamed. Suzanne Mubarak was literally yanked away from the table by her bodyguards, who bundled her outside. The wife of the Egyptian president was in such shock that she couldn't even cover her face with her hands.

Kamel Hannah rolled off the table and fell to the floor. Blood was everywhere. Uday, bereft of his senses, rushed him again, flailing away at his defenseless victim. Kamel Hannah tried to protect himself, attempted to raise the Kalashnikov, which he was still holding, but Uday shoved the weapon aside and beat him until he stopped moving.

Kamel Hannah's brother, a senior intelligence officer, tried to throw himself on Uday, screaming again and again, "I'll kill you. I'll kill you!" But Uday's officers held him back. They wrestled him to the floor, where they managed to hand-cuff him.

Uday seemed in a trance, oblivious to the screams. Breathing heavily, he stood astride the dying Kamel Hannah, drew his revolver, and pulled the trigger. The first 9-mm projectile ripped open Kamel Hannah's diaphragm. The second hit him in the breast.

The garden became absolutely quiet. The guests stared in shock at Uday and the body of Kamel Hannah, and no-body dared say anything. A few officers left the table and ran to the telephone to inform Saddam Hussein.

Uday stared for several minutes at his dying victim. He stood completely still above the man he hated so much. He then raised his head, his face expressionless, and looked at the faces of the party guests. But he didn't register the people around him. Uday was somewhere far away at that moment. He probably hadn't yet realized what had happened. Suddenly he grinned, dropped his weapon, and trotted back through the hedge into the other garden. From there he ran to one of the upper stories of the ministerial building and locked himself in an office. His bodyguards followed him.

Saddam Hussein arrived a few minutes later. He was wearing trousers, his shirt was open, and he had on shoes without socks. He looked as if he had taken only a few seconds to dress. Saddam was shaken. He ran to Kamel Hannah, leaned over his friend, shouted, "The doctor, where's the doctor?"

It wasn't more than a couple of minutes before the ambulance arrived. The medics put Kamel Hannah on a gurney, but it was too late. He was beyond saving. Saddam didn't want to accept the fact. He urged them on, climbed into the ambulance, and sped with his friend to the Ibn-Sina Hospital. Kamel Hannah was already dead when he was loaded into the ambulance.

I learned the subsequent events of that night only the next day from Azzam, Uday's first bodyguard. Uday, who was now officially a murderer, had tried to commit suicide with sleeping pills that he had brought to him by his bodyguards. "He swallowed a whole bottle," Azzam said. When he collapsed, gasping for breath, Azzam and his men took him to Ibn-Sina.

"The doctors told Saddam that his son had also been brought in," said Azzam, shaking his head and continuing, "Uday stammered, 'Don't tell my father. I want to die.' "

When told of Uday's presence, Saddam flew into a rage and burst into his son's room. The doctors were preparing to insert a tube down the throat of this self-described suicide case to pump out his stomach. Uday vomited, choked, a picture of misery. Saddam ripped the tubing from the doctors' hands, shoved them aside, and hit Uday in the face. He bellowed, "Your blood will flow like my friend's!"

Even Saddam Hussein couldn't cope with the murder of his friend. It was days before Uday was released from the hospital. No word emanated from the presidential palace. None of the newspapers reported anything. Within the palace, the official line was that Uday's violent deed was the act of a "completely normal but unstable, violent, and uncontrolled person. Uday has always let himself be guided by his aggressive feelings."

We all knew that this downplaying of the events was

nothing less than a bid to secure consensus in advance. Everyone in the palace knew it. Uday had always been an animal, a sadist who enjoyed violence and killing.

This slaughter, this tearing apart of an enemy, was more than finding an outlet for his violent emotions, however. In committing this act, Uday was carrying out an indirect command of his mother: "I want that Kamel Hannah, that dealer in women, destroyed," Sajida had said several times. No doubt she hadn't intended Uday to take it as a direct order. Yet, by repeating it, she managed to goad her son, who loved and idolized his mother, into greater fury.

As soon as he was released from the hospital, Uday flew with his clothes guru, Yassem, to Geneva. Saddam Hussein had him airlifted to Uncle Barzan al-Tikriti as "punishment." Although Saddam announced that Uday would have to stand trial and pay for his crime, he simultaneously brought pressure to bear on the family of Kamel Hannah, with the result that Kamel Hannah's brother, who had wanted to shoot Uday at the party, now "beseeched" the president to show mercy on the culprit. The accusation against Uday was withdrawn.

Nonetheless, family politics assumed a new dynamic during the discussions of this murder. For Saddam, the family had always been the chief instrument in maintaining control over state institutions, as it had been in Arab societies for centuries. Family politics, and the smoothness of family relations, were therefore of transcendent importance. Saddam had sometimes placed greater priority on clearing up obscure differences arising out of marriage negotiations than on conducting serious economic policy. He had strengthened political alliances through marriage. The most important members of the government had to have personal ties with him.

This had worked to his advantage until now. With Kamel Hannah's murder and Uday's departure for Geneva, however, open feuding broke out within the Saddam clan, potentially threatening his hold on power. What began with Samira's move into the palace developed into a tragedy along the lines of Shakespeare's *Macbeth*.

Sajida, her father Khairallah Talfah, and her brother Adnan Khairallah all severely reproached Saddam over the murder of Kamel Hannah, but the strongest response was Adnan Khairallah's. Adnan had been close to Saddam Hussein since childhood. If Saddam ever had a friend, it was his cousin. When Saddam became president, he made Adnan defense minister. At the end of the war against Iran, he also appointed him chief of the general staff.

Adnan Khairallah was beloved in Iraq. The people considered him a war hero — a great general who was also concerned about the well-being of his soldiers. After the ceasefire, he developed numerous plans to reintegrate war invalids into society. Soldiers who had been conspicuously brave and successful in battle received bonuses in the form of property, apartments, and tax benefits.

Such social programs made him a popular hero, a star. He had himself paid homage in Baghdad as the number-two man behind Saddam Hussein. That was his first mistake. But the acclaim was so great that this egocentric self-aggrandizement remained without immediate consequence.

Saddam's chief counselors made careful note of the "waves of support" for Adnan. But the president failed to react to those developments until the murder of Kamel Hannah — an unusual lapse. Saddam normally had no scruples in eliminating even the closest relatives when he considered them rivals.

Adnan's second great mistake was to raise the family argument to a level that made it appear as if he wanted to personally discredit or even topple Saddam Hussein.

Adnan referred constantly to the dishonor done by Saddam to his sister. He found it outrageous that Saddam should continue to live in the palace while Sajida had to move out, and he reproached Saddam for destroying the tranquillity within the family for the love of his mistress, Samira.

The conflict became so vehement that the bodyguards and the palace servants got wind of it. Neither Sajida nor her father appeared at the weekly family meetings. Sajida even warned her bodyguards to keep Samira far away from her villa on the palace grounds. In a conspicuous show of support, Adnan drove over to visit his sister almost every day.

Saddam Hussein reacted characteristically. First he sent Samira and their son, Ali, to Europe. Then he delivered the first blow against the family. The political police conducted raids on all the businesses owned by his adoptive father. Seventeen of Khairallah Talfah's managers were detained and pilloried. They were accused of cheating the people of millions of dinars through criminal activities. Everyone in Baghdad knew that Saddam Hussein was behind this act, but the day after the raids, in a televised speech, he had the nerve to praise Khairallah Talfah as an excellent businessman and politician.

The really mortal blow came a few months later, when Saddam invited the whole family to an "outing" in northern Iraq — Sajida, Qusay, his three daughters Raghd, Hala, and Rina, as well as Uday, who had returned from Geneva in the meantime. His daughters' husbands and Qusay's wife, Zainab, were also part of the group, along with Adnan Khairallah and Ali Hassan al-Majid, the man responsible for the poison gas attacks on the Kurds. They flew in several helicopters. Saddam sat in one, Sajida and their daughters in the other. Uday and Qusay took their private choppers. Ali Hassan al-Majid also had a separate helicopter, as did Adnan Khairallah. The joint departure was so spectacular it was shown on TV.

Twenty-four hours later, with Saddam and his close family still in northern Iraq, came the report on Iraqi TV's main news broadcast that Defense Minister Adnan Khairallah, who had been forced to return to Baghdad earlier than the others because of a pressing matter, had been caught in a sandstorm and crashed in his helicopter. He and his bodyguards had died in the accident.

The whole family attended Adnan Khairallah's burial. Sajida was supported by her father. Everyone wept. Even Saddam Hussein seemed dejected. The burial ended in a scandal, when Khairallah Talfah yelled at Saddam Hussein, "You have destroyed the life of my daughter and had my son murdered. I swear eternal vengeance!"

Over the next few days, Khairallah Talfah began disseminating his own explanation for his son's helicopter crash, which pointed to the conclusion that it was no accident, but murder.

First: There was no sandstorm anywhere in Iraq when Adnan Khairallah flew back to Baghdad.

Second: Adnan had no reason to return prematurely to Baghdad.

Third: He, Khairallah Talfah, had received indications that four explosive charges had been hidden on his son's helicopter.

Fourth: The explosives had been planted by an agent with the code name Karim.

Fifth: Karim had received instructions for the assassination from Hussein Kamel, who was married to Saddam's oldest daughter, Raghd.

Sixth: The operation was directed by Ali Hassan al-Majid.

Seventh: Karim had fled to Paris on an Iraqi Airways flight on the day of the assassination.

Saddam Hussein had nothing to say to all of these accusations. He and his bodyguards went bird hunting.

II

THE DUMB GIRL

AUGUST 1989. Uday was in a stir. Azzam had just brought him news of a shootout at the bus station in central Baghdad among fifty recently discharged border troops. Dozens of civilians had been killed, and the Republican Guards, aided by the political police, were trying to reestablish order. The fighting would continue all night.

The next day, Uday dispatched me to the station with my bodyguards to perform a simple but dangerous task: I was to inspect the scene in person and immediately report back to Project No. 7. Yassem brought me Uday's black uniform. I changed quickly, and our convoy left less than twenty minutes later in ten identical black Mercedes limousines. Calm had again been restored, and the bus station was surrounded by special units. Armored cars and soldiers were deployed on the square in front. Between the soldiers and the station milled hundreds of ragged people waiting for their buses, a dismal picture. The crowd retreated as our convoy drove up. I got out, along with my twelve bodyguards, and walked toward them. It was eerily quiet. The people stared at me, their gazes empty, their silence speaking volumes. Mistrust. I was last here exactly one year ago. The war against Iran had just ended, and thousands were celebrating tumultuously in the streets of Baghdad. The mood was of hope for change ahead, of boundless joy. And now?

The eight-year conflict with Iran had bankrupted our country. Our people were impoverished. Our army, which still numbered almost one million men, had seen better days. Unrest and criminality were rampant among the demoralized and jobless soldiers. Marauding troops were constantly involved in robberies somewhere. We in the palace had heard that such disarray existed, but we just didn't want to accept the facts. Now I saw the situation with my own eyes. The dead had been carted away already, but dried blood remained on the sizzling hot asphalt.

I asked four women waiting with their children how they were. They sank to the ground reverently before me. I had nothing to give them, so I asked about their concerns. "Oh, lord, we don't know how to provide for our children. Everything is so expensive."

I promised I'd take care of them, and had one of my bodyguards write down an address. My bodyguards then forced me into the car, and our convoy sped back to Project No. 7. As soon as I was back, I wrote a report for Uday, relating what the woman had told me, that they had no money to raise their children. I said I thought the soldiers behind the shootout must have it no better. After all, an ordinary soldier earned no more than twenty-two dinars a month, just enough not to starve.

Uday was indignant at my behavior. He whipped me in the face with his electric cable and raged, "That isn't true. Say it isn't true." He beat me again, screaming, "Why didn't you follow instructions? Why did you speak with the people? Nobody ordered you to do that! You're my fidai. Don't you ever forget it!"

A huge account of the events at the bus station appeared the following day in Uday's newspaper, *Babel:* POLICE ARREST CAR THIEVES, blared the headline. The story recounted a firefight between the Baghdad police and a group of car thieves that resulted in deaths and injuries. The television and radio news carried identical falsehoods. This official disinformation was obviously intended to maintain the fiction of a normal postwar life.

The reality was different. Saddam confronted severe social and economic problems maintaining his broad and highly developed military-industrial infrastructure while providing for a peacetime army of one million.

Iraq may have been bankrupt, but Uday didn't care. After the excitement over Kamel Hannah's murder, he was more concerned with showing Baghdad society that he himself had returned to normal: Uday Saddam Hussein, powerful son of the president. He had no sense of responsibility to the people. He followed the rule ascribed to Marie-Antoinette: "If your people have no bread, let them eat cake."

Uday displayed his riches more ostentatiously than ever. He told us he'd managed to complete his watch collection while in Geneva. And when he crowed that he now owned more than a thousand watches, he counted on our applause.

Gradually he resumed his daily routine, cruising the Baghdad clubs and hotels, drinking to excess, engaging in wild scenes with an entourage of twenty or more women. Uday found a new imaginary enemy during his expeditions. Earlier it had always been Persians, Jews, Egyptians, and bluebottle flies that he hated. Now those demons were joined by the Kuwaitis. Baghdad was overrun with Kuwaitis at the time. Thousands of them flew in from Kuwait City every Thursday to amuse themselves. Alcohol and prostitution were prohibited in Kuwait as in Saudi Arabia, and these sons of the desert took advantage of Baghdad's liberal atmosphere to party and have a good time. "They swarm into the hotels like hordes of locusts," Uday complained. "They flaunt their petrodollars and make their living by cheating us." The truth, of course, was different. Iraq had survived during the war with Iran only because Kuwait had supported Saddam's regime for years with billion-dollar credits.

On one of his tours, Uday ran into his old friend, Fahd

al-Ahmed al-Sabah, brother of the emir of Kuwait, in the al-Rashid Hotel. Uday had known Fahd for years and had always praised him. "He is my brother." As chairmen of their respective Olympic committees and presidents of their respective national soccer associations, the two were in regular contact.

I wasn't present at this meeting, but heard about it the next day. Uday had greeted Fahd enthusiastically and kissed him like a brother. But his effusions of joy lasted only briefly. Fahd, Uday's bodyguards told me, had bluntly confronted him about Iraq's national debt. "Iraq owes us eleven billion dollars. When are you going to pay?" he asked Uday to his face. Uday still hadn't stopped fuming about this unbelievable faux pas committed by his friend. "They're thieves, common, devious thieves. They've been stealing from us for years."

He paced around his office like a tiger. Munem Hammed entered and handed him a folder with background information about Iraqi-Kuwaiti relations. Uday sat down at his desk, read impatiently, turning documents, nodding in agreement. He jumped up and inundated Munem Hammed with a torrent of words: "You know as well as I do that they're stealing our oil. They're pumping off our oil in Rumeila. Rumeila belongs to us," he insisted angrily. "Say it, Munem. You know it's true."

The Rumeila oilfield is bisected by the Iran-Kuwaiti border. The greater part is in Iraqi territory, the lesser in Kuwait. Both sides exploited it, but because of their more efficient technology, Kuwaiti production quotas were conspicuously higher than Iraq's.

"That's right. They're stealing our oil from Rumeila, and then dare pose as the underwriters of Iraq," agreed Munem Hammed with unusual subservience. He added, "Lord, they're producing oil from a field that really belongs completely to us. The borders are drawn all wrong. Rumeila belongs to Iraq."

"The day will come when we prove it to them. Father has spoken of it several times."

Uday pulled out a map showing Kuwait as one of three government districts of the Ottoman Empire and part of what would later become Iraq. He stared at the map for a long time before quoting an entry on it: "We are going to expand the borders of Iraq to the southern part of Kuwait. Only the Iraqis and nobody else can sign treaties over Kuwait, and we thus consider the treaty between Kuwait and Great Britain as illegal from the day of its inception. Nobody, either in Kuwait or anywhere else, has the right to rule the Kuwaiti people, because they are the Iraqi people. The days of the sheikdoms are past."

This text was written by General Abdul Karim Kassem, the future president of Iraq, six days after Kuwait's declaration of independence. Uday didn't care that Kassem was a mortal enemy of his father and that Saddam Hussein had had Kassem assassinated. He cared only that Kassem's words lent support to his arguments and documented that Iraq's claim to Kuwait was long-standing.

A British protectorate since 1899, Kuwait was granted full independence on June 19, 1961, under the government of Abdullah al-Salem al-Sabah. There had been persistent border disputes between the sheikdom of Kuwait and Iraq prior to Kuwaiti statehood, and Iraq, which had joined the League of Nations as a formally independent state in 1932, had always justified its demands on Kuwaiti territory by the fact that Kuwait had been part of the formal Ottoman administrative district of Basra, and by the claim that Iraq was the legitimate successor to the Ottoman empire.

In 1961, Iraqi troops crossed the border to Kuwait and advanced as far as Mutla, twenty-five miles from Kuwait City. Six thousand British soldiers, dispatched to Kuwait with the greatest possible speed, threw the Iraqis back.

The attempted annexation didn't alter in any respect the imprecise definition of Kuwait's borders, going back to

Sir Percy Cox. In the period following World War I, Cox was the British high commissioner for the region known as Mesopotamia. He called the Uqair Conference in 1922 to put an end to scrapping with marauding Bedouins and egoistic rulers about supposed borders. Forcing all parties to a table, he took a red pencil and drew a line from the tip of the Gulf to the Trans-Jordanian border. Then he added two additional lines to create neutral zones, to be shared by Saudi Arabia, Iraq, and Kuwait.

These schematic borders, with their capriciously created, geographically ill-defined starting points, satisfied nobody. They gave a piece of Kuwaiti territory to Saudi Arabia and Saudi territory to Iraq, and the two neutral zones they created were to turn into a source of infinite quarrels and feuds. Yet those decisions stood from 1922 until now. Oil had come into the equation since then, however.

In 1963 after Kassem's fall, Iraq recognized Kuwait as a state, but not its borders. "It's true," said Uday, suddenly the international politician, "that we've sat with the Kuwaitis in the UN and the Arab League. But the borders are wrong, and the best thing would be to merge the two countries."

What he didn't say was that, with this policy of "bringing Kuwait home," Iraq would be rid of its sorrows in one masterstroke. The marauding soldiers would once again have something to do. And with the treasures of Kuwait's banks, Iraq could satisfy its people.

I remained silent during the conversation between Uday and Munem Hammed, stretched out on the couch, and listened, trying not to disturb them. I knew Uday was only parroting the words of his father. He concluded with, "There wouldn't be a Kuwait anyway if my father had been governing in 1961."

This was the first time they spoke openly in Project No. 7 about an invasion of Kuwait, but not the last time. But for now that was it. Uday once again turned to his search for pleasure.

I jotted down the most salient points of this conversation, developing them with extracts from Iraqi newspaper articles about Kuwait and the border problem. Their common message was that there had never been agreement about the borders between the two countries. Baghdad would accept the current border only if Kuwait was ready to cede the islands of Warbah and Bubiyan in the Persian Gulf, which Kuwait had always refused to do up to now.

Other articles denounced the boundless wealth of the Kuwaitis: "Emir Jaber al-Ahmad al-Sabah's private parking garage contains forty luxury limousines. For a hobby, the emir raises hunting falcons valued at $5 million. His palace has fountains of gold. The Dasman Palace is a pleasure dome with two hundred rooms in which the unbelievers devote themselves to wild orgies."

Inwardly, I had to grin at that. If this story was true, Uday's parking facilities alone were larger than those of the emir of Kuwait, and Uday indulged almost daily in orgiastic feasts, complete with his transvestite friends. Such newspaper reports were pure demagoguery, meant to distract attention from the poor economic conditions in Iraq and the excesses of the Saddam family. But not everything could be covered up, thanks to Uday.

One day in the fall of 1989, at the al-Rashid Hotel, Uday was extremely drunk, his bodyguards likewise. A little girl appeared, selling fresh flowers, accompanied by her mother. Her name was Linda, and her parents were Palestinians from Lebanon. Uday saw the girl, liked her, and ordered his bodyguards to take her. Everyone in the hotel witnessed how she and her mother were led away.

The bodies of the girl and her mother were discovered a week later in the vicinity of al-Mahgreb Street in Baghdad. Uday had violated the girl and left her mother for his bodyguards.

Uday threw a party a short while later in the al-Said Club. As usual, he ordered Adel Akle to sing the song about his father, "Saddam, Oh, Saddam You Great and Powerful One, God Keep You for Us, God Preserve Your Youth." Uday was humming along raptly, accompanied by his bodyguards, when Asra Hafez, a young, pretty girl, laughed out loud. She was drunk and clearly didn't know what she was doing. The president's son jumped up, grabbed her by the hair, and screamed, "Why are you laughing?"

Asra wasn't about to be cowed by his roughness. She laughed again, giggled, then asked mockingly, "How old is the young president Adel is singing about?" And she tried to push him away. Uday let go of her, and she straightened her hair. Throwing back her mane with a saucy motion, she stared at him as he stood before her, quaking with rage. She met his gaze. Nothing happened for a few seconds, then Asra couldn't hold it back any longer. She burst out laughing, almost bent double, and then tried to contain herself by pressing her hands to her mouth. She laughed so infectiously that others couldn't help but grin.

Not Uday: He grabbed her, dragged her out of the club, pulled out his pistol, and fired three bullets into her chest in front of the shocked club guests. She died instantly.

Everyone could see that it was he who had fired, but his friend Sirvan al-Jaf, who imported cars for him, was the one charged with the crime. Sirvan al-Jaf was sentenced to eight months in prison.

In my notes, I listed six other crimes committed by Uday:

Crime No. 1: It was a beautiful late-fall day, and Uday decided to drive to the Nineveh district with his friends. Saddam Hussein had a magnificent castle there, near the Nineveh Obri tourist hotel. As Uday's convoy was driving by the hotel, he ordered a short stop to check it out. He noticed a family with a pretty girl in the foyer. The girl was no older than fifteen or sixteen. Uday took a fancy to her.

And so, once again, the sadist set his horrible game into

motion. He ordered his bodyguards — this time led by Ahmad Suleiman — to kidnap her and bring her to him. The girl was taken to the Nineveh castle. Uday raped her, then threw her out, warning, "And don't even think of saying a word to anyone!"

She dragged herself back to the hotel. Only then was the true scope of the tragedy revealed. The girl tried desperately to explain what had happened, but she had been deaf since birth and managed only a few indecipherable words. She couldn't put a sentence together.

Uday's men observed the child frantically seeking help from the hotel guests, gesticulating, sobbing noiselessly. Nobody could understand her. The bodyguards abducted her again and took her to a nearby forest, where they gang-raped her. They then informed Uday that the girl had tried to report him at the hotel. Uday ordered her executed and buried in the forest, and the order was carried out.

Crime No. 2: On occasion, Uday used to invite Beda Abd al-Rahman to Project No. 7. Beda Abd al-Rahman was a successful singer and television announcer who had her own children's program. Uday supported and sponsored her, and Beda publicly described herself as Uday's lady friend.

One day, she turned up at Project No. 7 and complained angrily that Sana al-Haidari, a young student, also claimed to be having a liaison with Uday. Uday pretended to be furious, had his bodyguards fetch Sana from the university, and demanded of the girl, "Is what Beda told me correct? Are you telling everyone you're my girlfriend?"

Sana pleaded with him, imploring, "Lord, I never said that. It's a lie. I swear I never said I'm your girlfriend."

Uday listened quietly to the young woman's pleas, staring at her emotionlessly. Then he ordered, "Get undressed, lie down on the bed, and say you want me!" Sana undressed quickly and did as Uday said. Uday's electric cable whipped through the air several times, landing on the student's naked skin. She groaned with each blow, which was exactly what Uday wanted to hear. He was transported into a state of sexual excitement, and beat her as hard as he could, the cable slapping the skin, the tender skin ripping, blood flowing. He penetrated her. Then he screamed, "Bring me a razor." Two bodyguards had to hold Sana down while a third forced her jaws apart. Uday took the razor blade, pulled out her tongue, and slit it with one motion: "So that you can tell stories better."

But even that wasn't enough. The bodyguards took her away, loaded her into one of Uday's helicopters, and dropped her into the al-Sarsar lake, near Anbar district.

Crime No. 3: Uday was throwing a party at the al-Savarek Club in Baghdad, and all his underworld friends were invited. This time he assigned his bodyguards Namir al-Tikriti and Hilal and his procurers Muajed Aani and Ali Asuad the task of "rounding up as many pretty girls as possible."

About a hundred girls showed up, including Weam Tabet al-Kabisi, the daughter of one of Baghdad's richest businessmen. Her father advised Uday's mother, Sajida, in business affairs. Weam didn't come alone. She was accompanied by Uday's uncles, Maan and Luai Khairallah. Luai Khairallah was her boyfriend.

The party started, and Adel Akle sang for hours as usual. Uday danced with numerous women, behaving as always. He grabbed their breasts, danced as though he were having sex with them, was crude, licentious, and loud. He could have had any of the women present that evening except one — Weam. And she was the one he chose. He said straight out, "I want you, and you want me too," grabbed her hips, and tried to press his half-open mouth on hers. Weam recoiled, struggled to free herself from Uday's grasp. When he wouldn't let her go, she called her friend.

Luai threw himself on Uday and forced him from the dance floor, then three shots were fired. It was impossible to know who shot at whom, because Uday's bodyguards hustled Luai away, disappearing with him into the large park surrounding the club.

The president's son promptly left the party. Weam was "delivered" to him and spent the night, whether of her own volition I don't know. I just saw them speaking the next morning, and heard Uday exclaim theatrically, "I love women more than my father. I love them more than God!"

Weam was found shot to death a few days later. Luai had killed her. He couldn't stand the thought of her sleeping with Uday, and because he couldn't avenge himself on his nephew, he took revenge on the girl.

Crime No. 4: Baghdad, the Mansur district. It was between 6:00 and 7:00 P.M. We were on our way with Uday to the Olympic Club, when a car suddenly sped past our slower-moving column, a married couple sitting behind the wheel. Predictably, Uday began to seethe, because nobody had the right to leave his convoy in the dust. He radioed ahead to Namir al-Tikriti, Salam al-Aoussi, and Saadoum al-Tikriti and ordered them to head off the couple and bring him the woman, whatever the consequences.

They dragged the woman from the car and forced her into one of our cars. While Namir al-Tikriti took the man to a police station, the rest of us drove with the woman to one of Uday's farms on the edge of Baghdad. Namir al-Tikriti had the innocent man charged with "trying to harass the president of the Olympic Club."

The man — his name was Hassan Abd al-Amir Janabi — was imprisoned and tortured for six months. The woman was set free after a week. On his release, Janabi was warned, "Keep your mouth shut, or Uday's men will cut out your tongue!" But he swept the warning aside and tried to contact President Saddam Hussein, which he did in an incredibly naive manner, by simply announcing himself at the entrance to the presidential palace and informing the guards exactly why he was there. They of course notified Uday, who had him taken away. Passersby found his body three days later in the al-Umma Park. He had wanted to restore his honor and sought help from the supposed enforcers of the law. That was a fatal mistake.

Crime No. 5: A Miss Iraq is chosen every year. This is a major event, particularly for Uday. The sponsors of the pageant are his associates and business partners, and up to now Uday had propositioned every newly crowned Miss Iraq and gotten what he wanted. But when Ilham Ali al-Aazami, a student, won, she refused to indulge him. Uday reacted as always. A nod of the head, and Ahmad Suleiman, the karate expert, Muajed Fadel, and Mohammed al-Baghdadi knew what to do. Miss Iraq was sequestered at Project No. 7 for a week and raped repeatedly by Uday and all his bodyguards. He offered me the woman too: "Take her, she's good." I declined, but the others greedily availed themselves of the opportunity.

She was then thrown out, and Uday launched the rumor that Miss Iraq was a slut who had sex with "anyone who came along."

Ilham Ali al-Aazami was an only child. Her father was a respected businessman, who went out of his mind when he heard the rumors about his beloved daughter. First he killed her, and then he sought to confront Uday at the Olympic Club.

Uday let the man into his office, commiserated with him, offered him money, and advised him to "forget the little dead whore." Leaning back casually in his presidential armchair while drawing on his Cuban cigar, he grinned arrogantly and concluded, "God gave her so much beauty, but unfortunately no morals. She liked doing it."

That was too much for Ilham Ali al-Aazami's father. Until now too meek to raise his voice to Uday, he began to rant and rave. Uday looked to one of his bodyguards, Dafer

Aref, who knew what to do. Aref manhandled the desperate old man into an adjacent room. I heard two shots. The body was removed in the evening.

As I drew up my list, I had to pause several times to get a grip on myself. Uday, his crimes, my job as double, which I hardly ever performed — what had I done up to now? I went to the soccer stadium a few times, visited the troops twice. And as for the rest, I was nothing but a silent witness to a string of horrific crimes. I watched murders and intrigues, was a fellow traveler in horror. And now that I was tabulating everything, I had become the bookkeeper of horror.

Latif! I screamed at myself. *You've got to get out of here. You're twenty-five, you want to start a family, work in your father's company, take over his import-export businesses. And what are you doing instead? You're living with a psychotic criminal and wasting your time lying by the pool and watching idiotic videos.*

I'm sure I'd seen *The Godfather* at least thirty times, and all the porno films in Uday's video library at least as often.

But how could I escape this place? Who could I turn to? Uday? No, that was impossible. And flee where?

I started hating Uday for the first time. I hated him because he was a merciless criminal and yet nobody could do anything against him. I hated him more because he'd stuck me in this golden cage, which I could no longer leave. I didn't care that he beat me regularly with his electric cable or iron bar, because he determined that he had to "educate" me. The physical pain was bearable, a burning, stabbing wound that would heal.

But what about my soul? Had I become like Uday not only externally but also internally? No, I told myself, I was completely different, the exact opposite from him. My parents had raised me to be a warm and affectionate human being, imbued with goodness. As the oldest, I was respected by my siblings as much as my father, and I used to help them with their tasks and problems whenever Father was busy. We were always good to each other. Religion was a permanent fixture in our lives. I went regularly to the mosque to pray. And now? We didn't even observe the fast periods.

I lit a cigarette, inhaled the smoke deeply into my lungs. I never used to smoke. Father didn't want me to. And now? I smoked two packs of Marlboros a day. I also drank, sometimes to the point of losing consciousness. Drinking made this life almost bearable.

Why should I do anything but drink? My days were reduced to monotonous watching and waiting. Then I'd drive in luxurious limousines to various events, to act as a decoy for assassins. *Why wasn't I shot in Basra instead of the young officer?*

It was December 26, 1989, just before 4:00 A.M. After destroying my notes, I went into the bathroom and picked up a straight razor, first contemplating it for a while. I couldn't help but remember how Uday had used such a blade to slice open Sana's tongue. I could still see the blood, how it poured out of her mouth and onto her dress.

Slowly I cut into the vein in my right wrist. There was no blood at first. I cut deeper, then slit my other wrist.

The warm blood ran down my palms and fingers. I could hear it drip onto the floor. I lay down on the bed, wanting to cut my throat too, but I didn't have the courage or the strength. I started several times, but managed only tiny cuts that penetrated the skin but didn't reach the jugular vein. I tried once more, but again couldn't. I let my head fall to the pillow. I was breathing heavily when the telephone rang shrilly next to my bed. It sounded so far away.

I 2

THE KUWAIT RAID

AZZAM had to strip naked. My four bodyguards too. They did it without resisting, stood in front of Uday's large, baroque desk, and covered their privates with their hands. They held themselves slightly stooped, their shoulders hunched forward, head and eyes cast downward. Without a word, Uday moved from behind the desk, picked up his electric cable, drew it through his hand several times as if wiping it clean, then wound up. His body tensed like a spring. He followed through like a tennis player serving. There was a swishing sound, and the electric cable connected with Azzam's naked back. Uday beat him until he bled. Next he beat my bodyguards. His instrument of torture swished through the air again and again, ten times, twenty times, unaccompanied by his usual groaning.

Uday was punishing and humiliating the men because they hadn't prevented me from cutting open my veins. I'd probably be dead if Azzam hadn't called to inform me that Uday was planning to fly to Geneva in the next few days. I would have bled to death. I don't know how long I'd been lying on my bed when the telephone rang. I only know that I heard the ring very faintly, as if it were coming from another apartment.

When I failed to pick up the phone, Azzam had my apartment raided. They broke down the door, saw me lying on the blood-drenched sheets, and had me brought to the

Ibn-Sina hospital. The doctors closed up the wounds on my wrists with six stitches each. I was in pretty good shape two days later.

Now I was standing in Uday's office, watching him beat my bodyguards bloody. There was nothing he'd have liked better than to punish me as well. He probably would have liked to see me dead, but he needed me. My welfare wasn't his main worry during this incident; Uday was concerned strictly for himself. I was key to his security. Without me as his double, he'd have to expose himself to too many risky situations, and he had grounds to fear that such situations would be on the rise. It had been an open secret in the palace for weeks that something big was going to happen soon.

The mood was tense. Munem Hammed hardly had time for me anymore. In addition, new rumors had surfaced in the palace about the murder of Adnan Khairallah. People were whispering that there was a political dimension to the murder that went beyond Adnan's popularity and his open criticism of Saddam Hussein's mistress. As defense minister, Khairallah had reportedly cautioned the president in the strongest terms against an invasion of Kuwait: It would challenge the West too much. An invasion of Kuwait could never be justified as a protective measure against American imperialism in the Gulf region.

Saddam, however, had long ago decided to "bring Kuwait back home." His threats to that effect remained veiled, but we in the palace realized from snatches of conversation that his annexation plans had already been completed by 1990. He tried to hide this fact publicly. He whipped up emotions against Israel to distract the world from his intentions and to marshal the Arab world behind him, a clever diversionary move that few people outside the palace saw through.

He had Uday's newspapers and all other Iraqi media issue massive threats against Israel. He reminded the people again and again that the Jewish state had acted militarily against Iraq as early as 1981, when Israeli fighter-bombers destroyed the nuclear reactor at Osirak in a surprise attack. Saddam declared that Israel and America were now planning a new attack on Iraq, and challenged, "We will destroy the entire Jewish people with poison gas, should it come to that." Uday's newspaper *Babel* ran the headline, OUR ROCKETS STRONG ENOUGH TO REACH ISRAEL.

In his naive and egocentric way, Uday was becoming more and more reckless in his pronouncements. Once, with a glass of whiskey in hand, he told his amazed friends, "Everyone knows that Iran's aggression against our people led to a costly war. They forced war on us, but couldn't defeat Iraq. Now others want to starve the proud Iraqi people. It's a black plot against our nation, a plot concocted by the rulers of Kuwait."

Uday paused momentarily, picked up one of his newspapers, and quoted from a speech delivered by his father: "War is sometimes carried out with the use of troops — one side harms the other with explosives, steel, and attempted coups. At other times, war is carried out by economic means."

Everyone understood what Uday meant. Our country was bankrupt. We couldn't pay the debts we owed our main creditors, Kuwait and the United Arab Emirates. Either we could get our creditors to waive their claims, or we could demand further aid from Kuwait, which we would call compensation for the oil stolen from the Rumeila oilfield.

"As we all know," Uday went on, repeating his standard line on this theme, "Kuwait stole oil worth $28.8 billion back then. The southern tip of the oilfield lies only three miles on the other side of the border. We just need to push the border back a few miles and all our problems will be solved."

This comment proved that there were serious thoughts in the palace of going to war against Kuwait. Not even I could see Kuwait voluntarily agreeing to a change in the borders. Besides, Saddam was telling us daily that Kuwait was not only stealing our oil but also conducting a sneak attack on Iraq by means of its chronic overproduction of oil. As a result of this overproduction, the price of oil had fallen from twenty to fourteen dollars a barrel. "Our country loses more than a billion dollars a year through this single act of Kuwaiti aggression," Uday declared, and added, "It's like a stab in the back with a poisoned knife. It's a direct attack on my father."

I'd never seen him like this. All of a sudden he was politically engaged, and was even trying to glean a bit of knowledge about the situation. But his political engagement seemed to vanish two days after these statements, when he announced that he was going to fly to Geneva with Waadallah Abu-Sakr. I was surprised, though, that he'd picked Abu-Sakr to accompany him on his trip. Abu-Sakr was the supreme chief of security of the presidential palace, a powerful man. He directed all of Saddam Hussein's bodyguards and was responsible for their training.

They stayed in Geneva ten days. Their activities became public knowledge in the palace immediately after their return. Abu-Sakr had been on a secret mission to hire Cuban mercenaries, elite soldiers who were to be employed as extra bodyguards for the ministers and leading party members. The secretive Cubans moved into four stories of the al-Hayat high-rise on the palace grounds. The shooting range was off limits when they assembled for target practice. Any attempt to make contact with them was strictly forbidden. We heard that they were paid in dollars and not dinars. Supposedly they were earning millions, but no exact figures were mentioned, and I didn't try to find out more. It seemed dangerous to pry. The Cubans became another impenetrable piece of the spy machinery in the already overdeveloped security system of the presidential palace.

In June 1990, President Saddam Hussein began calling meetings of the family council strikingly often. Before, Uday used to reveal details about the meetings whenever he was drunk. Now he only dropped dismissive hints, such as: "Iraq has one million soldiers, Kuwait only seventeen thousand men, a ridiculous air force, and a pseudo-navy with twenty patrol boats. The navy's only there to help some princes smuggle alcohol into the country. The sons of whores of the al-Sabah family forbid alcohol for their people, but that hasn't stopped their own orgies, and they have a monopoly on smuggling the stuff.''

Every second sentence was meant to underscore Iraq's military superiority, and to disparage the Kuwaiti ruling family. Sheik Jaber al-Ahmad al-Sabah became the thirteenth emir of Kuwait in December 1977. The crown prince and head of government was Sheik Saad al-Abdullah al-Salem al-Sabah, the oil and finance minister Sheik Ali Khalifa al-Sabah, the foreign minister Sheik Sabah al-Ahmad al-Jaber al-Sabah, the interior minister Sheik Salem al-Salem al-Sabah, and the defense minister Sheik Nawwaf al-Ahmad al-Jaber al-Sabah. Every important post was held by family members. Uday became indignant about this, but his indignation seemed ludicrous, since the situation was no different in Iraq. Saddam surrounded himself exclusively with family members, though such family ties were no guarantee of survival, as Adnan Khairallah's example demonstrated.

Besides, unlike Iraq, Kuwait allowed the existence of a political opposition. Even open criticism of the emir was permitted. In Iraq, one careless word against the president could mean death. Thus, by Arab standards, Kuwait was one of the region's more open and tolerant societies. What was lacking was a national assembly that would give Kuwaiti citizens a right to have a say in matters of state.

Such a legislative assembly had existed once, but was dissolved by the emir during the Iran-Iraq war. In early 1990, however, many former Kuwaiti legislators began a massive campaign to compel new elections for a national assembly with increased powers. This was reported in detail in Iraq. There were accounts of mass demonstrations against the emir, rebellion, and radical suppression by the Kuwaiti police.

In June 1990, the al-Sabah family yielded to the pressure and granted permission for elections to a seventy-five-member national assembly. "What a farce!" Uday complained. "A third of them are supposed to be appointed by the emir. And the opposition is boycotting. We, Iraq, must support the opposition with every means at our disposal." Uday went into detail about how this should be done: "The people must demonstrate in the streets, because the greater the number, the greater the pressure on the government. If thousands take to the streets, they'll lose their cool and let the police fire."

Uday didn't say so, but I knew what he was thinking: Kuwait was a dwarf (6,880 square miles) compared to Iraq. Only 800,000 of its population of nearly 2 million were Kuwaiti citizens, and of these only 100,000 were "real Kuwaitis," members of the ancient Bedouin royalty. The al-Sabah family consisted of fewer than a thousand members. Foreign workers (1.2 million) made up the majority of Kuwait's population. More than a third of these (460,000) were Palestinians. The rest were Arabs from the whole region, as well as Asians, Europeans, and Americans.

This kind of population structure gave rise to great social differences, because only Kuwaitis had full rights as citizens. Massive resistance from the foreigners in Kuwait was therefore unlikely in the event of an invasion, especially not from the Palestinians, who generally had good relations with Iraqis, hated Israel, and considered Iraq the only power with the strength and determination to wipe Israel off the map.

"We must support our Palestinian brothers in Kuwait in all their struggles, because they're the true Kuwaitis. The country couldn't survive economically without them," commented Uday philosophically, adding, "They have to show their colors openly against the exploitive al-Sabah government."

Uday went so far as to mention names, confirming that Iraqi intelligence had been trying for months to prod

Kuwaiti politicians and opposition figures as well as the
Palestinians into open conflict with the "corrupt government." "We also spoke with Ahmed al-Sadoun," he said,
referring to one of Kuwait's best-known opposition figures.
Mohammed al-Qadri of the Democratic Forum was another
target. "They both share our opinion," he lied. "Both of
them openly demand an invasion by Iraq to topple the
satanic system."

Naturally, Uday concealed the fact that both politicians
had categorically refused all cooperation with Iraq. They
wanted no part in our game. "We're going to rush to our
brothers' aid," said Uday, "and drive out this corrupt government, who satisfy themselves on whores and homosexuals in
London."

He interpreted Saddam Hussein's battle plan as follows: First a lightning invasion of Kuwait in support of a
"revolutionary opposition group," which would have called
on Baghdad for help. Then elimination of the emir and
the whole government. The Republican Guard was to storm
the Dasman Palace as quickly as possible in order to seize the
Kuwaiti ruler before he could flee. If he agreed to cooperate
and remain in office as the head of a puppet regime taking
orders from Baghdad, his life would be spared. Should he
refuse, which was more likely, he would be summarily shot
for resistance against the allied Iraqi armed forces, as would
the rest of his clan.

Saddam Hussein had been one step ahead for quite
some time and had already begun to "come to the aid" of
Kuwait. This was at the end of July 1990. All of us in the
palace knew that the first troops, some thirty thousand men,
were on their way to the Kuwaiti border. Businessmen just
back from Basra in southern Iraq talked freely over gin and
tonics at the al-Said Club about having been constantly
bogged down in traffic jams on the al-Qadisiya freeway connecting Baghdad and Kuwait, because of tank and artillery

convoys rolling southward. Gigantic tent cities had been erected beside the road, they disclosed.

I asked Uday about these reports, and he confirmed that troops had been dispatched to the south. "Purely a protective measure," he contended, "should our Kuwaiti brothers need our help in their fight against the corrupt al-Sabah government."

"How many troops are being redeployed?" I asked.

"More than a hundred thousand," he answered.

That fact made it clear that the hour of action was very near. The countdown had begun.

August 1, 1990. Uday had driven off unusually early this morning, supposedly to the Olympic Club. He called me around nine at my apartment in the al-Hayat high-rise, where I'd been relocated following my suicide attempt, and said I should be ready in the next few hours. Because the phone connection was poor, I assumed Uday wasn't at the Olympic Club, since the lines there were always perfect. It sounded more as if he were farther away, in a bunker somewhere. I didn't waste any further thought over it, but my guess was confirmed by the afternoon radio news: Uday and the entire Iraqi leadership had withdrawn to secure locations. The news anchorman announced, "Negotiations in Jidda, Saudi Arabia, between an Iraqi delegation led by Izzat Ibrahim, vice-chairman of the Revolutionary Command Council, and the Kuwaiti prime minister, Crown Prince Saad al-Abdullah al-Salem al-Sabah, ended with an act of open provocation and aggression against Iraq."

The anchorman paused momentarily, then continued, "Kuwait failed to accept the Iraqi proposal concerning the cession of territory in the border region of the Rumeila oilfield. Kuwait further refused to pay reparations for the damages caused Iraq by its increased oil production, or to forgive the loans dating from the Gulf war with Iran. Negotiations were broken off after two hours."

Izzat Ibrahim immediately flew back to Iraq after the breakdown of negotiations. The borders between Kuwait and Iraq were closed when he landed in Baghdad.

All hell broke loose on the palace grounds. Convoys with ministers, party functionaries, and their bodyguards arrived every minute. Helicopters landed and took off. The security troops were placed on high alert: the guards at the palace gate had been tripled. All leaves were canceled, phone lines from the al-Hayat high-rise were blocked, and calls outside were possible only with the help of the operator. Everybody was tense, on edge, but not nervous. Everything was following a pattern that had been trained for and practiced hundreds of times.

In the evening I went to the shooting range with two of my bodyguards. It was empty except for a few members of the intelligence service. I practiced with my pistol and hit the target well. Shortly after midnight another of my guards came dashing in. He was excited and ordered me to return immediately to my apartment. On the way he told me, "Saddam is going to Kuwait. In the next few hours." "How do you know?" I asked. He said, gasping for breath, "We just got the word from Project Number 7."

Our tanks crossed the Kuwaiti border at al-Abdali on August 2 at 2:00 A.M. Three hundred fifty tanks charged toward Kuwait City at a speed of forty-five miles an hour. As predicted by Uday and expected by everyone in Iraq, there was hardly any resistance. I learned the next day that the Kuwaiti troops had run off in a panic. Firefights occurred only on the edges of Kuwait City, where isolated defenders tried to stop our armored columns but were rolled over inexorably. Even the Kuwaiti air force didn't resist. Their best pilots drove to their bases, fired up the thirty-six Mirage warplanes, and flew as a unit to Saudi Arabia.

That night I couldn't sleep a wink. I wanted to celebrate with my bodyguards, but we restrained ourselves, waiting tensely for news and orders from Uday. He didn't call all the next day. It was evening before he ordered me to Project No. 7. The villa was overflowing, and all of Uday's friends were there. Hundreds of vehicles were parked in front of the house. Azzam told me that Uday was planning a huge victory party at the al-Said Club, and that the masters of ceremonies had already prepared everything. We drove to the club in a gigantic convoy, with some revelers already firing wildly into the air with their Kalashnikovs as we started on our way.

At the club, everything was cleverly illuminated; the summer and winter pools sparkled in myriad colors. Buffets were set up in every corner, and liveried servants balanced champagne-laden trays through the crowd. The mood was jubilant.

Silence descended as Uday entered the club, accompanied by almost a hundred bodyguards, then loud applause broke out. Everyone clapped, bowed before Uday, and some even kissed his hand. He swam on the wave of enthusiasm. He was wearing his Ray-Bans and a black uniform with the inscription "Uday Saddam Hussein." He didn't walk, he strode. He held his Cuban cigar aloft in his left hand, waved to his subjects with his right, as if in slow motion. Sometimes he paused briefly, approached a woman, stroked her hair, and then continued on his way, followed by hundreds of gazes.

I remained in the background, dressed in my ordinary bodyguard uniform. It was strange, as always. Even though Uday and I looked extremely alike, hardly anyone even saw me when I was wearing my bodyguard uniform. All attention was focused on the beaming hero, the great son of the president.

After bathing in the adulation of the crowd, Uday reached for a microphone and shouted emotionally, as if he were declaring the Olympic Games open, "We have achieved our goal!" He then put down the mike, grabbed a bodyguard's Kalashnikov, and fired into the air until he had emptied the magazine. Screaming in exultation, he signaled that all the men should follow his example. In an instant all of them had weapons in their hands and were firing into the clear, starry night. The gunfire reminded me of the Iranian front, and it occurred to me that probably more shots were fired that night at the al-Said Club than during the entire Kuwait invasion.

The invasion was the number-one topic of conversation, of course. From different bits of conversation, I slowly pieced the situation together. Our troops had taken all key positions within four hours. They were able to celebrate their victory in the streets of Kuwait City within nine hours after the start of the attack. They controlled everything. The Dasman Palace was occupied. Radio and television stations had been secured and taken over by our people.

The only strong resistance had developed in front of the Dasman Palace, on the northern tip of the peninsula on which Kuwait City stands. It was Uday's friend, Fahd al-Ahmed al-Sabah, the emir's brother, who led the brave warriors against an overwhelmingly superior Iraqi force. When Uday learned of Fahd's death, he lamented cynically, "What an idiot. He was like my brother. Why didn't he submit to our will? He could have been my deputy! What did he want to prove with his stupidity?"

Fahd al-Ahmed al-Sabah had tried to rally the emir's palace guard to repel the attack, but as he appeared on the highest step of the palace, his gun at ready, he was killed by a burst from a twenty-one-year-old's Kalashnikov. The Kuwaiti resistance collapsed with his death. Our soldiers dragged his body through the streets, drove a tank over it, and deposited the remains at a curbside.

None of this moved Uday. "Such is war," was his comment. "We don't want to kill anyone. We just want to support the revolutionary forces in Kuwait."

Uday kept one secret that evening: The emir and all of his ministers had managed to flee. Even before our troops had reached the outskirts of Kuwait City, the duty officers were able to warn the entire government. By the time the

Republican Guards stormed the palace, the emir and his ministers were on their way to the Saudi Arabian border.

I learned of the second mistake the following day, August 4. None of the opposition figures contacted by our intelligence service was willing to participate in a new Kuwaiti government. Everyone in the palace knew what that meant. The grand declarations to the world media that Iraq was merely supporting a national revolution against a corrupt regime in Kuwait were thus given the lie.

Saddam Hussein didn't appear to care. He had a transition government installed in Kuwait on August 4, and Kuwait was simultaneously declared a republic. A news conference in Baghdad announced to the world that the head of this government was a certain Colonel Alaa Hussein Ali, an officer in the Kuwaiti armed forces. But a photo of this mysterious officer was never published.

We knew why, too: There was no Kuwaiti officer with that name. The officer in question was really Hussein Kamel al-Majid, who was married to Saddam's oldest daughter, Raghd.

I could hardly believe my ears! Hussein Kamel, known in Baghdad as "Saddam's loyal dog," had started out as an ordinary police sergeant. He later became the chauffeur of the former Iraqi president, Ahmad Hasan al-Bakr, and kept this job when Saddam Hussein "replaced" al-Bakr as president in 1979. (As mentioned earlier, officially al-Bakr died of heart failure, but in reality he was poisoned by Saddam Hussein's men. Everyone in Baghdad believed that Hussein Kamel was the one who mixed the poison into his master's food.)

Like Saddam, Hussein Kamel came from Tikrit. He was also distantly related to Saddam. Under the new president, after al-Bakr's death, his career took off like a rocket, which gave more credence to the supposition of his complicity. Saddam appointed him first bodyguard, a post that meant more than any ministerial position, and he was assigned the rank of first lieutenant, although he had never participated in officer's training. That wasn't important. Complete loyalty was the only thing that mattered. Saddam married Hussein Kamel to his oldest daughter in order to bind him even closer.

Hussein Kamel had two brothers, Saddam Kamel al-Majid and Hakim Kamel al-Majid. These two were made to marry into the Saddam clan so as to tie up loose ends and keep it all in the family. Saddam Kamel got Saddam's daughter Rina, and Hakim Kamel, the youngest, was married to the baby of the family, Hala. The three brothers were given magnificent villas within the palace grounds.

After Hussein Kamel's wedding with Raghd, he was awarded full responsibility for the armaments industry. A separate armaments ministry was created for him, and so Hussein Kamel, the former chauffeur, became a minister. He immediately absorbed the industry ministry, which before had been responsible for arms production. But that wasn't enough for the power-hungry Hussein. He also cast his eye on the oil ministry. To please him, Saddam Hussein forced his oil minister into public self-denunciation. The poor man was made to confess on the main television news program that he had broken Iraqi law and sold oil to enrich himself. He shook so badly as he was saying this that it was clear to everyone watching that he had been coerced. He died a short while later in a Baghdad hospital. "Heart failure" was listed as the official cause of death.

Hussein Kamel took over the oil ministry on the following day. He was also given the defense ministry, left orphaned by the death of Adnan Khairallah, as well as the transportation ministry.

Hussein Kamel, a man without a university education or any other special qualifications, had become minister four times over — and now suddenly the head of government of Kuwait.

13

EVERYBODY STOLE

DAYS after the invasion, Kuwait City resembled a ghost town. Our troops had secured the whole area, including the oil harbors of Shuaiba and Ahmadi, as well as the airport. Thousands of cars stood abandoned in the empty streets. They weren't even parked, just left there. Stores were closed, most of their owners having fled. In some sections of the city, the streets and sidewalks had been torn up by tank tracks. Television, telephones, and all other means of communication were under Iraqi administration. For sport, our soldiers were taking joyrides in luxury cars, mostly Mercedes. Battles flared only sporadically, when Kuwaiti snipers opened up on our military patrols.

All Kuwaiti opposition figures having refused to cooperate, the provisional government was made up exclusively of midlevel Iraqi officers. Nonetheless, Iraqi television proudly reported that, in an official communiqué to the Iraqi head of state, the head of the new Kuwaiti government, Alaa Hussein Ali, had indicated Kuwait's willingness to begin negotiations with Iraq about the location of the common border — smoke and mirrors, of course, because Saddam's son-in-law would never contradict Saddam. The border problem could now be solved by the family council. Izzat Ibrahim, another Saddam marionette, was appointed to head the Iraqi negotiating delegation. All high officers of the Kuwaiti army and police were simultaneously retired, effective August 4.

While this transparent drama was being played out, planning began behind the scenes for one of the greatest private episodes of plunder in modern times.

It was August 8, 1990, a memorable day. First, U.S. president George Bush demonstrated strength and resolve by sending the first contingents to respond to the crisis in the Gulf: troops from the 18th Airborne Corps. The aircraft carriers *Independence, Saratoga,* and *Eisenhower* were heading for the Persian Gulf, along with fifty escorts. U.S. F-11 warplanes were transferred from Britain to Turkish NATO airfields, and B-52 bombers were moved from their bases in the Indian Ocean to Dhahran, in eastern Saudi Arabia. The great arming of the Allies in the Gulf began.

Second, the independent state of Kuwait was officially dissolved in Kuwait City. In a televised speech, Saddam Hussein announced the union of Iraq with the former emirate: "Thanks to God's help, we are one people, one state, which will become the pride of the Arabs. The new Iraq extends from Zakhu [northern Iraq] to Ahmadi [Kuwait's oil harbor on the Gulf]." Frenzied celebration greeted his speech in Baghdad, and the party mobilized hundreds of thousands in the Street of the Palestinians to hold victory celebrations. The masses had no clue that the first U.S. troops were arriving in the desert of Saudi Arabia at the same time; the Iraqi media remained silent on that score. The people felt intoxicated, triumphant. Nobody seriously believed that the western world would wind up for a counterpunch.

But the most significant event for us was taking place in Project No. 7, where Uday Saddam Hussein had gathered all his bodyguards and friends to explain his own Operation Kuwait. He came in carrying written operational plans for the next few days, placed the documents heavily on his desk, stood before us, and began, "Kuwait now belongs to us. Its possessions are also ours."

He took his lists in his hand and strode back and forth in front of the desk, then stopped, turned toward us, took a drag on his cigar, gazed over our heads, and announced in a dramatic undertone, "We start Operation Kuwait tomorrow."

Uday paused to emphasize the importance of this moment. Then, like a chief executive at a directors' meeting, he explained what he meant by Operation Kuwait: "Azzam will immediately assemble teams of twenty men each," he said, and went on to assign the tasks of these teams.

First, the Car Team would confiscate every Mercedes and BMW left in Kuwait and transport them back to Baghdad on trailers. Uday emphasized that to begin with he didn't want Cadillacs or Rolls-Royces but only cars of German quality. Cars without keys should be started by shorting the ignition or simply lifted onto the transports with a crane. Any Kuwaiti car dealers or owners causing problems should be executed immediately for "resisting State authority."

Second, the Property Team was to confiscate all abandoned villas and put them under the administration of Uday's companies. Furniture, appliances, and especially air conditioners, marble floors, and objets d'art were to be loaded into trucks and brought to Baghdad. A subsection of the Property Team was in charge of taking apart and transporting hotel air-conditioning systems and kitchens, valuable medical equipment from hospitals, machinery, office equipment, computers, and telecommunications equipment.

Third, the Hi-fi Team was to comb all stores and supermarkets in Kuwait and remove in particular Japanese electronics equipment, but only the valuable components, not the cheap stuff.

Uday didn't even mention jewelry stores, which surprised me, because jewels and watches were easily transportable.

The operation commenced twenty-four hours later. I drove southward with my team along the al-Qadisiya highway, which was clogged with army vehicles transporting soldiers and military material toward Kuwait. We had no trouble getting through, though. Normally it was enough for my bodyguards to tell the checkpoints that our convoys were under the orders of Uday Saddam Hussein. If not, we also had certificates from the highest intelligence services stating that we were there to carry out "a special mission." Once, we were even offered a police escort, which I rejected with the explanation that my own escort was enough. Our convoy consisted of four identical Mercedes limousines and six car trailers that could carry loads on two levels, as well as five tractor trailers.

Our first objective lay only fifteen miles from the border. We parked our trailers in front of the Gahnem dealership, the city's largest, with a lot full of European and American cars.

Big cars were a common sight on Kuwait's streets before the invasion, because gasoline was extremely cheap. Also, there was no tax on cars, so each household had at least two or three. Most popular were the European luxury models from Mercedes, BMW, Porsche, Jaguar, or Rolls-Royce, and the heavy American cars. A total of 700,000 cars were registered in Kuwait before the invasion.

An officer guarding the car dealership approached our convoy as we pulled up. I got out of my car, with my bodyguards following, and my black uniform bearing the name of the president's son substituted for identity papers. The officer, a wiry man with dark skin, saluted and stammered out his report. I told him that I, Uday Saddam Hussein, intended to haul off all the Mercedes and BMW cars. The officer saluted again, kissed my hand, and bowed several times. Meanwhile I noticed several soldiers stripping the cars on the lot that were peppered with shrapnel. They were taking everything — radios, antennas, headlights, wheels, mirrors. Real hyenas. As soon as they noticed us looking at them, they dropped everything and disappeared behind the dealership offices. The officer knew that I'd seen the soldiers. It was clear from his self-conscious manner that he was in cahoots with them. My mouth moved to mimic a friendly smile, and I ordered him to get out of my sight immediately or I'd have him punished with his men. The wiry officer vanished as quickly as they had.

On the drive down, I had remarked hundreds of small trucks and buses going in the opposite direction, filled to overflowing with car parts. It appeared that every Iraqi occupier had called on relatives to come to Kuwait and return home with loot.

Kuwait had turned into one huge self-service store for all the soldiers, and apparently no officer had taken steps to stop it. They all obviously knew that everyone was stealing, but nobody reported it. To whom should they? Everybody stole, as if that had been the real purpose of the war. I didn't have the impression that we wanted to hold on to Kuwait. Would we be stripping it so brazenly if that were the case? Besides, not a single soldier seemed to worry about the fact that in the Saudi desert, just a few miles away, a powerful army was preparing to strike at our troops.

Nobody appeared concerned about that. Everybody just wanted to take as much as he could carry. I sympathized with the soldiers. Their usual pay of twenty-two dinars a month on the front, not even twenty U.S. dollars, was too little to live on, and too much to die. Now they had the opportunity to multiply their miserable wages a thousandfold if they managed somehow to get the goods out of Kuwait and into Iraq. The streets all the way to the border were crammed with soldiers and refugees. Asian and Arab guest workers, who earned their living in Kuwait, were evacuating the country in gigantic columns in one endless trek northward into Iraq. More than a million people were try to reach the Jordanian border to the west of Iraq, or the Turkish border to the north. Iraqi soldiers carrying plunder were interspersed among the refugees.

Thousands of Kuwaitis were trying to flee to Saudi Arabia. The Iraqi soldiers didn't hinder them; they simply asked for their papers and some kind of toll, thus profiting

from the people's misery. The whole campaign was an unbelievable, shameless spree of plundering. The only ones not
allowed to leave Kuwait were about six thousand "guests" —
Europeans and Americans, representatives of the countries
whose governments had sent troops to the Gulf — who had
to report to different hotels in Kuwait City and were then
transported in groups to Baghdad.

We loaded up with forty-two Mercedes 500s and the
most powerful BMWs. My bodyguards amused themselves in
their own way. After they hot-wired the ignitions of the luxury
cars, they took them for a spin, peeling rubber in the parking
lot. They loved it when a car was wrecked.

It took us two hours to load all the cars. The whole time I
felt as if I were being watched, but I didn't see a single
Kuwaiti. The area seemed deserted.

The next day we drove our prize to Uday's al-Rashdiya
farm in the al-Jasira al-Siahia district, where Uday bred his
attack dogs. He even had a young tiger and two black pumas
in cages.

Our transport wasn't the first to arrive. Azzam and his
men had worked faster than we, as had Captain Siad. The
booty was impressive. More than a hundred German luxury
cars had been collected.

Uday was satisfied with us and the other groups. There
had been no incidents, nobody had had to fire a shot. He
told us proudly that he expected more transports in the
course of the night, and that we should start out again the
following day.

On August 11, my men and I drove to Kuwait City's
Shuvaikh and Hawalli districts. This was where most of the
car dealerships were concentrated, we had been told, and
the information proved correct. There were problems, nonetheless. We ran into another group of Iraqi officers loading
cars in Hawalli — Hussein Kamel's men.

"What's going on here?" I asked the ranking officer,

and he reported, "Sir, we have instructions to bring European cars to the farms of Hussein Kamel in Tikrit."

I said nothing and turned away, thinking, *Hussein Kamel is also one of these hyenas.*

Fortunately, there were enough cars for both teams. We began to load and watched as an officer from the other group stopped a Kuwaiti who happened to drive by in his car, ordered him out, and chased him away. The man took off without a word, probably happy that he hadn't been shot.

We needed substantially less time to load the cars now; my men had developed a certain routine in breaking open the locks and shorting the ignitions.

On my return, I told Uday about the incident with Hussein Kamel's men. He suffered one of his choleric attacks, ranted and raged, and in doing so divulged an important detail: "It was agreed exactly who could confiscate which cars."

That made everything perfectly clear. All of the Hussein clan was participating in the plunder of Kuwait. But they were so greedy that they were trespassing on each other's territory, like wild animals fighting over prey. Still, a certain pecking order prevailed here too. First came the hyenas (the Hussein clan), then the vultures (the ordinary soldiers) to take what was left.

Saddam Hussein reserved the biggest haul for himself. He had 3,216 gold bars, sixty-three tons of gold coins, and whole helicopter loads of foreign currency transported to Iraq, as well as all the cultural treasures of the National Museum.

Either directly, through relatives, or indirectly, via the market, the common folk also benefited from the raids. These days one could find everything in Iraq, even though the United Nations had imposed an economic embargo. Baghdad, like other Iraqi cities, was literally awash with consumer goods from Kuwait, many still bearing Kuwaiti price stickers. There were chicken-liver pâté and Norway salmon, alcohol-free beer, which you never used to be able to find, and canned meats from all over the world. There were cameras, both video and still, VCRs, and all kinds of appliances, from mixers to hair dryers, from washing machines to light switches. Everything was available, and everything was for sale at bargain-basement prices. The UN embargo was thus rendered completely ineffectual. There were enough food items in storage in the Kuwaiti supermarkets to feed Iraq for months.

Most of these stores were under the grip of Hussein Kamel's men. He had assigned entire companies of soldiers the sole task of pilfering the supermarkets in Kuwait and bringing back the wares to Iraq. A business worth billions.

Our own troops were more discreet, but just as effective. By September 10, we'd managed to transport more than ten thousand luxury vehicles from Kuwait to Baghdad. There was no more room on Uday's farms for cars. Even the parking lots and the garages at the Olympic Club were overflowing. The other stolen goods, like electronic appliances, cosmetics, and furniture, were partly sold in Iraq and partly smuggled to Jordan by Uday's business associates, the dealers Mohammed Kora Ghauli, Khaled al-Kabisi, Said Kammuneh, and Dureid Ghannaoui.

Now came the next step: The stolen cars had to be sold. Full-page ads began to appear in the Baghdad newspapers: "Auction of Mercedes and BMW luxury cars." The stolen cars were offered at clearance-sale prices and sold from the parking lots in front of the Olympic Club high-rise. The terms of payment were cash on the barrelhead, in U.S. dollars. Azzam and I took turns conducting the auctions. Uday remained discreetly in the background, keeping watch from his office in the Olympic Club. We unloaded an average of sixty to seventy cars a day.

The buyers didn't mind that we didn't have ignition keys for the cars. We offered to short the ignition for them so they could drive to the nearest garage and have keys made there. Obtaining new car papers and license plates also posed no problem. New plates cost a hundred dinars. The first auction brought in profits of $8 million. We threw the bundles of money on Uday's desk in his office in the Olympic Club. The whole club became like one enormous bank vault, and everyone helped himself, because Uday and his financial managers had long ago lost control over the glut of money.

Fresh girls appeared daily at the club, and every day was a drunken party. The offices degenerated into venues for wild orgies. If Uday and his men had led dissolute lives before, now they went completely overboard. Screeching naked women intertwined on the floor with the bodyguards. Uday had one girl jump up on a table covered with various lamb dishes for a buffet. She rolled around in the rice with raisins, smeared curry and all kinds of sauces on her breasts, and demanded lasciviously that we lick it off. Some did.

By September 10, Uday had made the unbelievable profit of $125 million from the car sales. Mercedes and BMWs, formerly a rarity on Baghdad streets, were a common sight. Uday used to punish everyone who drove a showy car, but now he was inundating Baghdad with just such cars. Jaguars, Rolls-Royces, and big American cars or all-terrain vehicles had also become commonplace.

Unfortunately, the oversupply led to a drastic drop in prices.

Hussein Kamel's men in particular were selling the cars at monster discounts: Chevrolets for five thousand dollars, Cadillacs for four thousand dollars, BMWs for eight thousand dollars. As a special incentive, they offered free license plates, which the buyer could pick up directly at the Interior Ministry. Hussein Kamel's car-sales stands in front of the People's Stadium in Baghdad turned into real bazaars, attracting thousands.

This was tough competition for Uday. He had Hussein Kamel's people observed, and discovered a scandal. His

enormous earnings from the sales of cars, electric appliances, and cosmetics were not enough for Hussein Kamel.
Assuming that anything goes in times like these, he had also
installed printing presses on his farms in Tikrit, and was
printing twenty-five-dinar, fifty-dinar, and hundred-dinar
notes. About 80 million counterfeit dinars from Hussein's
workshop were in circulation in Baghdad alone.

Saddam Hussein had already announced severe measures against counterfeiters on Iraqi television, not knowing
of Kamel's involvement. Two Baghdad businessmen, Make
al-Dalimi and Naser al-Basrani, were detained and charged
with counterfeiting. When Saddam learned shortly afterward that his own son-in-law was behind it all, he drove to his
farm in Tikrit. Seven counterfeiters, all members of the intelligence service, were arrested and displayed on the evening
news. They were executed one week later. The president shot
them personally, with the revolver of his bodyguard Abed
Hamid al-Tikriti.

Simultaneously, the fourfold minister was relieved of all
his responsibilities. Iraqi television announced that Hussein
Kamel had no more authority. All of his property was confiscated, and he was forced by Saddam to divorce Raghd, the
president's oldest daughter.

But these radical measures were rescinded shortly there-
after, following some internal discussions among the family.
Supposedly all of the other ministers had expressed support
for Saddam's son-in-law and protested his innocence. Another television broadcast was arranged and used to announce that Hussein Kamel had resumed control of his
ministries. The divorce was annulled, and the president
demonstratively expressed full confidence in his son-in-law.

But back to Kuwait. Saddam Hussein had made Kuwait
the nineteenth province of Iraq on August 28, 1990. Two
weeks later, on September 15, 1990, Ali Hassan al-Majid
became the governor of Kuwait province.

Thus one evildoer followed the other, and Ali Hassan al-

Majid, the Chemist, who had ordered the poison-gas attacks against the Kurds in 1988, brutalized Kuwait even more frighteningly than his predecessor. Al-Majid ordered harsh measures against suspected resistance fighters. Saddam Hussein had given him carte blanche, and he applied martial law ruthlessly.

When an Iraqi patrol was fired on in a residential area, they ordered all residents out of their houses. Men and women were made to line up in separate groups against the building walls. An officer counted off the women and ordered every tenth one to step forward. Another counted off the men and had every fifth one step forward. The ones selected were lined up against another wall, and a jeep with a mounted machine gun drove up. Several bursts and it was over. An officer ordered the survivors to remove their dead.

In another punitive action, fifteen Kuwaitis were butchered, and the survivors were beaten on the bottoms of their feet until bare bone was exposed, then their heads were dunked in a tubful of water and human waste — until they drank so they wouldn't be drowned.

Al-Majid also ordered the torture of all Kuwaitis who refused to declare themselves Iraqi citizens. It was enough to be caught in possession of the abolished Kuwaiti currency to be considered a traitor or instigator.

Al-Majid's people had complete freedom to act. They weren't bound by the strong disciplinary rules of the army. They murdered, raped, burned. Al-Majid was in his element.

In Baghdad we heard almost nothing of these depredations. We were much too busy plundering. Now we were taking cars of all makes that we considered to have some value. We'd also abandoned our former restraint and were acting exactly like Hussein Kamel's men. We stopped cars in the open street, rousted the drivers, and the deal was done. Or we forced our way into businesses and confiscated everything.

Of course I realized I was committing crimes. But my excuse was that I had to carry out Uday's orders.

We quickly progressed beyond stealing cars. Uday ordered me one day to ransack the private villa of a jeweler in the Kuwait City district of Shamiya, which was reported to be the hiding place of large amounts of gold — more than half a ton — along with loose diamonds, jewels, and watches.

But when we stormed the house, another band of plunderers was already there. They had killed the jeweler, who was lying in a pool of his blood. A coffin stood in the middle of the room, and the men were packing it with all the jewelry. Their leader was Ali Hassan al-Majid, governor of Province 19. While his men believed I was Uday Saddam Hussein, al-Majid realized immediately that I was only his double. He yelled at us and chased us off, but I still managed to see how they had draped an Iraqi flag over the brimming coffin.

The next day the coffin was transported to Baghdad with official honors, accompanied by an officer and two soldiers. The media celebrated "THE RETURN OF A HERO." In reality, the coffin's final resting place was on Ali Hassan al-Majid's farm, outside of Baghdad.

The officer and soldiers detailed to accompany the coffin were hanged two days later. Al-Majid had accused them of robbing a jeweler in Kuwait. Their bodies hung for seven days in Baghdad, in full public view, as a warning. Images of the dead were sent around the world. Al-Majid declared that every soldier caught looting would be executed immediately and without a trial.

Uday was unimpressed. He knew, just as we did, that this applied only to common soldiers and officers, not to members of the president's family and their employees.

By now the bodyguards of Uday's mother were also participating in the sack of Kuwait. Already considered one of the world's richest women, Sajida had truckload after truckload of marble brought to Baghdad. She had erected a high-rise near the Babel Aubouri Hotel shortly before the invasion, and now was having the walls and floors sheathed with marble from Kuwait. Exclusive business offices were placed on the market at 300,000 dinars per unit.

I heard little about the developments in Saudi Arabia and the gathering of the Allied troops. We all knew what names such as Desert Shield meant, and that new troops were steadily flowing into the Gulf. But none of us really believed there would ever be a massive attack against Iraq. I noticed that Saddam Hussein was constantly calling for "holy war" against the West, and that he wanted to lure the Israelis into the conflict with his threats to fire poison-gas missiles against them. But I didn't take his threats seriously, believing they were diversionary. Moreover, we still had the six thousand western hostages — a guarantee that nothing would happen.

Most of these "special guests," as Saddam referred to them, hung out at the bars of the large hotels, passing the time by playing cards, and hardly anyone paid any attention to them after a few weeks.

When not in Kuwait with my team, I was either at the Olympic Club or taking part in the auctions. The trade in stolen goods had reached such dimensions in the meantime that it couldn't be kept hidden from foreign journalists staying in Baghdad. There were only a few representatives of the world media here at that point, and their freedom of movement was strictly limited, but the numerous Rolls-Royces, Jaguars, Mercedes, and Cadillacs on the streets of Baghdad spoke more clearly than words. Reports on the situation soon appeared in the West. And everyone in Baghdad who retained a bit of decency and self-respect began to get incensed about the despicable way in which the president's son was lining his pockets.

This was a precarious situation for Uday. On the one hand, we still had lots of cars to sell; on the other, public pressure was mounting from day to day. Even western politicians, who came to Baghdad in supplication to win the hostages' release, heard about the dealings of the president's son, and the Information Ministry was busily trying to cover up the facts with lies such as that the goods were brought to Iraq by refugees.

What was more, these reports had drawn Saddam Hussein's anger. The whole Gulf region was confronted with a war of unpredictable results — and here he had to deal with accusations that his own son and his closest associates were guilty of robbery.

Besides, criticism was being voiced within the army of the fact that common soldiers were summarily hanged or shot if caught looting, while Saddam's son could plunder openly, without fear of punishment. Uday had always been hated, but now his reputation sank beyond redemption.

Uday realized this. He spoke openly in late September of 1990 of having me disappear. "The simplest thing," he suggested once in a conversation with Azzam, "would be for you to kill Latif and send his body to the bottom." My death sentence? No, not exactly — a quiet death wouldn't help. Azzam replied, "That wouldn't improve anything. The people would continue to talk, and your reputation wouldn't be salvaged, sir."

In Iraq and in the West, Uday would still be considered the main culprit responsible for the plundering.

He had to find another solution. The day after his conversation with Azzam, which I overheard from a neighboring room, Uday summoned Munem Hammed and all the other officers who had trained me to discuss how to stop the talk about him and his looting of Kuwait. Shukr al-Tikriti, an intelligence officer, came up with the lifesaver, an idea at once bizarre and brilliant. His train of thought went as follows: Uday had all the media in Iraq under his thumb. "With the help of the media," he explained, "we should be able to pull you out of this mess." Uday was skeptical and started to interrupt, then let him continue. His friend elaborated, "You never showed up anywhere in person, did you?"

Uday shook his head. "What's that got to do with any-thing?"

"Wait, I'll explain in a minute. You were never in Kuwait, and you never stole cars and auctioned them off. Thus no-body could have observed you, Uday Saddam Hussein, en-gaged in any kind of criminal activity." Al-Tikriti paused briefly, stroked his mustache with his left hand, and contin-ued, "If it wasn't you who plundered Kuwait, then you can't have personally enriched yourself — understand?"

Uday and the other officers still didn't get what he was driving at. What he said next made my blood run cold: I, Latif Yahia, should appear on the main newscast of Iraqi television and declare that it wasn't Uday Saddam Hussein who had plundered Kuwait, but me. I, Latif Yahia, had ex-ploited my likeness to the president's son to deceive honest officers and bring thousands of cars to Baghdad.

Uday was speechless, as were Munem Hammed and the officers. Then they burst out laughing and showered Shukr al-Tikriti with compliments. "Brilliant!" was Uday's judg-ment.

He got up, planted himself in front of al-Tikriti, grabbed him by the shoulders, embraced him, kissed him three times, and exulted, "My brother, that's just brilliant. And we're also going to publish that evil scoundrel Latif Yahia's deposition in all the papers, along with his picture. I want the whole world to know that I was robbed of my honor by a malicious impostor."

I didn't know what to say. They had me where they wanted me. Uday grinned, clapped my shoulder, hissed, "We're going to sentence you to death, Latif, and you're going to play along." All of them stared at me, laughing boisterously. I grinned in embarrassment.

Preparations began the very next day for my television appearance. My apartment in the al-Hayat high-rise was made over as a television studio. Shukr al-Tikriti composed the text that I was to commit to memory:

"I, Latif Yahia Latif, born June 14, 1964, exploited my resemblance to Uday Saddam Hussein to steal goods from Kuwait in his name and sell them in Baghdad. In reality, I did this all for myself. I enriched myself, not Uday Saddam Hussein. Uday is completely innocent. He is the most honest person in the world."

I had to practice this text twelve days in a row. We made hundreds of video recordings with me always sitting in a moderator's chair in front of a gray screen — wearing Uday's uniform, of course. They wanted me to place particular emphasis on the word "I" during my performance.

First we rehearsed without props. I sat up straight in my chair and said what I had to say. But Uday thought it would be better to have me hold a Cuban cigar in one hand and sit in an armchair, with my legs crossed. Then everyone would see immediately how closely I resembled the president's son and that I'd even adopted his mannerisms to betray him.

We repeated the scene several times. I had to hold the cigar demonstratively in my left hand, loll in the armchair, take an occasional drag, and then give my little speech. Everything was recorded on video and analyzed. Uday always found fault with something. Either I was puffing too hard, or I was lounging too much. Finally they agreed that while saying my speech I should only hold the cigar like Uday, not puff on it.

It was November 9, 1990, and I was being made up by Ismail al-Azami, Uday's private hairdresser. He cut my beard, my hair, every hair individually in his finicky way, paying attention to the least detail. Then it was the turn of Yassem al-Helou, the dresser. He arrived with a brand-new uniform bearing the Iraqi eagle and the name of Uday Saddam Hussein on the breast. It took slightly less than an hour to get me into shape.

Then I was ready. I sat on the moderator's chair, with the cameraman facing me. He gave me a sign, and I began. I held the cigar prominently, my legs crossed, my gaze steady on the camera. Though completely relaxed, I made a mistake on the first take: "I, Latif Yahia Latif, born June 18, 1964, in Baghdad —" Al-Tikriti interrupted, "Idiot, you weren't born on June 18, 1964. Uday was!"

We laughed, tried again, and this time I got it right. I didn't make a single mistake, and nothing about me was artificial or tense. I appeared relaxed, tranquil, not at all as if someone had forced me to make this statement.

It was absurd: Here I was declaring myself guilty before the world, and at the same time I was proud of having done so perfectly, without fault. I worked hard, cooperated, did everything my master asked me. "A real fidai," I told myself miserably.

On November 11, 1990, on the evening news, the newscaster announced in a sonorous voice, "A criminal named Latif Yahia Latif, son of a rich Baghdad businessman, has been taken into custody. Latif Yahia Latif is responsible for smuggling large quantities of stolen goods from Kuwait and selling them in Baghdad. This scion of a rich family exploited his resemblance to the president's eldest son to carry out his criminal activities. By his actions, he has sullied both his family's name and that of the great son of the president." Then came the video we had recorded the previous day.

I was sitting with Uday, the bodyguards, and Shukr al-Tikriti in Project No. 7 when it was broadcast. They all bent double with laughter as they watched.

After my self-denunciation, the newscaster concluded in a sepulchral tone, "With this crime, Latif Yahia Latif has done irreparable harm to the reputation of Uday Saddam Hussein and has consequently been sentenced to death by hanging. The execution will be carried out in the next few days."

Over. That was it. Uday and the bodyguards hooted, applauded, congratulated each other for this great show.

I felt awful, because Latif Yahia was officially dead as of

that announcement. Forever. Not only did I not exist anymore, I had become a dead man. Until now, as far as my friends
were concerned, I had simply disappeared, but with my confession I became someone who had been both disgraced and
executed. And the disgrace extended to my family. My father,
my mother, my brothers, my sisters — had they seen the
broadcast just now? What was my mother going to think? If
she hadn't seen it herself, she'd hear about it from her friends
and neighbors. She'd be called up and told that her son had
just confessed on television to being a criminal. I don't want
to present myself as better than I am. I too went crazy over all
the goods in Kuwait. I also admit that I diverted several cars
for myself. But Uday never found out about that, and I have no
scruples about it because Uday was the real criminal. He was
the mastermind. It was his idea; he ordered us to carry it out.

"What's going to happen now?" I asked him. "What's
the next step after this TV show?"

"You'll be told." He laughed. Before he left the room, I
asked him if I could contact my parents and tell them I was
still alive. Uday responded with a sharp "No! As of this
moment, you're not allowed to leave the palace and the
grounds around the al-Hayat high-rise."

I realized in that instant that I could no longer remain in
Iraq, should I ever manage to escape alive from Saddam's
clan. My ordinary existence could never resume. It had been
destroyed, and that was worse than death. I called to mind
the hundreds of transparent show trials, clinging to my belief
in the intelligence of the Iraqi people: The people would
never believe this story. They had to realize it was all a cheap
show to clear the name of the president's family. Everyone in
Baghdad knew that Uday had enriched himself. He did it for
months. How could I have done it without his knowledge? It
was impossible. My parents and friends would never be
fooled by this fabrication!

For the first time, I contemplated fleeing, but things
developed differently.

14

THE BOMBS FALL

ON BAGHDAD

I'D been more or less under house arrest since my public declaration of guilt. Bodyguards kept me under closer watch than ever. I could still go to the pool and the shooting club, but received little information about what was happening in the outside world.

For instance, I didn't learn that the situation in the Gulf was becoming increasingly tense, although Saddam had freed the western hostages. My bodyguards informed me only that the Security Council of the United Nations, "a pseudo-council blackmailed by the Americans," had given Iraq an ultimatum. Our troops had to withdraw from Kuwait by January 15, 1991, or the Allied forces would strike at Iraq to free Kuwait by force.

In their blind arrogance, my bodyguards parroted everything that was fed to them. Like Saddam Hussein, they spoke of a jihad, a holy war, although they had no idea what that meant. Laughing and brandishing their Kalashnikovs, they threatened "to strangle every American soldier who falls into our hands," promising, "If Bush attacks, we'll teach the aggressor a lesson. We'll triumph in the mother of all battles."

I didn't put much stock in their slogans, especially since I knew the men felt differently in reality: "Nothing but empty words. How are we supposed to win against the rest of the world?" Just about everyone in Iraq felt the same way. Everybody feared war, and nobody wanted to obey "him, up there."

And because I knew that Saddam recognized the mood of the people, I expected him to pull back from Kuwait at the last instant, because he couldn't trust his subjects anymore. He was like a poker player who bluffs as long as he can, but then folds because he has the inferior hand. Saddam had to realize that more and more people were leaving Baghdad for their summer houses in the countryside. They were afraid and believed their chances of survival were greater there in the event of an attack.

On one occasion, I heard from my bodyguards that unbelievable numbers were circulating in the West concerning our fighting strength. "The American media," they said, "report that more than half a million Iraqi soldiers are sitting in Kuwait, equipped with thousands of tanks and all sorts of sophisticated weaponry. You were in Kuwait. What's it really like?"

My answer disappointed them. "Yes, I was in Kuwait, and all I can say is, there can't be more than a quarter-million Iraqi soldiers dug in there. Probably less. Their positions are primitive, and none of them want to fight. They'd like nothing better than to throw away their weapons and run home."

These remarks could have spelled death if my superiors had found out about them. But my guards kept my unique outburst of frustration to themselves. They probably thought the same way I did.

In January 1991, I chanced to meet Munem Hammed in front of the al-Hayat high-rise. When he asked how I was, I said I was relatively fine, but would be happy for new tasks. "I've done nothing for weeks. Absolutely nothing," I complained.

He nodded in commiseration, answering cryptically,

"You'll have missions enough sooner than any of us would like." Then he walked away.

I couldn't make sense of his answer. What did he mean? What did he know?

Days passed before I found out: it seems that almost all of Saddam Hussein's family had already fled Iraq via Jordan from one day to the next. Uday and his bodyguards drove off in one convoy; his mother and sisters Raghd and Rina in another; in a third, the youngest daughter, Hala, with her husband, Hakim Kamel. The families of numerous ministers had also slipped away. The whole clan proceeded together from Jordan to Algeria, and from there to Brazil. Uday flew from Brazil back to Geneva, to his uncle Barzan al-Tikriti. The ministers' families fled to Mauritania. Only Saddam Hussein and his son Qusay remained in Iraq.

This information was confirmed by the statements of several bodyguards, even if they didn't agree in all the particulars. One asserted that Uday flew directly from Amman, Jordan, to Switzerland, another that he first flew with his family to Brazil, and from there to Geneva, but such details didn't matter. The only important thing was that the families had decamped, because it confirmed that Iraq's leaders now reckoned with a war, and that the negotiations conducted by Foreign Minister Tariq Aziz in Geneva and UN Secretary General Perez de Cuellar in Baghdad had become irrelevant.

Saddam Hussein didn't want to withdraw from Kuwait. He wanted war, and once again threatened to attack Israel with missiles in the event of an Allied attack.

My thoughts went to my parents: *Where will they go? There aren't many air-raid shelters in Baghdad, and the few that do exist are reserved for party members. I hope they go to relatives in northern Iraq or book a room for the next few days in a tourist hotel outside Baghdad.*

When I again pressed my bodyguards about the threat

of war, I wanted to know what was happening around the country. They acknowledged that for days the television had been showing instructional films about how mass evacuations were supposed to be conducted, and suddenly they weren't as cocky as they had been just a few days before. "My father," confessed one, whose name I don't want to mention because he always treated me properly, "said that Iraq can't possibly survive a second war, that we don't stand a chance of survival. The Americans and Europeans will destroy us." He actually admitted that some of his family had tried to emigrate and stay with relatives in Amman, but couldn't obtain documents for the trip. I noticed for the first time that fear was on the rise.

January 16, 1991: a fateful day. The countdown began. The Allies' ultimatum had expired. War could start any minute now. My bodyguards brought back the television they had taken from me weeks ago. One of my keepers even had a short-wave radio. We turned it on to hear what the world was thinking, but were only able to home in briefly, once, on Radio Monte Carlo. We couldn't find the BBC World Service.

We switched on the television. We couldn't get CNN, of course, and had to depend on the Iraqi news. The anchor reported that President Saddam Hussein was in his bunker at his headquarters, and that the Iraqi people would deal "deadly blows to the aggressors." I couldn't stand any more of this lousy propaganda. I could even hear the fear in the voice of the newscaster. Sure, our people had become familiar with war, with the terror of missiles striking and bombs exploding. But this time? Us against the whole world? Where the hell was *my* personal bunker?

My bodyguards calmed me down, reassuring me that we were unlikely to remain in the high-rise should it really come to an attack.

We turned to the television images once more. They showed thousands of demonstrators marching along the Street of the Palestinians, waving pictures of Saddam Hussein and screaming, "Down Bush! Down Bush!" Youths were pointing their Kalashnikovs into the air, as if they could shoot down fighter-bombers with them. Amid the demonstrators we could see party cadres who were goading them on. The hacks disgusted me: Fear was obvious in the people's faces! Couldn't they even see it? And they didn't even know that Hussein's whole family had long since absconded. They had no idea that the important military units had been withdrawing from the palace grounds for days. Project 2,000, Saddam's headquarters, was deserted. Documents were being removed around the clock by special units.

A tense air of expectancy prevailed. Everyone was nervous, but nobody wanted to admit he was afraid of what was about to happen. My main fear was, How is Israel going to react when we fire our Scud missiles at Tel Aviv? Will the Israelis resort to the nuclear bomb if Saddam deploys poison gas?

The phone rang just before 7:00 P.M. One of my keepers picked up the receiver. He turned deathly pale and shouted, "We have to go right away to the bomb shelter next door."

I asked, "Why?"

"Our intelligence people in Saudi Arabia have received word of increased activity at the airport in Dhahran. They may be planning to bomb Baghdad tonight."

On our way from the al-Hayat to the bunker, I could see Baghdad and the palace building still illuminated. Why light up everything if they were expecting an attack? That defied logic. Didn't they take the information from Saudi Arabia seriously? Once again, doubts surfaced in my mind. "Are they really going to do it?"

They did it. There were sixteen of us in the shelter. The mood wasn't bad, although we knew that the palace grounds would be one of the main targets of the assault. They'd bomb this part of Baghdad to smithereens. We were hiding in the devil's headquarters.

After torturous hours of waiting, the first explosion

rocked the palace grounds at 2:40 A.M. It must have been a powerful detonation, because our bunker shook and there was a smell of gasoline. "We'll never leave here alive," I told myself. Then a second detonation, a third, a fourth. The bombs must have fallen in the immediate vicinity, probably on Project 2,000. We could only imagine what was happening above us. We were sitting under a six-yard-thick concrete ceiling in a nuclear-bomb-proof bunker, and only the vibrations enabled us to guess whether the missiles had landed nearby or farther away.

The attacks came in waves five minutes long, with a detonation every second, then a short pause, then again this vibration every second. None of us dared admit it out loud, but all of us were scared. We did our best to cover it up. We laughed, joked, and played pool, although the electricity had been cut in the meantime and we had only emergency lighting. Someone remarked sarcastically, "Hopefully the French didn't skimp on the concrete."

Another dull thud, followed by shaking. It was as if the concrete walls were magnifying the thuds, making them even more muffled and menacing. One wave after another rolled over us until five in the morning. Then there was sudden quiet, as quiet as death.

An officer entered the bunker. He ordered us to take off our uniforms and exchange them as quickly as possible for the brown djellabas brought to us by other soldiers. We were ready in less than five minutes. They led us up. A thick cloud of smoke hovered over the palace grounds. There was a burned smell, but, amazingly, the destruction appeared minimal. Judging by the noise in the bunker, everything should have been leveled to the foundations. But only Project 2,000 was destroyed. An officer said that Saddam's palace was hit by the first bomb.

We were rushed onto army trucks and driven off the palace grounds. A ghostly silence reigned. We went in the direction of al-Dejel, a little town about fifty miles from

Baghdad. All the way, very little destruction was evident. "What's the deal, what did they bomb?" I asked the officer, but he didn't answer.

In al-Dejel, we were quartered in a little community of town houses. Nothing in its appearance indicated that it was a military base. The houses looked like private homes, and were furnished like private homes. But underneath the single-story buildings were shelters with outlets somewhat outside the settlement and so cleverly concealed by trees that one couldn't spot them from the air, although they were big enough for tractor-trailers to drive into.

We stayed in al-Dejel until early February. Four days after our arrival, we heard a rumor that Saddam Hussein was also here, and Saddam Hussein did truly come to al-Dejel. Like us, he wasn't in uniform. His convoy consisted of only four ordinary compacts, no Mercedes limousines, no attention-getting escort. Only four compacts, but I'm convinced it was Saddam Hussein himself, and not his fidai, Faoaz al-Emari.

Saddam remained for three days in al-Dejel. Then he left suddenly, for where we didn't know.

At the end of January 1991, the air war was in high gear. We had long since gotten used to the waves of attacks. Fear had been replaced by a kind of apathy. We had heard reports a few days earlier that Saddam Hussein had visited his troops in Kuwait despite the incessant attacks by the Allies, who controlled all of Iraq's airspace. It was no secret they did. American fighter-bombers roared over our territory in extremely low flights, and our antiaircraft defenses watched them almost powerlessly. The weather seemed our sole ally. The air activity lessened somewhat on days of poor weather.

Only when Scud missiles targeted Saudi Arabia or Israel could our soldiers rejoice. We didn't know back then that these Scud attacks had no military significance. We were only told that another major blow against the Zionist enemy had been delivered and that each hit was celebrated ecstatically by our Palestinian friends. The reports about the celebrating Palestinians were meant to remind people in Iraq that we had friends.

Nonetheless, morale within the army fell by the day. It was simply frustrating to have to witness the death of thousands because we had almost nothing to counter the air attacks.

We heard reports that the morale of our troops in Kuwait was almost zero. Word was they weren't getting supplies because the supply routes were constantly bombed. Some of our men had apparently deserted. I learned nothing precise. The fact was, however, that morale was poor generally, not only in Kuwait but in Iraq. More and more people were finding out that almost all of Saddam's family had gone abroad.

Western short-wave programs reported several times that Uday was having a good time in a Geneva nightclub while people in Iraq were dying. Iraqi radio responded: "Pure propaganda from western intelligence services and their broadcasting facilities in Saudi Arabia."

These Saudi facilities really did exist, and their signal could be received in Iraq. They were urging us all the time to put down our weapons, surrender, and publicly oppose Saddam.

On January 28, 1991, Rokan al-Tikriti, one of Saddam Hussein's closest associates, picked me up in person and brought me to a subterranean bunker about twelve miles from the international airport in Baghdad. The entrance to the bunker was expertly camouflaged near some private homes. Trees stood before it. We were in the midst of a war, but the area radiated unbelievable tranquillity. Not a single building was damaged; not a single bomb crater was visible.

Rokan al-Tikriti escorted me inside. First there was a large hall where two MiG-29 fighter-bombers stood, beside them several army personnel carriers. We crossed four rooms separated by steel doors painted reddish brown. Then we went down a set of spiral stairs one story deeper, to a checkpoint of the kind I last saw when I was introduced to Saddam Hussein. I was searched briefly, then taken to a kind of conference room with a large table and two dozen wooden chairs with dark green upholstery. The door to an adjacent room was open. I could see electronic equipment, telephones, computer screens. Rokan closed the door. I waited.

The door to the adjacent room suddenly opened again. Qusay Saddam Hussein entered, followed at short intervals by Hussein Kamel and the president himself. All of them sat down, Hussein Kamel to the left of Saddam, Qusay to the right. I was standing next to Rokan, about five yards away from Saddam Hussein. He gazed at me, and I was shocked at how poorly he looked: eyes sunken, face swollen, hands trembling slightly.

The president said only, "I want you to go with Hussein Kamel to our troops in Kuwait. Perform your duties well, my son." Saddam's normally quiet, whiny voice sounded even weaker, like that of an old man. He spoke shakily, exhaustedly, as if fighting for breath.

Rokan then escorted me out. Saddam remained behind. As I was leaving, I saw him lean toward his son and explain something.

On January 29, shortly after 9:00 P.M., our mission to Kuwait began. We drove in a convoy, under battle conditions. That meant without headlights, with only the lead driver illuminating the road briefly again and again through the narrow slit left on his taped-over headlamps. The other vehicles followed the brake lights of the car in front of them. A driver was allowed to flash on his lights briefly if he got disoriented, but our drivers were such experts at operating under battle conditions that the moonlight was almost enough for them to avoid any accidents.

Hussein Kamel and I were accompanied by seventy-five bodyguards. There were no incidents during the drive. Occasionally we saw the orange glow of fire on the horizon, as if the sky itself were burning — the sign of bomb attacks against the Republican Guards, who had retreated from Kuwait back to Iraq.

We reached Basra in the early hours of the morning. The city had sustained major damage. From there we proceeded toward Safwan, the large Iraqi air base near the border with Kuwait, but we halted at a camp outside the base. I was wearing the black uniform of the president's son and my Ray-Ban glasses. Only the cigar was missing.

We were met by the ranking officers in the camp. I kept to the background, as I had been instructed, and we were taken to the underground command post, which seemed relatively undamaged, although attacks had been flown daily for more than two weeks against these positions. Hussein Kamel listened to the commander's report about the condition of the troops, and was given several plans and documents in a brown leather briefcase. He scanned them briefly. None of the officers mentioned that the men's morale was understandably poor and that the resupply of food was catastrophic. Terrorist attacks conducted by Shi'ite deserters against their own units were also left unmentioned.

We were served tea and shown the food rations and weapons issued to the troops. The commanders also spoke of Tabun and Sarin, chemical ordnance, which could be fired off by any number of weapons from a mortar to a SAM missile. But not a word about the fact that none of the common soldiers had gas masks.

Before we left, our propaganda team had to do their job. We were filmed by two cameramen. Four newspaper photographers recorded the whole visit as well: Uday speaking to the troops, Uday manning an antiaircraft battery, Uday using a radio, Uday eating with the soldiers.

My cameramen were careful to choose those soldiers whose uniforms were relatively clean and who didn't look too haggard. The men obligingly screamed, "Saddam Hussein! Saddam Hussein!" into the lens, and "Down Bush!

Down Bush!" I gave a brief, prepared speech before the soldiers, exhorting them to hold out. While I was speaking to the 11 Magavir company, I noticed a former comrade with whom I'd fought on the Iran-Iraq front. He'd been with me at the observation post in the swamps of Basra. My friend stared at me for a long time, literally fixing his gaze on me, and his face held a look of recognition. I returned his gaze, turned up the corners of my mouth to smile, and he smiled back. I thought of embracing him for a second. I didn't.

Every Iraqi newspaper ran pictures of my visit to the front. *Al-Iraq* and *al-Thawra* provided the most thorough coverage, devoting a special layout to the president's son's visit with our valiant troops. Uday's bravery was lauded. All of the papers mentioned how, unafraid, he ate together with the soldiers during the hellish air attacks that were a crime against the Iraqi people. This was to suggest that the men had enough food supplies. UDAY, THE GREAT SON OF THE PEOPLE, JOINS OUR VALOROUS TROOPS FIGHTING AGAINST THE IMPERIALISTIC AMERICAN ENEMY, proclaimed one headline. Lousy, unimaginative propaganda.

We spent the next night in a school several miles from Basra. Hussein Kamel was avoiding the city, which had been the site of unrest for several days. Fundamentalist Shi'ites had been targeting the Republican Guards relentlessly. Accused attackers were arrested by the dozens and either summarily killed or hauled off to Baghdad's prisons. The Shi'ite revolt was led by Ayatollah Mohammed Baqr al-Hakim, who was living in Iran. Yet not a word was printed in the Iraqi newspapers about any problems with the Shi'ites in the south.

The night was quiet. It was still dark when Hussein Kamel departed. He wanted to return to Baghdad as quickly as possible to report to the president. I remained behind, along with seventeen bodyguards.

We drove to Basra the next day, which we knew was a risky undertaking. We'd been advised at a checkpoint that several resistance groups had formed within the city and that there were also street demonstrations, but we wanted to go into the city nonetheless. Then it happened. Suddenly we began taking fire from the sand hills next to the road. Submachine guns rattled, hand grenades exploded. We stopped, returned fire.

The vehicle meant to protect my left flank was hit by a hand grenade and went up in flames. Then came a loud bang, and the armored windshield of my car burst into a thousand pieces. I, Uday Saddam Hussein, hated son of the president, was hit by grenade fragments. On the shoulder, on the right hand. Two fingers of my right hand were hanging by only a few strands of tissue. There was blood everywhere. I felt no pain, heard the coughing and rattling of my bodyguards' Kalashnikovs.

I collapsed under the steering wheel. Through a gray fog, I saw someone ripping open my door. Bodyguards yanked me out of my Mercedes and into their car, and we took off, heading toward Baghdad. It was only now that I started feeling the burning sensation in my shoulder, my head, my hip, my right hand.

My bodyguards stopped after ten or fifteen miles and bandaged me provisionally. Worst was my hand wound. They tied my arm high so I wouldn't lose too much blood.

I had no idea how long the trip back to Baghdad lasted. They brought me to an ordinary hospital, where I was operated on. When I came out from under the anesthesia, the doctors told me that they'd probably have to amputate the little finger on my right hand.

A catastrophe — not for me, but for Uday Saddam Hussein, who was still amusing himself in Geneva.

I was operated on three more times in the following days. The surgeons tried to save my finger with all their skill. The operations went well, they said, but the hand became badly infected because of the poor hygiene in the hospital.

Even worse, however, was the fact that the attack on the

president's son's convoy had become public knowledge. The Shi'ite rebels apparently reported their success to their head-quarters in Iran, or to the Americans. In any case, the Voice of America and Radio Monte Carlo, both of which broadcast into Iraq, reported about ten days after the attack that "the son of the Iraqi president, Uday Saddam Hussein, was killed in a firefight with Shi'ite rebels in Basra." These reports were picked up by all the major international news agencies and created panic in the propaganda department of the presidential clan, first, because they gave the rebels hope; second, because they proved irrefutably that there was open resistance to the president, something that had always been denied; and, third, because our troops in Kuwait were about to be targeted by a massive ground offensive, and there was nothing Saddam needed less at such a time than reports that might shake the myth that the president's clan was invincible.

15

THE AGONIES OF TORTURE

CAPTAIN Sabri Kamel Matar was a good man. Now he was dead. As were First Lieutenant Hussein Fath-Allah Mohammed, Lieutenant Bashir Yunes al-Tikriti, and Lieutenant Nazem Hilal al-Douri. These four men had guarded me since my televised self-denunciation in November 1990. "Guarded" is possibly not the right term; they lived with me, were my bodyguards and my keepers, my friends and jailers at the same time. We were together in the bunker when the bombing of Baghdad began; we fled together to al-Dejel; they were with me when I visited our troops in Safwan; and it was they who returned fire when we were attacked in Basra in an ambush by Shi'ite rebels.

The four officers died because they sought to protect me. They jumped out of their cars and tried to storm the hills behind which the rebels had entrenched themselves. First to fall was Sabri Kamel Matar, hit by a salvo from a Kalashnikov. The other three were so badly wounded by shrapnel that they couldn't be helped. I still don't know today how many rebels were killed by my bodyguards. And I wouldn't even know that these four officers died, had not two of my bodyguards visited me and told me the whole story of the incident in Basra.

I remained in the hospital. The inflammation in my right hand hadn't improved, but my head and hip wounds had more or less healed.

Rokan al-Tikriti pressured the doctors. "Latif has to be

ready for action as quickly as possible." If there was no other way, I'd have to return to the front with my hand in a cast. Saddam needed successes, positive media coverage, and part of that was for the president's son to be seen with the soldiers. But Uday still lingered in Geneva, although the urgent dispatch demanding his return to Baghdad at once must have reached him long ago.

In the hospital, in all of Baghdad, everywhere in the country, people were talking of soldiers deserting daily and crossing over to the enemy. The reports we got from the front were awful. The Allies were flying as many as eight hundred sorties a day against the Republican Guards and the frontline positions of the regular army. The soldiers were forced to hole up in their bunkers for days. They'd dug into the sand, just like the units I visited in Safwan. All the artillery, all the tanks — everything was dug deep into the sand.

I learned another detail in the hospital. The Fifth Motorized Division had conducted tank attacks against Allied positions on three parts of the Kuwaiti-Iraqi border while I was in Safwan on January 29. One column of tanks was beaten back relatively quickly, but the other two were able to penetrate as far as al-Khafji, an oil refinery on the Saudi coast, seven miles south of the Kuwaiti border. This was the first time that Iraqi units had occupied Saudi territory. And our troops were able to hold the city of Khafji for several days. They defied the world. Saddam sent almost four hundred tanks and armored personnel carriers into this pocket in an action that was completely senseless militarily but perfectly exploitable politically. First the images of the son of the president visiting the troops at the front, then the report that Iraqi troops had taken Saudi territory, even occupied a city. Nobody in Iraq knew at the time that al-Khafji was a ghost town whose twenty thousand inhabitants had fled.

Saddam's propaganda machinery continued to work perfectly. Only the attack on me confused the overall propaganda strategy somewhat.

On February 16, 1991, Uday was ordered back from Geneva to Baghdad. He flew via Rome to Amman, Jordan, where he was met by Iraqi security people. In an ordinary car, they brought him to Baghdad over the highway connecting Jordan with Iraq. The road was heavily damaged from the numerous bomb attacks, but still drivable, even though it was extremely dangerous because of frequent air raids. After meeting with his father, Uday came immediately to the hospital. His interest wasn't in me or the numerous other wounded, of course, but in my little finger. He paid a visit to the doctors who had treated me. They'd been on the job permanently for weeks, had operated on and helped thousands. He didn't care a bit. He had them explain in detail what the problem was with the treatment of my little finger. The doctors reiterated several times that only complicated plastic surgery could save it.

They didn't say so, but it wasn't difficult to guess what they must have been thinking: "Children, women, soldiers, are dying here, and we should save a little finger?"

Uday remained completely calm during the whole conversation. He faked interest. Then he got up and declared in his unique high-handed way, "If you can't save this little finger, I'll kill all of you. With my own hands." Then he disappeared.

His threat didn't spring from worry for me. He was only concerned for himself. If his double lost a finger, wouldn't they have to amputate one of his too?

Four days later, on February 20, 1991, they picked me up early in the morning at the hospital. I was still weak, but they ordered me to put on the black uniform of the president's son. We had to return to Basra. Even a visit to the positions of the Republican Guards in northern Kuwait was projected, should the situation allow it. The Tavakalna, Hammurabi, and Medina armored divisions had been under intense fire for more than a month, and a personal appearance at this unit,

the spearhead of the Iraqi army, would be of utmost importance, my commanders told me. But that wasn't to happen. It
took us until sunset the next day even to get close to Basra. We
had to leave the road repeatedly, because the Allies were
flying one attack after the other. It was utter chaos. Everywhere we encountered units retreating from their positions
on the Iraqi-Kuwaiti border, and the retreat was not orderly
but planless, hasty, more like headlong flight. Nobody could
tell us which bridges were intact, whether there was still a
chance we could reach the Republican Guards.

We heard on our car radio that Foreign Minister Tariq
Aziz had returned from Moscow and declared Iraq's readi-
ness to withdraw from Kuwait. The same newscast announced that the Americans had demanded Iraq's
unconditional surrender. One of the cameramen, a serious
man who had already filmed several poison-gas attacks in the
Iran-Iraq war, commented, "We Arabs accept no ultimatums.
We'd rather die."

The cameraman was right. Our president refused to
capitulate. With that, it was clear that a ground offensive
against our troops lay directly ahead.

Another indication that the Americans were about to
attack was the leaflets fluttering down from the heavens to
cover the whole length of the road. They instructed exactly
how the Iraqi soldiers should surrender, promised that nothing would happen to them as prisoners of war, and claimed
that thousands of our soldiers had already gone over to the
Americans and Saudis. One leaflet even contained schematic
drawings showing the proper way to surrender.

We never reached the Republican Guards, and instead
remained for only about two hours at a base on a small hill
near Safwan. We hardly had time for our photo and film
shoots, as the area was under constant air attack. The soldiers
told us that the Americans were still flying pattern-bombing
sorties with B-52 bombers because of the stationary Scud

missile emplacements near the hill. It was from here that Iraqi missiles were launched in the direction of eastern Saudi Arabia.

The way back to Baghdad was less difficult. My arm hurt, though, and I was exhausted. The footage taken by our cameraman was broadcast no more than two hours after our return. The newscaster's voice-over reported that I had urged our valiant soldiers to continue to hold out. There were no close-ups of me. The bandaged right hand, which I had to carry in a sling, was shown only once and briefly.

It surprised me that the report was not more detailed, since, after all, we had put our lives in danger to make these shots. But a short while later I realized why. While we had been driving south, the real Uday was filmed carrying his arm in a sling, too, and with a bandage around his head, declaring in a firm voice, "The rebels' bullets hit me, but only caused slight wounds. As you can see, I'm not dead."

I watched his pathetic performance from the hospital. The newspapers flogged Uday's resurrection ad nauseam — a pointless exercise, first, because there was hardly any electricity anywhere in the country, so most people were unable to watch the televised speech; and, second, because the ground offensive against our troops began on February 24. The Allied military machine rolled over our proud army with lightning speed. Almost twenty thousand Iraqi soldiers surrendered to the enemy on the first day alone. We heard nothing about this on our news. There was almost no information coming out of Kuwait. Communications between Baghdad and Basra had apparently been severed. The bomb attacks on Baghdad itself had ceased, although U.S. fighter-bombers continued to overfly the capital at extremely low altitudes day and night. They approached at supersonic speeds and broke the sound barrier directly above the city. It was an infernal psychological game: the supersonic booms sounded like detonating bombs. The Americans were playing cat-and-mouse with us.

State radio carried a speech by Saddam Hussein every hour. He proclaimed in a whiny voice, "The despicable Bush and the traitorous Fahd began their ground offensive this morning. They're attacking our people on the whole breadth of the front. May disgrace cover them. But they'll discover that the great, heroic Iraqi people is superior to them. Fight, oh, valorous people of Iraq. Oh, you sons of the mother of all battles, fight to protect your women and children, for you are on the threshold of the highest glory, God's honor. The weapons they have built to fight against us will fall from their hands, and then it will be only a fight between believers and unbelievers. Fight them. Be merciless against them. Have no pity on them. For God wants the believer to defeat the unbeliever."

I shuddered as I listened to this the first time. The doctors, who, like me, had waited breathlessly in front of the radio (the speech had been announced), remained silent after Saddam had stopped talking, and the sound of military music and patriotic songs filled the air.

In any case, Saddam's "moving words" were to no effect anymore. The Gulf War that destroyed our country ended four days later. Sixty thousand of our men gave up without a fight. Negotiations over a cease-fire began on March 3, 1991, in Safwan, the same position on the Kuwaiti-Iraqi border that I'd visited during my first tour of the front. Saddam sent the completely unknown three-star generals Sultan Hashim Ahmad, deputy chief of staff in the Defense Ministry, and Salah Abud Mahmud, commander of the Third Corps. Meanwhile, in Baghdad, another campaign began: Saddam wanted to clean house of his enemies.

Our army stationed in southern Iraq seemed to dissolve. Command structures ceased to exist, formerly loyal officers mutinied, and enraged soldiers ripped the gigantic portraits of Saddam Hussein from the walls in the Basra pocket, where opposition against Saddam had already surfaced during the air attacks, and where the army had suffered some of its worst defeats. The offices of the Ba'ath party were attacked everywhere, and mutinous soldiers hunted down party functionaries and secret police officials. For a few days it appeared as if these rebellions might develop into a powerful revolution that could sweep away the hated Saddam regime. Insurgent troops in Basra successfully stormed the prisons and opened the detention camps. A kind of spontaneous liberation movement was formed, and the unrest spread rapidly. The whole south and southeast of the country threatened to succumb.

The rebellion in the south, to the extent it was organized, was led by the Supreme Council of the Islamic Revolution in Iraq. The leader of this movement was the political head of the Iraqi Shi'ites, Ayatollah Mohammed Baqr al-Hakim. In northern Iraq, the Kurdish Pesh Mergas, led by Massoud Barzani and Jalal Talabani, attempted to bring Iraqi Kurdistan under their control.

The situation was so confused, however, that almost no one was in a position to say which areas were still controlled by Saddam Hussein and his Republican Guards, and which were already ruled by rebels and mutineers. Only one thing seemed sure: it was only those garrisons stationed in the Baghdad region during the whole war, as well as the majority of the Republican Guard, who remained truly loyal to the president. When the unrest spread to the region around Karbala, not fifty miles from the capital, Saddam Hussein convened the men in Baghdad he could still trust blindly in such a situation: his sons Uday and Qusay, his sons-in-law Hussein Kamel and Saddam Kamel, his cousin Ali Hassan al-Majid, the Chemist, and General Bashar al-Sabaawi, director of the Mukhabarat intelligence service.

Those six men and Saddam Hussein himself formed the supreme command in the fight against the rebels. Every means available was to be used to suppress the revolution. Qusay Saddam Hussein and Bashar al-Sabaawi assumed command of all intelligence services. Uday was promoted to chairman of the Journalists' Union and thus became the head of all Iraqi media. His first act in office was to increase journalists' salaries by twenty-five percent. He also gave journalists property to build houses and declared, "My goal is to preserve and protect free speech and to keep an eye on unwholesome publications." Everyone in Iraq knew what he meant by "unwholesome publications." Anyone not heeding the rules issued by the palace and not ready to write propaganda for Saddam Hussein would be liquidated.

Hussein Kamel and Saddam Kamel each controlled ten intact divisions that hadn't been involved in the Gulf War. Ali Hassan al-Majid had eight regiments of the Republican Guards under his command. This army proved sufficient to defeat both the Shi'ites in the south and Kurds in the north. The means were so brutal as to be almost beyond description. First, communiqués whose clarity left nothing to the imagination appeared in the government organs *Al-Iraq* and *al-Thawra:* "Warning to all who think they can challenge Iraq's national integrity. The authority of the state and the people will crush you! Anyone attempting to subvert the security of the Iraqi revolution is a traitor and a soldier of the enemy. All traitors will pay. Their punishment will find them wherever they may hide."

The unrest continued despite this proclamation, even enveloping parts of Baghdad. Roadblocks were set up and houses covered with anti-Saddam slogans. The revolutionaries desperately wanted to mobilize the capital in order finally to topple Saddam from the throne. But Saddam delivered a counterpunch.

Units of the Republican Guards, under Ali Hassan al-Majid, went on the rampage in Basra and Karbala. Mutinous soldiers were summarily shot, their leaders either hanged in the streets or brought to the prisons of Baghdad. One hundred six Shi'ite leaders, among them Abu al-Kassem al-Khavai, were given special treatment by Ali Hassan al-Majid

and Qusay Saddam Hussein. They were particularly interested in al-Khavai, considered the religious leader of Iraq's
Shi'ites, whom they ordered to tell the Shi'ite rebels to submit immediately to the regime and surrender all their
weapons. The ninety-five-year-old man refused, replying,
"I'll tell my men instead, 'Rip up the tyrant's pictures. Destroy his statues. Lock the godless out of the mosques.' "
That was his death sentence. They poured gasoline over him
and set him ablaze.

When they sought to learn the names and command
structures of the Shi'ite revolutionaries from other prisoners, they ran into a wall of silence. Qusay Saddam Hussein
lined the prisoners up, had every tenth one step forward,
and sprayed nerve gas into his face, which paralyzed the
breathing apparatus — a terrible death. Others' eyes were
ripped out, or their ears and noses, arms and legs, were
lopped off.

Saddam Kamel, husband of Rina, the second-oldest
daughter, was in charge of the al-Daghil and al-Radvania
prisons. On April 1, as the fear of assassination turned into
paranoia within the president's family, I was summoned by
Uday's brother, Qusay. Unlike Uday, who had completely
withdrawn himself over the last few days, Qusay was an active
participant in the fighting against the rebels. We drove together to al-Radvania, one of the most infamous secret-police
barracks.

Conditions in the prison there were catastrophic. The
cells were filled to bursting with Shi'ite and Kurdish rebels.
The men were skeletal, covered with lice, most of them
hardly able to stand. It was stifling, unbearably hot. The stink
of urine and feces was pervasive, and the sweetish smell of
decay wafted from some cells. Everywhere could be heard the
sighs and groans of the dying and the screams of men being
tortured. I couldn't begin to guess at how many people were
being kept here like cattle before slaughter.

Qusay was sweating, and I noticed that he could hardly bear the stench. His hands were clenched into fists; his gaze was fixed straight ahead. We marched into the director's office, where Saddam Kamel was sitting. He appeared swollen and breathed heavily. As we entered the room, he stood up, and I could see the sweat rings under his arms as he shook Qusay's hand briefly and embraced him. We went out into the prison courtyard.

The director knew what to do. He ordered two upholstered chairs brought and placed in the middle of the dusty prison yard. Saddam Kamel sat, with Qusay to his right. The director then had a group of prisoners brought in. They were all Shi'ites from Karbala, allegedly the leaders of the revolution against the president. They were supposed to have painted anti-Saddam slogans on house walls.

Saddam Kamel held a pistol in his right hand, in his left documents about the traitors who faced questioning under the scorching midday sun. But the interrogation was a farce. "Say that Saddam is the greatest," he hissed at the prisoners. None of them abased themselves in front of Kamel. "You're miserable cowards. Beg for mercy, and then we'll let you go free!" He immediately shot anyone who pleaded for mercy. His comment: "The president doesn't like cowards."

He shot fifteen prisoners on that day alone, while sitting in his armchair. It was supposedly almost one hundred another day. This repellent procedure, which allowed him to rid himself of his pent-up hate, went on for four hours. His dull love of killing left me in shock.

He had the corpses thrown into the collective cells of the other prisoners. The dead were removed only after they had begun to decompose and the stench became so overwhelming that even the guards couldn't stand it. Saddam Kamel collected a bounty of twenty thousand dinars for each murder from Ali Hassan al-Majid. Saddam Hussein also gave him a Mercedes and several office buildings in Baghdad for his loyal service.

Saddam Kamel, known by now as the Butcher of Baghdad, was ambushed in mid-April 1991 on his way back from a
mass execution in the al-Karada district. Youths tried to assassinate him with nothing more than small arms. Saddam Kamel remained unharmed, and his bodyguards were able to
arrest three of the attackers. Saddam Kamel killed them during their interrogation in the intelligence service building.

Saddam Hussein participated personally in these orgies
of killing. I was eyewitness to one such instance. Uday had me
picked up from the al-Hayat high-rise, which had remained
unscathed by the war. We drove to Project 2,000, Saddam's
formerly magnificent palace, now a ruin. A convoy of Mercedes, the president's cars, was parked out front, while Saddam inspected the devastation with his security officers
Rokan al-Tikriti, Shabib al-Tikriti, Abed Hamid, and Saddam
Kamel. Qusay was also present. The president was furious.
Minutes passed while he stood silently before the ruins, then
he ordered Rokan al-Tikriti to fetch prisoners.

More than five thousand people were being kept in the
prisons on the palace grounds, serving as a kind of protective
shield against the rebels. It didn't take long for Rokan to
return with thirty prisoners. They were Kurds. Saddam shot
them one after the other, from close range. Uday, Qusay,
Arshad al-Yasin, Abed Hamid, Shabib, Saddam Kamel, and
Rokan kicked the bodies. They were wading in blood. Everywhere was red. Those not killed instantly were finished off by
the security officers, who put guns to the prisoners' heads
and fired.

But this massacre wasn't enough for Saddam. He had
thirty more prisoners brought, and murdered them too. He
had Rokan bring him a new magazine every time his was
empty. When it was over, he seemed liberated by the orgy of
bloodletting. He laughed resoundingly, with the laugh of a
madman. "Now I feel better," he shouted.

I felt sickened and miserable, although a few days after
this butchery Saddam gave me a dark blue Mercedes 500,

200,000 dinars in cash, and a house he called Hero's House as a reward for my "heroic deeds." I hated Uday. I hated Saddam Hussein. I despised my life and myself, and wanted out of this madness.

I can't say how many people were murdered and tortured to death by Saddam's bloodhounds after the war. There were thousands, and hardly any family in Iraq remained untouched.

The campaign of slaughter resulted in most of Iraq returning to Saddam's control by June 1991. Uday reverted to his old lifestyle. Although chief of the journalists, he continued to pursue his other business interests as well. He controlled most of the real estate in Baghdad through his companies, as he did the supply of food and other goods that had to be smuggled in from Jordan because of the embargo. Children were dying in hospitals because there wasn't enough medicine. Hundreds of thousands of soldiers and war invalids had no idea how they were going to feed their families. Uday didn't care. He continued to party, openly, shamelessly, in full view of the public.

June 18, 1991: Uday's birthday. The cleanup of the palace grounds was still under way, yet the magnificent swimming pools of the presidential palace looked as if the war had never happened. Uday invited more than three hundred young girls and women to the party, and all of his underworld friends. His car dealers, pimps, and of course Adel Akle, the singer, were there. Champagne, whiskey, French wines, and even German beer were served, along with a fantastic buffet offering all the delicacies one could wish for. Here was the old dreamworld, the lens that distorted reality. People outside the palace were starving, while inside, the war profiteers, the cheaters, the murderers, the unscrupulous exploiters, were having a good time. Alcohol flowed in streams. The party was loud, lewd, vulgar. All were drunk, without restraint.

Uday behaved the worst. He jumped onstage, ripped the

microphone from Adel Akle's hand, and commanded with
an obscene giggle, "Hihihihi, all women get undressed. I
want to see the females naked, completely naked."

Some obeyed. Others were reluctant. The uninhibited
head of the Journalists' Union, observing the bizarre spectacle from the stage, once again seized the microphone. This
time he didn't grin. "I said everybody. Without exception.
Whoever refuses spends the night with my bodyguards."
They followed his orders like sheep. Peeled themselves out of
their dresses. Uday amused himself splendidly when they
were all naked. He lit a cigar, took two puffs, then continued,
"Now the men. Undress, you sons of bitches!" They com-
plied too.

The rest of the evening was one gigantic orgy of jerking
bodies and screeching women. They did it shamelessly and
everywhere, in the pools laid out with mosaics, on the thick
lawn, in the lawn chairs. Adel Akle's music drowned out the
gasps.

Uday summoned me the next day and accused me of
bothering Beda Abd al-Rahman at his party. Beda was the
television announcer and singer, one of Uday's longtime
girlfriends, who had denounced the young student Sana al-
Haidari and instigated her murder by Uday. She was a star, an
important cog in the insane machinery of mass manipulation of the Saddam clan, in which everyone knows about the
lies, and yet everyone remains silent — out of fear or pure
hunger for power. It was true that Beda had spoken to me.
She knew I was Uday's double, and she also knew that it was
strictly forbidden for me even to talk with Uday's girlfriends,
yet she asked me with a giggle whether I wanted to go out
with her and a friend. An absurd question. "No, I don't want
any problems with Uday," I replied.

Uday didn't want to hear my explanation. I couldn't be
sure, but I suspected that he had sent Beda to provoke me.
He knew I hated him. It was obvious that I did my job only
because I had no choice. "Why are you pestering my girl-

friend? Why are you sneaking around after her?" Uday ranted. His hands shook with rage. He was breathing hard and screamed, "I can tell you despise me, that you want to get away. But I have you in the palm of my hand. You're my fidai, my bondman. Don't you ever forget it. I'm going to have to educate you again."

"Education" meant torture, fear, psycho-terror. Uday had realized long before that I, too, was disloyal. It was getting more and more difficult to hide my contempt for him, and the fact that I was his enemy turned into an open secret. I was sure he was already secretly planning my liquidation — because there was no way he could simply let me go. I knew too much about him. Besides, he still needed me. But because he knew I was an enemy, his only choices were to kill me or make me subservient forever. The incident with Beda was thus only an excuse. He wanted to humiliate me and prove to himself that he had me under his thumb.

That same day, I was taken away for "education" at the special facilities in the al-Radvania secret-police barracks. I was one of among more than five hundred political prisoners interned there. It was a nightmare. The whole block of buildings lay exposed to the burning sun, and in this region the temperatures climbed above 120 degrees. The cells were small and had no windows, only small slits with bars. There were almost no sanitary facilities; the toilets were latrines without flush mechanisms. My special attendants were two felons who had been sentenced to death but pardoned by Saddam Hussein to serve in the camp as torturers. They had to obey only one command, and only their obedience saved them from the gallows: "You must torture whoever is brought to you. Even if the delinquent is the son of the president." Now it was me who was delivered to their clutches.

Everything had its precise order in this camp of horror. Rise at four, roll call at five, naked to the waist, then punishment from 6:00 to 10:00 A.M. They beat me with electric cables and whips. Always twenty lashes on the back, then a

pause, more whipstrokes, another pause. Then I was told to
kneel down. They plugged my nostrils so I could breathe only
through my mouth. They forced me to do pushups until I
couldn't do any more. If I collapsed, they shoved needles
under my nails and forced me to do more pushups. Break
from 10:00 to 11:00 A.M. Then more "education" from 11:00
to 2:00 P.M., followed by another break, then more torture
from 3:00 to 6:00 P.M., during which the prisoner had to lie
facedown and be worked over by his torturers.

The skin on my back broke open quickly, but the torturers had strict orders to continue despite pain or infection.
The open wounds were smeared with dirt. If I lost consciousness, I was usually thrown into a tub of dirty water, and my
torturers would urinate into it. During the first two days I
tried to resist them. I wanted to be a man, tried to block out
the pain, so as not to give them the feeling they could break
me. They increased the dose. I was not merely whipped, but
they tied my ankles to a fanlike device attached to the ceiling.
I hung with my head downward, and the fan was switched on
and began turning, slowly at first, then more quickly. They
started beating me with their electric cables. I took a terrible
blow to the nose and lost consciousness. Another time they
locked me into a kind of windowless niche in the wall. The
temperatures were murderous, and it was too tight for me to
sit down. I had to spend two days in that hole.

I shared my customary cell with a man named Sabah
Merze Mahmoud, who had already been here for seven
months and was completely broken in spirit. It took four days
for him to start trusting me. At first he wouldn't speak with me
at all. Then he poured his heart out to me: "I was with Saddam
in Samarra as a sixteen-year-old. I was his friend," he lamented.
Mahmoud later rose to the leadership of the Ba'ath party in
Iraq, and even served as Saddam Hussein's first bodyguard.

He fell out of favor after a dispute in the al-Said Club in
Baghdad. Mahmoud was at a gala for leading party and
government members, the high point of which was an ap-

pearance by the Iraqi singer Mahmoud Anwar. As Anwar was performing a hymn of praise to Saddam Hussein, Ahmad Hussein, then head of the presidential chancellery, jumped up and threw a whole bundle of dinar notes at the singer. Mahmoud was incensed. He yelled at Ahmad Hussein, "All of you can throw your money around like that because you stole it!" The music abruptly stopped, and Ahmad Hussein's oldest son came after Mahmoud, who pulled out his revolver and fired several shots in the air to warn him off.

The next day, Ahmad Hussein complained about the incident to the president. Mahmoud was summoned to report to Saddam, and Saddam ordered him to apologize to his rival. "I refused," Mahmoud told me in our tiny cell. That was enough. Saddam had him brought to the reeducation camp at al-Radvania. "You stay there until you apologize!"

I asked Mahmoud why he didn't apologize long ago.

"Because I'd rather die than serve that animal any longer."

I squatted in that miserable cell for twenty-one days with Mahmoud. He recounted how he used to roam the streets of Baghdad with Saddam as a common thief, how they'd rob pedestrians and then visit a bordello in Baghdad's al-Rahmanija district that was run by Amira al-Maslavia and Manal Junes. That house of pleasure was a favorite meeting place for the leaders of the Ba'ath party. After Saddam Hussein took power, he appointed the madam chairwoman of the General Federation of Iraqi Women.

On the twenty-first day our torturers entered the cell, and one of them grabbed hold of Mahmoud, who was at the end of his strength. The other shoved a hypodermic needle into a vein in his wasted right arm. Then they dragged him out. I could only think of his angry words: "Why do you cooperate with those criminals? Don't you have any honor? They'll do the same to you as they did to me. They'll discard you when they don't need you anymore." Those were the last words I heard him utter.

16

FLIGHT

I'D been in the cell in the al-Radvania camp for more than three weeks. Mahmoud was gone. I was only waiting for my torturers to come and work me over before I finally gave up. I was finished. Emaciated, maltreated, skeletal — a wreck, physically and psychologically. My back burned like fire. The wounds weren't healing and were filled with pus. My shoulder joints ached with every movement. I could hardly endure the heat in my cell, and they gave me water only once a day. I felt dehydrated, listless, without will.

I no longer felt anger or revulsion when they came to get me in the morning for "education." I was apathetic and weak. I could hardly stand, and they had to drag me by the arms to the torture chamber, where I bore the pain they inflicted as if in a trance. At night I could hardly sleep, because the wounds on my back were so inflamed. I lay on my stomach or scrunched up on my side like an fetus.

"Maybe they'll do the same to me as they did to Mahmoud," I sometimes mused. "They'll hold me firmly, stick a needle in my arm, and I'll slowly fall asleep. It's over, done. Simply sleep . . ."

Or maybe they'd shoot me. Step up to me, blindfold me, aim their weapons, pull the trigger. They'd throw my body, along with others, into a mass grave and bury me like a dead dog. They probably wouldn't even tell my parents that I'd been executed only now and not back in November.

How many people had simply disappeared in Iraq since Saddam came to power? Thousands? Tens of thousands? Maybe even hundreds of thousands? Probably nobody knows the exact number.

Merely the list of victims that I was aware of was long enough: Ali Jaafar, poisoned; Mohsen al-Sahab, poisoned; Munem Hadi, starved to death; Ahmad Saleh, beaten to death. Hamed al-Dalimi: they first broke his legs, then cut off his penis. Saleh al-Saadi had his eyes ripped out and was beaten to death. They let Sabri al-Hadisi starve. His brother was forced to dance on his corpse before they let his relatives bury him.

Saddam purged not only little people, but his leading politicians as well. He would liquidate any minister who became too powerful. Three economics ministers were murdered, as were two industry ministers, three foreign ministers, and three defense ministers. They shot Saddam's deputy, Hardan al-Tikriti, along with fifty-nine members of government.

The horror surpassed the Gulf War in mortality. Saddam had killed more people since Operation Desert Storm than the number who lost their lives during the weeks of war.

The president's lackeys once "cleansed" a so-called Village of Leaders north of the Euphrates. Only party and government members lived in the Villages of Leaders, where all their needs were entirely subsidized. The following rivals to Saddam were murdered in the village of Kubeisi: Khaled Abd Osman al-Kabisi, a former minister; Rahim al-Sattar Sulaiman al-Kabisi, a government employee; Abd al-Hanan al-Kabisi, an architect; Nafel Hussein al-Kabisi, an officer.

There was similar butchery in Hadisa. Cleansed and lying in the village cemetery are Kordi Said Abd al-Baki al-Hadisi, Ba'ath party member, hanged; Abd al-Asis al-Hadisi, army general, shot; Shokat Dakom al-Hadisi, government employee, shot; Murtoda Said Abd al-Baki al-Hadisi, former minister, shot; Mohammed Sabri, deputy minister, shot; Nisan al-Hadisi, officer, shot.

"Why did they have those people slaughtered like cattle?" I asked myself, sitting on the wooden bench in my cell. "Is there nobody intelligent in this country who can kill Saddam?"

These thoughts I soon sublimated, because otherwise I would have had to ask myself the same hard question. Few outsiders had gotten as close to the Saddam clan as I. I'd seen how they lived and how they behaved with others, how they raised people to the top like lightning and then destroyed them just as quickly. Uday once told me that when he was in power, he would be crueler than his father ever was. Why didn't I kill Uday to free my country of this tyrant? He used to lie drunk in front of me, would force me to watch while he beat women, dragged me along when he tested his cars. All I ever had to do was pull the trigger, but I didn't do it.

Why? Because I knew what would have happened next? Because I didn't want to be a martyr? Or because I, like everyone else, stood by with the requisite adulation and watched the bloodthirsty terror that had the people by the throat, just so I could snatch up my own share of the booty?

The simple truth was that, while Saddam fears the people, the people also fear Saddam. Anyone who values his own life had better play along — even when this absurd drama of power and might plunges an entire people into misery.

Everyone in Iraq has long since seen through the tawdry Saddam show. The cheers have frozen on everyone's lips, but nobody can extricate himself from the system, or wants to. The stool-pigeon machinery continues to function perfectly. And Qusay, named supreme security service director by Saddam Hussein on March 2, 1991, has even expanded it!

Qusay's first act in office, two days after his appointment, was to have First Lieutenant Sulaiman Harb al-Tikriti shot. The official statement purported that he had been an opposition spy. In reality, Qusay wanted to invest himself immediately with authority — and you're convincing in Iraq only if you can use force unscrupulously.

The security apparatus, consisting of six different branches (secret service (Mukhabarat), national security service (Amn al-Khass), military intelligence (Estikhbarat), intelligence (Amn al-Amn), Ba'ath party security (Amn al-Hizb), and palace security (Amn al-Qasr)), had already been a gigantic octopus, reaching into the country's farthest corners, before Qusay's appointment. Qusay made the octopus stronger. Thousands of new workers were recruited. Wages were increased and social benefits improved. Besides this, as of March 2, all branches were responsible to al-Khass director Qusay.

They had worked independently up to then, with each branch observing, denouncing, and spying on the others. Now all directors had to give their reports and documents to Qusay. An unbelievably bureaucratic procedure! Each director depended on the other. Each mistrusted the other and was panic-stricken that he would be caught up and spit out by the system.

On my twenty-third day in al-Radvania, my torturers woke me at four in the morning. At five they dragged me, naked to the waist, to roll call. Everything began as usual. This time, though, they didn't take me to the regular torture chamber, but rather to a special room. They tied me to a chair that was bolted to the floor. I didn't ask what was coming next, avoided the men's gazes, and stared at the wall in front of me. It was absolutely quiet in the room. All at once, one of the torturers asked, "Do you want to know what we injected Sabah Merze Mahmoud with?"

I nodded. The man laughed, showing his rotten teeth, got up, walked over to me, and squeezed my right forearm with his massive hand. He pulled a pencil out of his breast pocket with the other and poked the tip into the crook of my arm. He drew it back and forth, as if he were looking for a vein. Once again he gave his filthy grin: "Thallium. It was thallium. Do you know what that is?" I knew what thallium was. Thallium is worse than death itself. It eats you from the inside. First your hair falls out, then your hands begin to tremble. It interferes with all of your movements, like Parkinson's disease in its final stage. The poison isn't immediately fatal. It destroys you slowly with attacks of fever, paralysis, and impediments of speech and sight. You can hardly eat, you lose control over your sphincters, and you turn into a zombie — the living dead.

Numerous high-ranking officers who had "proved themselves not sufficiently loyal to the regime" during and after the Gulf War were given the "special treatment" with thallium. They could thus be rendered harmless fairly simply and without creating a stir. The substance was mixed into their food; they suddenly fell ill, had to be discharged from the army. Naturally, they were honored for their magnificent work on behalf of the Iraqi people prior to their "retirement," and showered with bonuses.

The burly creep pushed the pencil into my vein for ten or fifteen seconds. He pressed steadily, as if he wanted to drive the point through my arm, breathing deeply through his nose all the time and hissing, "Thallium," as if he were crazy. I turned my head away, couldn't stand his stinking breath anymore. I felt like spitting in his face, ramming my knee into his groin (my legs were not bound). But what would be the point? There was none.

He left off only at the sound of voices and steps in the hall. "Stop it, they're coming," said the other. The door was flung open, I saw Azzam first, then Uday. He was in uniform, carrying his thick, black electric cable, and was accompanied by about a dozen bodyguards. The men, also wearing black uniforms and Ray-Bans, crowded into the room, surrounding him as if I could still pose a threat to their master.

Uday smiled at me, stepped up, and asked, "How did you like your education? Was it enough, or should we leave you here a few more weeks?"

He stared at me and wound up with the piece of cable.

He followed through all the way — but let it fly just past my face. Then he turned on his heel, took two steps, remained with his back to me, and asked, "Have you had enough?" I didn't know what I should say. He could see what I looked like. I weighed little more than a hundred pounds, my ribs protruded, my lips were broken open and full of pus like my back.

Uday didn't wait for an answer. He wheeled toward me and beat my naked chest. "Say it!" he screeched.

"Lord, I can't take it anymore. Lord, oh, lord, I'm your fidai, and always will be. You can do what you want with me, and I'll always do what you order me to. May Allah protect and keep the powerful son of the president," I pleaded. I didn't have the courage to confront Uday and defy him, although I had nothing left to lose. I was sure he was about to kill me or have his bodyguards do it.

But it didn't happen that way. Uday summoned one of the bodyguards, ordering him to treat me like the "ape faces." "Shave him like the sons of African slaves."

The Shi'ite rebels of southern Iraq were dubbed "ape faces" and "sons of African slaves." Supporters of the radical Islamic Dawa party, they had retreated by the thousands to the swamps between the Euphrates and Tigris rivers after the war, and from there dealt painful pinpricks to Saddam's security forces. The regime had burned down whole forests of reeds and drained whole swamps to be able to deal more easily with the "ape faces."

Captured rebels were hanged or shot. Their supporters were punished in a special way. Their whole pride was singed off: beard, eyebrows, hair.

To me they did something different. One of Uday's bodyguards first cropped my hair closely with a pair of scissors and trimmed my beard. Then they lathered me up. They flung the shaving cream at my face, cursed me, called me — a Sunni — a "Shi'ite ape face." Uday and his bodyguards doubled up with laughter. They howled, made faces, and slapped their thighs with glee.

It was demeaning and humiliating. For the climax, Uday took over. He pulled out a straight razor and laid the blade against my throat. At that, everybody hooted with laughter. Then he waved the blade in the air like a conductor's baton. They hooted again. He put the blade to my skull and started to shave my head. Like an actor imitating a hysterical hairdresser, he shaved off all my hair, only stopping to wipe the lather on a bodyguard's uniform, then my eyebrows, then my beard. After he finished, he slapped my bare head with his cupped hand. This humiliation was worse than death. It was like being emasculated. "Please, lord, kill me," I whispered.

Uday didn't. To this day I still don't know why he didn't. Because he believed this humiliated, disfigured skeleton, this crawling, half-dead creature, could never again do him harm?

He dropped the straight razor on the floor, turned, and left the room.

Two of his bodyguards untied me, grabbed me under the arms, and yanked me out of the chair. I was too weak to stand. They dragged me outside into the fresh air, where I was lifted onto the backseat of their car. We didn't drive to the palace but to the al-Azamiya district in Baghdad. The driver slowed in front of my parents' house, and the bodyguard next to me opened the door and shoved me out of the moving vehicle. The dark limousine peeled off, tires squealing.

My head and shoulder struck the asphalt. I was stunned but didn't lose consciousness. I lay on the street for several seconds, then dragged myself to the entrance, rang, knocked, rang again. It was so unbelievable, so unreal. Uday let me live. He only threw me away like a miserable piece of filth. Like a broken toy.

I wanted not to lose control, pressed my lips together hard, but it all burst out anyway. I sheds tears of anger, shame, total exhaustion. I hadn't noticed that I was bleeding. The blood mixed with the tears.

Through the blur I noticed that the door was opening. It was my mother.

I hadn't seen her since the summer of 1988. She didn't recognize me. Why should she? I looked like a ghost, or worse. My face was smeared with blood, my skull bald. She recoiled, was going to slam the door, taking me for one of the thousands of beggars left in the wake of the Gulf War.

"Mother."

She began to scream and weep when she recognized my voice. Her whole body trembled as I tried to embrace her. Shouting, she ran inside, calling my siblings Jotie, Robie, and Omeed. My brothers helped me inside, brought me to the living room. Jotie turned to my mother, for whom the shock had been too great. She whimpered, gasped for air, and Jotie had to have her lie down on the couch and bring her a glass of water.

"We need a doctor for mother and Latif," he shouted. "We need to get them to a hospital."

The doctor arrived within thirty minutes. He was a friend of mine. He too didn't immediately recognize me. He injected my mother with a substance to stimulate her circulation. After examining me, he said, "What did they do to you, Latif? You have to go to hospital right away."

"That's impossible," I replied.

"Why?"

"Please don't ask. Just help me."

"I can only help you if I have the means."

He first dressed the bleeding wounds caused by the fall from the car. Then he examined my back. Again he said, "It's senseless. You have to go to a hospital."

They took me to a private clinic and registered me under a false name. I stayed there until October. My pelvis had been broken, as well as my left ankle. Vertebrae had been displaced by the powerful blows. I had problems with my spine, and the pain was insufferable. But the pus-filled wounds on my back were the worst. My general condition was dramatic, but slowly I was brought around intravenously. It was weeks before I was halfway there.

My family visited rarely, and only at night. I was certain in any case that Uday had my family watched and already knew which clinic I was staying in. Were it not so, he'd simply have had them detained and tortured until they revealed my hiding place. We tried nonetheless to be as discreet as possible. I wanted to avoid riling him and his lackeys with any stupid actions.

I was silent whenever my parents and brothers asked me about my injuries; I gave no reply when they asked me about the death sentence announced on television; I didn't offer the smallest clue concerning what had happened to me over the past several years.

I also kept my escape plans to myself. I didn't share them with anyone, informed no one how and when I wanted to leave Iraq. I realized that I had one chance: only if I could make contact with sympathizers of the Kurdistan Democratic Party would I be able to pull it off. I knew the party's chairman, Massoud Barzani, from before. And while a university student, I had been in touch with friends and acquaintances of Jalal Talabani, the head of the Patriotic Union of Kurdistan.

I was able to organize an escape car with secret documents I sent from the hospital. The next step was to wait for the best moment.

That came on December 9, 1991. I took very little with me, in order not to attract undue attention at possible checkpoints: a bag with clothing, notes about my time as fidai, one million dinars, and photographs showing me and Uday. I knew the photos could be worth more than cash. *If I can reach the Americans with these photos, they'll help me,* I told myself. *They're my life insurance, my capital.*

I left Baghdad in the dead of night. My first objective was a small community near Mosul, a city two hundred miles north of Baghdad. From there I wanted to go to Dahuk, in the Allied protection zone in northern Iraq. I knew from Kurdish friends that the Americans had a base in Zakhu, a Kurd city on the Turkish-Kurd border.

But the most important and immediate thing was to reach the vicinity of Mosul. "You'll be expected there by Kurd friends," I was promised in Baghdad — by guides who had already brought numerous Kurd refugees over the demarcation line.

I made it to the meeting place without being stopped once, a small wonder. As prearranged, I parked my car in a forested patch and waited. It was two hours before my helpers appeared. We hiked for eight hours straight, with only short breaks, following donkey paths carved through extremely difficult, snow-covered, mountainous terrain. After a rest, we continued, again on foot, until we came to a position held by Massoud Barzani's soldiers. The fighters deposited me in a rickety van and brought me to Dahuk. From there we started out for snowbound Zakhu.

I was safe for the first time.

More than a thousand refugees were waiting in the border town for passage to the West. Hardly any of them would manage to secure a transit visa for Turkey. For me, it was another matter. After telling the guards my story, I immediately jumped the line. An American soldier, Palestine-born Saad Adin Halim, led me to his commander, Colonel John Nab.

John Nab was a tall, slender man with snow-white hair. His face was slightly florid, his handshake firm. He received me cordially and offered me tea and cigarettes. His office, in the main building of the American base, was a mixture of living room and radio room. I watched as he and Saad Adin talked for several minutes, but couldn't understand a word because they were speaking English. Nab appeared calm. He nodded his head occasionally, stroked his chin with his well-groomed hands, reflected.

"Latif," he said and looked me in the eyes, "Saad Adin has just told me who you are. That's okay, that's good, very good in fact. I think we should talk."

Our first conversation lasted two hours. Nab asked me

about everything: my family, my relationship with Uday, my job as fidai, my life in the palace, Saddam Hussein. Saad Adin acted as interpreter. Nab got up several times while we were speaking, went to the phone, talked at length and in a calm manner. I had no idea who he was calling, although occasionally I thought I heard the word "Washington."

When the colonel finished, I asked him whether he really had spoken with Washington. He only smiled, said something, and Saad Adin translated, "Latif, you're going to have to stay with us a few days." He didn't go into details.

Saad Adin led me to a side building. They assigned me a small apartment with two rooms and a kitchen. It was furnished with a beige couch and armchair and a comfortable bed, and they brought me a VCR. I also received new clothes, T-shirts, underwear, and brand-new, rugged boots. I didn't have the feeling of being observed by the Americans in the next few days. The only noticeable thing was that I was always surrounded by soldiers. They brought me videos, drank tea with me, made sure I had plenty to eat. I met women soldiers for the first time: Mary and Susie. Both were officers, helicopter pilots. In our army, pilots are heroes, proud sons of Iraq, haughty and almost untouchable in their grandeur. Mary and Susie were the exact opposite. We understood one another well, although we could hardly speak with each other. They were relaxed, uncomplicated — ordinary people. An unbelievable impression for me.

Two days later I was again escorted to John Nab's office. Saad Adin told me I should take all my documents with me.

Nab wasn't alone. A tall man, no more than thirty-five years old, was sitting next to him. The new man stood up as Saad Adin ushered me into the room and shook my hand with a wide grin. Unlike Nab, he wasn't wearing a uniform. He had on jeans, a black T-shirt, a thick burgundy jacket. A lockable briefcase of shiny aluminum stood next to his chair.

Nab opened the conversation. There was a note of caution in his voice. "My colleague has come directly from the

U.S.A. He was flown in over Turkey. You will tell him every-thing, in detail. The talk will certainly last eight or nine hours. Be prepared for that." Nab didn't mention his col-league's name, and when I asked if he was from the CIA, his response was, "Latif, I think it's better if I ask the questions."

The unidentified man proceeded to squeeze me dry. He asked me about every detail, wanted to know things that up till now seemed completely innocuous: "Which cologne did Uday use?" was one such question, as was "Do you know his favorite color?" The questioning went on without interrup-tion until the evening. Several times Iraqi citizens, intro-duced as being from Baghdad, entered the room. They would ask a few questions and then disappear. The whole conversation was tape-recorded, though the man in civilian clothing jotted down occasional notes.

I gave him all my notes and documents. I wanted only to keep the photographs of me and Uday, and suggested that copies be made, but John Nab persuaded me otherwise, claiming, "We don't have the technical facilities for that here. It'd be best if you gave my colleague everything. You'll get it all back after my colleagues have evaluated it."

When the interrogation was over, after nine hours, I felt drained but not bad. The whole conversation had taken place in a friendly atmosphere. My interlocutor got up first, shook my hand, and said, "Good, Latif. It was very good that you came to us." He slipped my documents and the photos in his aluminum attaché case, asked Nab if the helicopter was ready for takeoff, and wished me good-bye. He said to me, "You couldn't know this, but we already knew about you."

"How?" I asked.

I received no reply. To this day, I don't know who that young man was, whether he was truly from the CIA, or what he did with my documents and photos.

When Saad Adin was taking me back to my apartment, I heard the sound of the rotor blades chopping the air as the helicopter lifted off. "What's going to happen now?" I wondered.

Nothing happened at all for the next few days. I waited, waited, waited. John Nab summoned me several times, tried to persuade me to emigrate to America. I declined, however, and named Austria as my preferred destination, although I wasn't quite sure exactly where in Europe Austria was.

The main reason I chose Austria was that I had family there. A cousin lived in Vienna, where he worked as a respected doctor in one of the leading clinics. Besides, my father had recommended it. "It's a neutral country where many of our friends live. They'll take care of you." Maybe I would have done better to give in to Colonel Nab's urging, but a gut feeling that's difficult to rationalize said to me, *Decide for Europe. It's better that way.*

Meanwhile, Nab had forwarded my paperwork to the United Nations, which, in turn, had applied for an entry visa to Austria. "I can't say how long this will take," Nab warned me, "but probably several weeks."

At the end of February 1992 Colonel Nab informed me that Austria had agreed to grant me political asylum. A diplomatic bargain had been struck between the Austrian Interior Ministry and the United States, at the urging of the Americans. Austria pledged to take me, and in exchange a family of Iraqi Christians who had been waiting in Vienna for months was allowed to emigrate to the United States. "We're only waiting for the papers from Vienna," Nab said. "Then we'll take you to Turkey."

So everything was arranged. Nothing could go wrong now. I can hardly describe the mix of feelings that I experienced. Elation, relief . . . I was in seventh heaven, wanted to shout my happiness out loud and tell everyone. I wanted to express my gratitude. To Nab, to the other Americans — and to my Kurd friends, especially to Nishevan Barzani. Nishevan was twenty-two and the son of Idris Barzani, who was the brother of the leader of the Kurdistan Democratic Party, Massoud Barzani. I couldn't have escaped without his help.

On March 1, 1992, the Americans in Zakhu received a positive reply from Vienna. The very next day I was taken to a temporary airport, and a U.S. helicopter ferried me to the Turkish city of Diyarbakir. A second helicopter escorted us. Thousands of other refugees remained behind.

In Diyarbakir, I was taken to UN headquarters under heavy guard by UN soldiers and Turkish troops, then installed in a five-star hotel. Twenty-four hours later, on March 3, 1992, a senior UN officer drove me back to the airport. I flew on to Ankara, where I received a UN passport issued by UN High Commissioner Brain, with a visa for Austria, and was put up in the Conac Hotel pending my flight out.

I landed on March 9, 1992, at Vienna's Schwechat Airport. It was 1:30 P.M. My reckoning with the regime in Baghdad had begun.

As Latif Yahia landed in Vienna, radio stations in Turkey reported his defection. The largest Turkish daily, Milliyet, ran the headline THE DOUBLE OF THE IRAQI DICTATOR'S ELDEST SON HAS FLED TO THE WEST. International news agencies, like Reuters, followed suit: THE DOUBLE OF UDAY SADDAM HUSSEIN, HATED SON OF THE IRAQI DICTATOR, COULD FLEE TO EUROPE. On March 11, 1992, the Austrian Press Agency published the story.

EPILOGUE

So Did Saddam Hussein Win?

THE war had ended. In Washington, President George Bush announced to the world press, "It's over. We destroyed Saddam Hussein."

The same day in Baghdad, millions of Iraqis heard their leader, Saddam Hussein, proclaim, "It's over. I am the winner."

Who was right, Bush or Saddam? It is still too early to say. The Gulf War has all but disappeared from the news, except for an occasional story on Gulf War syndrome, and the "new world order" that Bush spoke of has long been forgotten. But Saddam Hussein remains. With his amazing will to prevail, and a regime built on brutal repression, the dictator has survived Desert Storm and all subsequent attempts to depose him. This epilogue demonstrates how a tyrant can continue to rule with an iron fist despite international pressure against him, and despite his failure to keep even his family in line: After his sons-in-law Hussein Kamel and Saddam Kamel defected, they were lured back to Iraq and put to death. Uday and his brother, Qusay, oversaw the executions, which were carried out on orders from Saddam Hussein, who said in justification, "The treacherous branch must be severed from the family tree." Saddam and his sons have neutralized with equal effectiveness threats from all fronts of the Iraqi resistance, including a campaign of bombings and assassination organized by the CIA.

A few months after the murders of Hussein and Saddam Kamel,

Uday himself was the target of an assassination attempt. In an ambush in al-Mansur, one of Baghdad's most exclusive neighborhoods, he was caught in a hail of Kalashnikov fire, and was hit fourteen times. Despite several operations by an international team of surgeons, he apparently remains, at the very least, paralyzed in one leg.

Latif Yahia, who has survived two assassination attempts since his escape, now lives in Germany, where he runs an import-export business. He said, when he heard about the severe injuries Uday sustained in the attack, "It gives me great satisfaction to know that Uday is no longer a whole man."

August 8, 1995, almost exactly five years since the invasion of Kuwait, just after midnight. Under the cover of darkness, twenty-five armored Mercedes-Benz limousines and two Toyota Land Cruisers sped down the four-lane highway that leads out of Baghdad toward Jordan. The highway was virtually deserted, and the border guards on the Iraq side of the Trebeil crossing had retreated into their guard boxes. Before the war, the Trebeil crossing had been a desolate checkpoint with a few dilapidated buildings and a tearoom where truckdrivers sat out the time it took for their wares to clear customs.

Now everything was different. After the war, Saddam Hussein had Trebeil built into a showpiece of victorious Iraq's newfound self-confidence. A duty-free shop was stamped into the desert sand, a dozen customhouses were erected, and the roadway was given a new asphalt top and new granite curbs. There was even an ostentatious VIP center, where liveried hosts stood ready to welcome occasional foreign visitors. Inside, the walls were covered with kitschy portraits of Saddam Hussein by his artist laureate, Yahia al-Darraji.

The mysterious convoy stopped, horns blaring, in front of the VIP center. Astonished, the officers on duty poured out onto the blacktop, but no one emerged from the cars.

Only the driver of the lead car nonchalantly let down the tinted glass of his window. "Hussein Kamel and Saddam Kamel," he announced curtly—Saddam Hussein's sons-in-law.

None of the officers dared inspect even one of the cars, whose passengers included the two men's wives. Hussein Kamel was married to Saddam's eldest daughter, Raghd, Saddam Kamel to her younger sister, Rina. "We're on a secret mission," was all Hussein Kamel would tell the ranking officer at the crossing.

Just five minutes later the barriers opened and the convoy filed past, then raced across the three-mile-wide no-man's-land to the Jordanian crossing at Ruweished. The unthinkable had occurred. For the first time, members of Saddam Hussein's inner circle, two of his closest relatives, had defected. Both men had detailed knowledge of the workings of Saddam's regime. Hussein Kamel, whose most recent posts included that of armaments and industry minister, was responsible for Iraq's entire arsenal, including its atomic and chemical weapons programs. His brother Saddam, head of Saddam Hussein's personal bodyguard, knew the dictator's hideouts like no one else alive.

Jordan's King Hussein had chosen not to oppose Baghdad during the Kuwait crisis and the Gulf War. Within five minutes after the convoy had arrived in Jordanian territory, he learned what high-ranking guests he was about to receive, when Hussein Kamel called him on the hotline at the border crossing.

King Hussein's first move was to grant the two men and their wives political asylum. He then ordered a special unit of his border guard to escort them to his royal palace. He also informed Washington. At this point, King Hussein was absolutely convinced that "the time is ripe for a coup in Baghdad." Even Yasir Arafat, president of the Palestinian Authority, came to the same conclusion when he heard that the "two thugs in Armani suits" had defected. "This is the end of Saddam Hussein," he said.

By now Baghdad was on maximum alert, and Saddam Hussein had summoned his sons, Uday and Qusay, to a crisis meeting in the presidential palace. While this triumvirate was deciding what to do next, Washington was also taking precautions. Alarmed by satellite photographs showing "troop movements" in Iraq, President Clinton ordered the aircraft carrier *Theodore Roosevelt* to the waters off the Israeli shore. Its announced mission was to protect Jordan from possible reprisals by Iraq.

In a televised address, U.S. Secretary of Defense William Perry assured the public that the United States had enough Tomahawk cruise missiles in the region to respond to any move by Saddam Hussein. The feverish political and military activity soon swept up Iraq's neighbors as well. The atmosphere on the Jordanian border was reminiscent of the days immediately before the outbreak of the Gulf War. American GIs took up position in Wadi Ram, a desert valley near the Red Sea, and American helicopters patrolled the airspace above Kuwait and Saudi Arabia.

"A storm is brewing," American special envoy Robert Pelletreau declared when he rushed to Amman. "Saddam Hussein has gone off the deep end again."

This was a fundamental misapprehension. Saddam Hussein is a gambler, and he has often lost bets in the past, but he isn't a madman. The troop movements inside Iraq—first along the border with Jordan, then near the newly defined border with Kuwait—were nothing but a diversionary tactic.

Saddam Hussein and his two sons were preparing a brilliant operation: the methodical destruction of Hussein Kamel and his brother Saddam Kamel. While the Kamel brothers were calling for Saddam's removal from power at press conferences in Amman, exactly as Saddam expected, Uday, working on his father's orders, was mobilizing the entire Iraqi press against Hussein Kamel. HISTORY WILL STONE HIM, screamed the headlines on the front pages of Iraqi newspapers the next day. "Our enemies will squeeze him dry, then put him on the street," Saddam Hussein predicted. For page after page, the papers described the hoard that the two brothers had purportedly taken with them to Jordan: from ten to eighty million dollars in cash and gold, depending on the source. "These traitors used foreign fronts to rob the Iraqi people of millions of dollars," Saddam Hussein charged during an appearance on Iraqi television. "It would have been better if they had died, rather than to live in disgrace."

In the Arab world, honor and shame are more than mere words, and whoever disgraces his family is punished in accordance with an unwritten code of honor. The traditional punishment was to be banished to the desert and left to perish in the heat of the sun. In Iraq, where the honor of a clan is perceived as synonymous with its hold on power, jeopardizing that power is the worst of all possible crimes. When his sons-in-law called for his ouster, Saddam saw this not just as high treason, but as an offense against blood kin—a crime that could be paid for only with the culprits' blood.

The people of Iraq have no trouble understanding this way of thinking; it reflects a belief system shared by everyone. For days, Uday saturated the Iraqi press with the most outlandish stories about his two brothers-in-law and their high-flying lifestyles. Almost overnight the anger of the masses, who could scarcely get enough to eat, became focused on Hussein Kamel and Saddam Kamel. Gone was their irritation with Saddam's clique; now it was the two defectors who had betrayed the Iraqi people.

The smear campaign against the brothers had an arresting effect on public consciousness, eclipsing for a while the conspicuous contrast between the wealth of the ruling class and the suffering of the people. No one remembered the forty new palaces Saddam Hussein had built after the war, when the average family couldn't even afford to renovate an apartment. No one complained about the delicacies from

Harrod's, the exclusive London department store, that Uday's European operations had flown in via Jordan.

While Uday went about his propaganda work, Qusay was active on two other fronts. He ordered the Estikhbarat, the military intelligence service, to organize troop movements throughout the country over the next several weeks—not for military reasons, but to foil any attempt at a coup. The Saddam clan had dealt with the threat of revolts before, and knew how to keep its opponents off balance.

Simultaneously, Qusay directed members of the Mukhabarat to remove all documents and records from Hussein Kamel's offices. As minister of armaments and industry, Hussein Kamel was responsible for the nuclear sector, and for the production of chemical and biological weapons. Within twenty-four hours, Mukhabarat agents had gathered enough material to fill 148 six-by-three-foot metal cabinets—over 650,000 files, videotapes, and computer diskettes, which documented Iraq's entire biological and nuclear armament programs.

Qusay was also in daily contact with his Mukhabarat agents in Amman, who reported on Hussein Kamel's every move. When Hussein Kamel met with American, Israeli, British, and French intelligence agents, Qusay knew when and where the meeting took place, and who attended. He also had a complete list of the American agents and officials who arrived with special emissary Pelletreau in Amman the day after the escape from Baghdad.

Qusay had enough information to predict almost without fail what Hussein Kamel would do next. When he learned that in his first meetings with western intelligence agents Hussein Kamel had revealed details of Iraq's biological and atomic weapons programs, he decided it was time to go on the offensive.

On the night of August 10, 1995, he had the 148 metal cabinets smuggled onto Hussein Kamel's chicken farm on the outskirts of Baghdad, where his men unloaded them into a barn and covered them up with straw. It was meant to look as though Hussein Kamel had hidden them there himself.

The next day, Qusay placed a phone call to the Hotel al-Canal in Baghdad. The al-Canal was originally a first-class tourist resort with 130 rooms, ten suites, a swimming pool, a nightclub, and a fitness center. Since the war the hotel had served as UN headquarters in Iraq. UNSCOM, the UN unit responsible for finding and destroying Iraq's chemical arms, set up its offices on the second floor, in the rooms that had previously housed the hotel management.

The entry to the UNSCOM suites looked like a high-security wing in a military complex: armored doors with combination locks, bugproof telephones, bulletproof windows. Seventy experts worked here under the direction of Göran Wallen, a wiry former admiral in the Swedish navy. Wallen's political superior was Rolf Ekeus, also a Swede, who happened to be out of town when Qusay called.

Qusay had amazing news for Wallen. "We've accidentally discovered 148 metal cabinets on Hussein Kamel's chicken farm and are unable to determine exactly what's in them. But we suspect they contain secret documents relating to atomic and biological armaments. None of us, not even the president, knows what these documents mean. Obviously, Hussein Kamel was operating without our knowledge. Please investigate. We'd like to know more." Göran Wallen was so astonished he had to take several deep breaths before he could find his voice.

Under the UN Security Council's Resolution 687, after the war Iraq was required to allow access to all its nuclear, chemical, and biological arms installations. The UN specialists began work in May 1991, and to date had disposed of almost 100,000 gallons of mustard gas, 20,000 gallons of nerve gas, and more than 300,000 gallons of the substances used to manufacture these tools of destruction. They had also destroyed 40,000 poison-filled bombs, rockets, and grenades. Together, these arms would have sufficed to extinguish human life from half of the Middle East. Hussein Kamel had built the largest of his chemical weapons factories in al-Muthanna, seventy miles north of Baghdad. Hundreds of subterranean arms shelters were discovered in a six-by-eight-mile section of the desert.

The shelters, which were joined by a network of tunnels, were where Saddam concocted his poisons. For years, European, Russian, and even American specialists had overseen production of chemical weapons of all sorts, such as the infamous "S-Lost" grenades. "S-Lost" is a skin irritant that, when inhaled, dissolves lung tissue the way hydrochloric acid consumes a sponge. A few drops are enough to cause the skin to break out in boils for which there is no known treatment.

In other underground shelters Tabun and Sarin were made. A minuscule dose of either gas paralyzes the central nervous system, causing immediate death. Wallen's experts destroyed these weapons of terror with so-called mobile incinerators. Gas stored in conventional drums was burned at 1,200 degrees centigrade, but gas-filled grenades, rockets, and bombs posed greater difficulties. First, a hole had to be blasted open in the shell by means of a special explosive, then the gas could be vacuumed off. When the shells were empty, the gas was incinerated and the shells, with whatever trace chemicals remained in them, were blown up.

Wallen's men used the same methods in dealing with Iraq's nuclear weapons programs. The installations at al-Thuwaitha, al-Athir, al-Furat, and al-Hateen were demolished with explosives. High-tech instruments for the enrichment of uranium were rendered useless by filling them with concrete or mangling them with welding machines. Nuclear power stations were fitted with video monitoring systems, so that any attempt to alter the function of such plants for military purposes would be immediately obvious to UN officials. By August 1995, Wallen and his team believed that all atomic and chemical weapons installations in Iraq had been discovered and destroyed.

And then came the call from Qusay. The Swede could scarcely believe his ears. Had they still not found everything, after four years of searching? Had the Iraqi high command been deceiving UNSCOM the whole time?

Wallen notified his superior, Rolf Ekeus, and quickly assembled a team of specialists to investigate Hussein Kamel's chicken farm. They found the metal cabinets. Some were locked, some had been broken into. There were signs everywhere that the cabinets had not been sitting there for months, but had just been moved a few days before. Only a few of the cabinets were covered with a layer of dust. How could metal cabinets sit for weeks on a chicken farm in the desert without gathering dust? Göran Wallen soon realized that Saddam Hussein had had the cabinets brought to the farm in order to discredit Hussein Kamel. But although he had plenty of clues, he had no real proof.

Despite Wallen's suspicions, the plan that Qusay and his father put in action had begun to achieve its intended goal. All of the secrets Hussein Kamel could possibly reveal to agents in Amman were now available to the UN authorities on paper and diskette. This meant that Hussein Kamel was of much less interest as an informant than had originally been supposed. Also, by cooperating with his enemies, Saddam Hussein could blame everything on Hussein Kamel. It now looked, at least superficially, as though Hussein Kamel, not Saddam Hussein, were responsible for deceiving the UN specialists for so many years.

The documents were shipped off to the UN's International Atomic Authority in Vienna, where Wallen's men made a horrifying discovery. "The documents and diskettes show beyond any doubt that Iraq had access to everything it needed to make an atomic bomb," David Kyd, spokesman for the Atomic Authority, declared afterward. Putting an end to any talk about the uselessness of the Gulf War, he told reporters, "If it were not for the war, Saddam would now be in possession of at least one atomic bomb. And he would be capable of dropping that bomb on Israel or on Saudi Arabia at any time he chose. We have always suspected this was the case. These records are the irrefutable proof." But the documents also revealed something else. They were embarrassingly explicit about the names and addresses of the companies and technicians who had supplied Saddam Hussein with billions of dollars' worth of arms. Even after the invasion of Kuwait in 1990, western firms had sold advanced nuclear technology to Iraq. "After the invasion," David Kyd explained, "Saddam Hussein was willing to do anything to get the bomb."

Saddam Hussein had set more than 10,000 technicians to work on his atomic bomb program. A hundred-centrifuge uranium enrichment plant was to be built in al-Furat, one of the five nuclear installations in Iraq. The plant had almost been completed. By the end of 1991, perhaps even earlier, high-tech centrifuges could have begun to enrich uranium for use in atomic bombs.

Iraq's secret nuclear armament program originated in the 1980s—in Austria—when German nuclear technician Karl Heinz Schaab contacted the Iraqi embassy in Vienna. At the time, Schaab had a high-level position at URENCO, a German-Dutch company and the leading manufacturer in Europe of uranium enrichment technology. Schaab was responsible for a line of centrifuges called the TC-11. The product of a top-secret development program, the TC-11 was reputedly the most efficient system of uranium enrichment in the world—exactly what Saddam Hussein and his minister of armaments and industry Hussein Kamel were desperate to have.

Iraq was never a Third World country as far as nuclear energy was concerned. It is rich in uranium deposits and has been mining them since the late 1940s, when Iraq first began to develop nuclear technology. There are reactors in Mosul, Sharqat, Tramiya, Thuwaitha, and Athir. Al-Thuwaitha is one of the largest nuclear plants in the world. Officially, all of

Iraq's reactors were being monitored by the International Atomic Authority in Vienna, but as Göran Wallen said, "Baghdad has been involved in secret programs from the start, the true extent of which is only now coming to light."

Saddam Hussein kept the pressure on his son-in-law to produce results. "Iraq tried for decades to enrich its own uranium ore," David Kyd explained. "But it never succeeded."

Hussein Kamel needed experts from abroad. He found what he needed in Karl Heinz Schaab, whom he soon put in charge of the entire operation. Schaab left URENCO at the end of 1989. Either he took a complete set of data about the centrifuge program with him, or he managed to smuggle the data out before he left. Judging from what was found in the metal cabinets in Iraq, he must have carted away crates full of plans and designs.

He handed them over to Iraqi agents in Geneva and in Vienna. In return he received a first installment of $350,000 sometime in the early 1990s. Under an assumed identity, Schaab himself went to Iraq just as the first bombs were falling on Baghdad. Working feverishly alongside Iraqi scientists, he tried to complete work on the centrifuge system in al-Furat before it was too late. At one point he tried to speed things along by using fuel removed from working reactors.

But Saddam Hussein lost the war before his nuclear scientists could complete their work. By late February 1991, all activity in al-Furat was stopped. Karl Heinz Schaab left Iraq for Austria and moved into a little house in a town called Reichraming, in Upper Austria. No one there knew anything about the kind old gentleman's previous life, or suspected that this modest man had been Saddam's nuclear mastermind.

On the same day that Hussein Kamel defected to Jordan, Karl Heinz Schaab disappeared from his house in Austria. "He told everybody he was going to his vacation home in the south." Karl Heinz Schaab has never been seen since.

Police in all parts of the world have put out a warrant for his arrest.

It took the UN experts two weeks to sort through and analyze the documents Qusay had handed over to them. When they were done, Göran Wallen and his superior, Rolf Ekeus, left Baghdad for Amman to discuss the findings with Hussein Kamel. But Hussein Kamel had nothing to tell them that they didn't already know. The former armaments and industry minister lost no time protesting that it was Saddam Hussein and his sons who had carted the documents onto his chicken farm, but this didn't render his testimony any less obsolete.

Qusay's shrewd move had paid off. Now Hussein Kamel's value for western intelligence services and for the UN was reduced to zero. He could no longer blackmail former associates by threatening to reveal their identities. Consequently, the West had no further use for the high-ranking refugee.

There was no one left to whom Hussein Kamel and his brother could turn, except perhaps the opponents of Saddam Hussein's regime living in exile. But for the most part, they too gave Hussein Kamel the cold shoulder. "The brothers have too much blood on their hands," said some of them. Hussein Kamel had been involved in mass executions in northern and southern Iraq. Other dissidents suspected that Hussein Kamel and his brother had staged the entire escape in order to spy on resistance groups in Amman and elsewhere.

Among those who doubted the two brothers' sincerity was Shadi Ahmed Pire, the minister of agriculture in the Kurdish rebel organization Patriotic Union of Kurdistan. Led by Jalal Talabani, the Patriotic Union of Kurdistan (PUK) is one of two Kurdish groups in northern Iraq. About sixty percent of the four million Kurds living in Iraq belong to or support the PUK. The other Kurdish group is the

Kurdistan Democratic Party, under the charismatic leadership of Massoud Barzani.

Pire has no trouble explaining why he didn't trust Hussein Kamel and his brother: "Hussein Kamel was working
secretly with the Iraqi opposition even before he defected,"
Pire claims. Hussein Kamel made himself available to covert
agents who had been sent to Baghdad by the Iraqi National
Congress (INC).

The INC was created in 1992 under the aegis of the CIA.
The first organizational meetings took place in Vienna, in
the SAS, a five-star hotel on the Danube. The men from CIA
headquarters in Langley envisaged an umbrella organization
large enough to include all of the opposition groups in Iraq:
the Kurdish groups in the north, the Shi'ites in the south, the
Sunni underground in Baghdad, as well as former Ba'ath
party members who had defected and were now living in
exile throughout the world.

The INC was to be a full-fledged alternative to Saddam's
regime in Baghdad—a kind of Iraqi government-in-exile. As
head of state, the CIA chose an Iraqi banker who had grown
up in the United States and was now a Jordanian national,
Ahmed Chalabi. Chalabi's father had been a powerful man
in Baghdad and president of the Iraqi parliament.

The CIA gave Chalabi $15 million in immediate direct
aid. The money was handed to him in a black suitcase on the
day the INC was founded in Vienna.

Chalabi's official mandate was purely political: He was
asked to establish a twenty-five-member "executive committee" that would function at the head of a 250-member parliament. But entrusting Chalabi with this task was a mistake that
put the whole operation in a bad light from the very beginning. Ahmed Chalabi had a flawed reputation. He had been
mixed up in a corruption scandal and was said to have
defrauded Jordanian banks of millions of dollars. Although
his guilt was never proven, his reputation had suffered con-
siderably. Also, Chalabi was a Shi'ite Muslim, a fact that could

only rub Barzani and Talabani the wrong way. "The Americans were never really interested in achieving a political solution to the Iraqi problem, let alone helping us to found a Kurdish state," Jalal Talabani says in explaining why he had reservations about the INC from the start. "They were following an agenda set by the CIA and used us merely as a spearhead against Saddam Hussein. The CIA wanted Saddam's head, and the INC was their means of getting it."

Despite the Kurds' misgivings, the CIA proceeded with its plans and continued to pour money into the INC, whose leaders met regularly with high-level American officials. In 1992, Chalabi had several private meetings with Secretary of State James Baker. After Clinton's victory in 1992, Vice President Al Gore, Secretary of State Warren Christopher, and National Security Adviser Anthony Lake continued the talks in Baker's place.

Officially, these meetings concerned aid for reconstruction north of the thirty-sixth parallel, as well as political support for the government-in-exile. Warren Christopher called openly on Saudi Arabia and other neighboring states to recognize the INC as the legitimate governing body of the Iraqi resistance.

But Christopher's plea fell on deaf ears. The Saudi royal family, mistrustful of the Kurdish elements in the INC, founded its own opposition group, the Iraqi National Accord, based in Amman. Ayad Alawi, a physician from Baghdad and a former high-ranking member of the Ba'ath party, was tapped to lead it. The CIA also backed this group, but limited its initial support to $10 million.

Direct intervention by the CIA was organized from within the INC. On a hillside near the northern Iraqi city of Salahaddin, twenty-two agents set up operations in four different buildings. CIA headquarters was in Arbil, in a building on Ain-Kawa Street. Officially these agents were part of "Operation Provide Comfort," the international aid program established in northern Iraq after the war. But their objectives, listed below, were anything but humanitarian:

- *Recruiting.* More than six hundred former Iraqi military officers who had deserted were hired, as well as journalists, writers, doctors, and former Iraqi government officials. Ultimately, there were eight hundred people on the CIA's payroll.
- *Propaganda.* The agents set up radio stations powerful enough to be picked up anywhere in Iraq. There was also a TV station that broadcast eleven hours of programming a day critical of Saddam Hussein.
- *Disinformation.* A printing press turned out flyers that could be dropped over Iraq. Forged issues of *Babel,* Uday's newspaper, were produced by the hundreds of thousands and smuggled into Baghdad.
- *Surveillance.* In Salahaddin, tens of millions of dollars were invested in a computerized command center equipped with highly advanced satellite communications and surveillance technology. The installation was capable of monitoring all radio and television communications in Iraq.

But the greatest emphasis was put on the deployment of covert agents inside Iraq. "They were planning an attack on the army and on Saddam Hussein and his sons," Ahmed Pire says. There was to be a constant string of bomb explosions in all parts of the country, first in Baghdad, then in Basra, then on the Syrian border. "They wanted to keep Saddam's army busy all the time," Pire remembers. "The idea was to keep Saddam's counterintelligence services so busy they wouldn't be able to trace the source of the terror."

The decisive blow against the regime in Baghdad was planned for the end of August 1995. To the American strategists, the time was right to act. The regime was drained and weak, and the populace had lost all patience with the ever-worsening standard of living. Even Iraqis who had been wealthy before could now scarcely afford the basic necessities. The gap between the elite groups that profited from the defeat and the great majority, who suffered terribly from the UN sanctions, grew unconscionably wide. A problem was that Saddam's propaganda machine had redirected the aimless rage of the masses against the UN and the United States, holding them responsible for refusing to lift the sanctions. But popular discontent was a constant source of trouble for the regime, and it seemed to be on the rise. The people could turn against their rulers at any time.

"It was at around this time that a bomb attack on Saddam Hussein was supposed to be carried out, right in his palace in Baghdad," Pire explains. A "member of Saddam Hussein's inner circle" was to have let the assassins into the palace. Who this person was, Pire does not say. The plans for the attack had been worked out to the last detail at CIA headquarters in Langley. The idea was that once Saddam was gone, the people's fear of the system would dissolve, setting off a popular uprising in the army and in the public at large. The plan seemed foolproof. "Within six months, I'll have Saddam's head on a silver platter," CIA chief John Deutch is reported to have said.

Nothing came of it. News of the plan leaked to Saddam Hussein. The assassins, who had already infiltrated Iraq and were in Baghdad waiting for the signal to go ahead, had to abandon their mission. The regime knew that they were in the city. What it didn't know, or at least didn't know for sure, was the identity of the traitor inside the palace: "Who is the spy in our midst who is working for the Americans and the Kurds?"

It could only have been one of Saddam's closest relatives, for only they were allowed anywhere near the president. Was it Hussein Kamel? Saddam Kamel? Or even Wathban Ibrahim? Wathban was Saddam's stepbrother and Iraq's min-

ister of the interior. He had two brothers, Sabaawi and Barzan. Barzan, Iraq's UN ambassador in Geneva, is still in
charge of the Hussein family's foreign holdings. It was a
poorly kept secret that these three stepbrothers, members of
the al-Tikriti clan and born into Baghdad's high society, were
all power-hungry. They felt they had been slighted in favor of
Hussein Kamel and Saddam Kamel, whom they considered
"crude arrivistes and toadies." Hussein Kamel and Saddam
Kamel, members of the al-Majid clan, had been officers in
the police. By marrying Saddam's daughters, they and their
brother Hakim had gained entry into Baghdad's most exclusive circles. The two clans had been at each other's throats
ever since.

To calm the waters, Saddam married his son Uday to
Barzan al-Tikriti's eldest daughter. The match was nothing
but a marriage of convenience. Uday and his wife never set
up residence together, and Uday led the same debauched
existence as he had before—which didn't exactly endear
him to his father's three stepbrothers.

News of the foiled plot to assassinate the president put
an end to the delicate balance between the clans, and caused
widespread panic in the palace. Uday's reaction was the most
volatile and emotional. In early August 1995, at the festivities
celebrating Mohammed's birth, he got in an argument with
Wathban Ibrahim and shot him in the leg.

The official explanation was that Uday was shooting
celebratory rounds into the air and hit Wathban by accident.
But Hussein Kamel later confirmed from his exile in Amman
that Uday had aimed not only at Wathban but at Hussein
Kamel himself as well. "Uday wanted to kill me because he
thought I was a double agent," Kamel confided to a Jordanian business associate in Amman.

A few days after Uday's attack on Wathban Ibrahim,
Hussein Kamel and Saddam Kamel fled to Jordan with their
wives. The defection was likened to a split in the holy family,
and it further aggravated the conflict between the clans.

There was speculation that it was Hussein Kamel who had collaborated with the assassins.

For a brief time, Saddam Hussein seemed to observers like a stunned boxer who wavers but doesn't fall. With Hussein Kamel and Saddam Kamel gone, the only member of the al-Majid clan who remained in a key government position was Defense Minister Ali Hassan Al-Majid, the so-called Chemist, notorious for having overseen the gassing of the Kurds. Saddam Hussein threw him out of office. At the same time, he threatened to wipe out the entire al-Majid clan at the slightest sign that any one of them intended to betray him.

As countless occasions in the past had made clear, Saddam's brutality toward potential opponents knew no bounds. An example was his persecution of the al-Dulaimi clan. The al-Dulaimis were based in Ramadi, a city on the Syrian border. They had always been one of the main pillars of Saddam's power. The patriarch of the family was the highly decorated air force pilot Muhammad Maslum al-Dulaimi, an Iraqi war hero.

After the Gulf War, however, General al-Dulaimi made no secret of his opposition to Saddam Hussein. The regime in Baghdad even suspected him of plotting to overthrow the president and assume power himself. Other sources claim that he was working with the National Accord in Amman. Baghdad's reaction was not long in coming. Troops from the elite Republican Guard stormed the al-Radami district on May 18, 1995, and arrested General al-Dulaimi. He was tortured over a period of several days and forced to reveal names of other possible conspirators. Then he was murdered. Uday and Qusay were both present as al-Dulaimi was being tortured. Afterwards, Uday had the gruesome idea of sending the dismembered body and the severed head of the general to the family as a present. One hundred fifty other members of the clan were also executed.

Saddam's merciless pursuit of rival clans was an effective way of destroying his rivals, but it was of no real help to him politically. The UN Security Council, which had been considering lifting or at least easing the sanctions that were devastating his country, decided under the circumstances that it was better not to budge. Yet Iraq was economically dead. Agriculture was a shambles, oil production was at a standstill. Unemployment was at seventy percent, and even high-ranking officials earned only six thousand dinars a month— the equivalent of about two dollars. Just before the war, the exchange rate was two dinars to a dollar; now, on the black market, a dollar cost 2,500 dinars.

The situation called for something spectacular, something Saddam could exploit to show Iraq and the world that the country was willing to change. What he came up with was in keeping with his character. In October 1995 he staged a bizarre plebiscite to shore up his own position. The people were called to the polls to vote on whether he should remain in power. There was no alternative candidate; ballots could be marked only yes or no. Saddam invited journalists from all over the world to Baghdad for the occasion. They arrived, and were treated to a farce. Paid extras streamed through the streets roaring, "Naam, naam, Saddam" ("Yes, yes, Saddam"). Not a single critic of the regime could be found anywhere in the country. The result of the plebiscite was as expected: 99.99 percent of the vote was for Saddam. In Baghdad, a city of millions, just forty-five voters had enough trust in this "election by secret ballot" to vote no.

Not once during the campaign did Saddam Hussein himself appear in public. The only event worthy of notice occurred four days before the vote, at a match between the Iraqi national soccer team and the team from Qatar. In the presidential box sat a noticeably diminished Uday Saddam Hussein. Normally, Iraqi television made a point of glamorizing Saddam's son and heir, showing him as a cigar-smoking demigod dressed in fashionable silk suits. But this time Iraq's television spectators looked on in astonishment as the camera came to rest on a dejected, pensive-looking Uday. The announcer explained why he looked so depressed: Saddam Hussein himself had set fire to his son's garages. A hundred brand-new Mercedes, BMWs, Porsches, and Ferraris had gone up in flames. The reason for Saddam's fit of anger? He wanted to punish his son for attacking Wathban Ibrahim. He also held Uday responsible for the defection of Hussein Kamel and Saddam Kamel.

Actual pictures of the burnt-out luxury cars were never shown. In all likelihood, there never was a fire at all. The whole affair was nothing but a propaganda exercise and a thinly veiled lie designed to make it look as though Uday were being pushed out of the inner circle. The truth is that he was not relieved of a single one of his duties. In fact, he was actually given more responsibility: in addition to his position as head of television and of the press, he assumed command of the Fidaijun Saddam (Followers of Saddam), a paramilitary organization supporting the Republican Guard. The Fidaijun Saddam consisted of young, unemployed men who were paid 25,000 dinars a month, eight times the average salary of a physician.

From now on, Uday worked from behind the scenes. His major goal was to persuade his sisters to return to Iraq. He called Raghd and Rina almost every day in Amman, and often spoke with the six nieces and nephews who had gone with them. In these conversations he soon learned what diplomats in Amman had known for some time: Hussein Kamel had no idea what to do next. Saddam's opponents would have nothing to do with him, and no one was about to accept him as an alternative to Saddam Hussein. Even the other countries in the Gulf rejected his overtures. The emissaries he sent to Saudi Arabia and Kuwait returned home without having seen a single government official.

Ahmed Chalabi, president of the Iraqi National Congress, had nothing but disdain for him. "He wants us to work with him and to follow him. No one in the resistance takes him seriously; he's just a war criminal. But we're not shutting the door in his face; we just ignore him."

To make matters worse, Hussein Kamel had a falling-out with his host, King Hussein. King Hussein had proposed that Iraq be transformed into a federation of smaller states, and Hussein Kamel had publicly ridiculed the idea. In an interview with a Jordanian newspaper, he went so far as to call the proposal "absurd." Later he denied using that word, adding that he would "make mincemeat out of the journalist" who had misquoted him.

But the damage was already done. Hussein Kamel and his clan were transferred from the king's Hashemiyah Palace to one of his guest houses. A few weeks later they were bluntly informed that these quarters too were needed for other, more important guests, and they were unceremoniously transported to simple apartments on the road that led to the airport. This demolished whatever was left of their social standing.

The disgrace made a profound impression above all on Raghd and Rina, who until this point had been entirely loyal wives. They called their mother, Sajida, in Baghdad more and more frequently. Jordanian intelligence agents reported that "the women were on the phone with their mother for hours at a time every day. They told her they wanted to return home." Raghd burst into tears once, because her nine-year-old son, Ali, was becoming increasingly withdrawn. He had stopped painting nice pictures—for Grandpa Saddam.

By now, Hussein Kamel had lost all self-control. He would walk for hours through Amman's parks in his shirt-sleeves, even through the rain and cold, whispering feverishly into his cellular phone. "Once," Jordanian diplomats reported, "he went totally berserk, hit himself in the stomach with a cushion, and cried out, 'I'm a man, I'm a man!' Then he fell to his knees in tears, moaning that he was going to kill himself."

The final blow occurred on February 15, 1996, when

Crown Prince Talal of Jordan paid a visit to Hussein Kamel's apartment. After a brief, formal greeting, he told Hussein Kamel that he was "free to go." They were throwing him out. Kamel strapped a pistol around his hips and drove his Mercedes to the private residence of the Iraqi ambassador. The two of them had a shouting match in the doorway. Then they drove together to the Iraqi embassy in Amman near the Hotel Intercontinental. From there, Hussein Kamel called his father-in-law in Baghdad.

Twenty-four hours later, on the afternoon of February 16, a courier arrived with an urgent delivery for Hussein Kamel: a videocassette from Baghdad. "I promise that I have forgiven you," Saddam Hussein said on the tape. "Come back, we'll have a great celebration. The whole family will be there. . . ." He also said he would send a signed pardon.

Although friends warned the son-in-law that he was going to his death, Hussein Kamel summoned his wife, his family, his brother, and his brother's family and announced, "We're going home." Raghd and Rina swore on the Koran that they would commit suicide if, despite Saddam's promise, anything should happen to their husbands.

The signed pardon arrived on February 17. A few hours later the same convoy of Mercedes-Benz sedans that had fled to Amman six months earlier set off again, this time in the opposite direction. It was going back to Baghdad. "Saddam has forgiven me. I'm going to serve him till the end of my days," Hussein Kamel announced at a hurriedly organized press conference before his departure.

At the Trebeil crossing, a smiling Uday, wearing sunglasses and a custom-made silk suit, was waiting for the convoy. When it arrived, the two sons-in-law were immediately separated from their wives. They would never see them again. On the evening news the next day, Uday's television station Shahab announced that the president's two daughters, Raghd and Rina, had sued for divorce from the two traitors and that their request had been granted. The divorce was performed by a mullah in Rathbag, just outside of Baghdad.

After a brief interrogation, Hussein Kamel and Saddam Kamel were set free. They were even allowed back into their villa, the family residence of the al-Majid clan in Baghdad's Saydida district. It was a perverse trick.

Seventy-two hours later they were dead. What Uday's newspapers and television stations described as the "al-Majid clan's battle to recover its family honor" was nothing but a contract murder. Qusay and Uday promised Ali Hassan al-Majid that he would be fully reinstated if he carried out this special assignment. Operating under his command, troops surrounded the al-Majid villa at sunrise and closed off all the exits.

The sons-in-law learned of their condemnation on television. Shortly afterward, a hundred soldiers and policemen opened fire on the villa. Machine-gun bullets riddled doors and bodies. There was blood everywhere. At least four children were killed in their pajamas, including Ali, who had been painting nice pictures for his Grandpa Saddam just a few days before.

Ali Hassan al-Majid's Mercedes was parked right by the front gate of the villa. He was on his cell phone with Saddam Hussein throughout the attack. "We have seventeen bodies. Saddam and Hakim are dead, only Hussein is missing," he reported. Saddam replied, "I want his head."

Bulldozers started to raze the villa. Suddenly, Hussein Kamel jumped out of his hiding place. Naked from the waist up and bleeding, he brandished a pistol and a machine gun.

He fired . . . and was shot to pieces. His body was showered with bullets. Then everything was still. Ali Hassan al-Majid walked up to the body, bent down, and emptied his handgun into Hussein's head. Then he grabbed hold of his foot and dragged the corpse through the dust. "This is what happens to a traitor. . . ." The bulldozers finished their job.

That evening, Uday's TV station broadcast the al-Majid family's declaration of loyalty to Saddam Hussein: "The treacherous branch of the family has been severed. The family's honor is preserved." Then a band played the national anthem, patriotic songs praising Saddam Hussein, and a medley of military marches. Commenting on this display of cynicism, Madeleine Albright, the American ambassador to the United Nations, said, "I have long since given up trying to understand Iraq's leaders."

The attack put an end to Saddam Hussein's problems with the al-Majid family, but the threat posed by the Iraqi National Congress remained. Working on Qusay's orders, both the Mukhabarat and the Estikhbarat stepped up surveillance of American activities within Operation Provide Comfort. Iraqi double agents had been present at the very first organizational meetings at the SAS Hotel in Vienna. Additionally, Qusay had cleverly planted sleepers in the so-called peacekeeping force in northern Iraq, which consisted mostly of Iraqi army deserters recruited by the United States. From their various agents, Baghdad knew virtually everything about the Americans' activities in Salahaddin. Qusay's men knew exactly what computers, modems, and satellite receivers had been delivered. They even knew the computers' serial numbers.

One major source of information was Necherwan Barzani, the young nephew of Kurd leader Massoud Barzani. Necherwan Barzani is a cheap copy of Uday Saddam Hussein. He too is crazy about cars and watches. He has the only fire-red Ferrari in Kurdistan, owns countless restaurants and hotels in north Iraq, and is said to be completely unpredictable. Necherwan never wears the billowing pants of the Pesh Merga, the Kurdish fighters; he prefers to be seen in western attire, which he has flown in through Turkey.

Qusay and Uday have known Necherwan for years. They invited him to Baghdad, gave him money when he needed it.

A profound, mutually advantageous friendship grew up between them. Necherwan favored a rapprochement of the Kurdish groups with Baghdad. In return, Qusay promised to help him and his uncle Massoud Barzani in their struggle against the other Kurdish group, the Patriotic Union of Kurdistan under Jalal Talabani.

The two groups had agreed to a truce after the Gulf War, and both of them received massive military assistance from the United States. But despite—or perhaps because of—this aid, Talabani and Barzani remained enemies. Corruption and power struggles kept them at each other's throats. "Barzani was never interested in the fight against Saddam Hussein," Talabani claims. "He just wanted money and power, and Washington gave him all the support he needed." Barzani and his nephew Necherwan maintained tight control over almost all black-market trading between Iraq and Turkey, collecting millions of dollars in customs fees. They also had nearly exclusive control of the oil and gas market in the north.

Barzani replies that "Talabani is nothing but a puppet of the regime in Tehran. He even planted Iranian agents in northern Iraq in order to gain control of Kurdistan."

More and more, the CIA was becoming entangled in this web of petty jealousies and territorial battles. To keep control of what was happening in Kurdistan, it increased the number of operatives in Salahaddin from twenty-two to forty. Yet by this time the Americans' eight-hundred-man team in northern Iraq was so infiltrated with double agents that no move could be made without Qusay knowing.

The worst setback to the opposition came in November 1995, when Saddam's agents used a four-hundred-pound bomb to blow INC headquarters to pieces. Twenty people were killed. A short time later, Barzani and Talabani broke with each other definitively. "We noticed," Talabani claims, "that from this time on, Barzani received arms not only from the CIA, but directly from the Estikhbarat, Qusay's military intelligence."

The situation in Salahaddin was totally chaotic. On the one hand, Langley couldn't very well dissolve its enormous spy network from one day to the next; the network had taken four years to build. On the other hand, it was senseless to continue the operation under these circumstances. A decision was made to transfer a large number of CIA agents to Amman, where they were assigned to work more closely with the National Accord. The $200 million that Langley had invested in the INC operation was irretrievably lost. Just twenty American agents remained in Salahaddin.

U.S. intelligence sources failed to notice when Saddam Hussein and Massoud Barzani formed an all-out alliance six months later. The top-secret meeting took place on the night of August 22, in one of Saddam Hussein's palaces in Baghdad. Present at this decisive meeting were Qusay, Uday, Saddam Hussein, and Necherwan Barzani. The foursome worked out a deal whereby Saddam Hussein would place troops from his Republican Guard at Barzani's disposal; Barzani would be free to use them in his fight against Talabani's forces. In return, Barzani would help destroy the INC's presence in northern Iraq.

The agreement was put into action on the morning of August 31, when Saddam's tanks rolled into Arbil. "The first thing the elite troops did was to storm the building on Ain-Kawa Street," Talabani's men remember. But the Americans were already gone. Just a few hours earlier, during the night of August 30, they had taken their jeeps and fled through Zakhu to Turkey. They had so little warning that they had to leave all of their equipment behind—as well as all of the records of their covert activities.

Saddam's henchmen recovered an exact list of everyone who had worked with the Americans. Names and addresses in hand, death squads went systematically from house to house, searching cellars and garages for the dissidents on their lists. In the meantime, Mukhabarat specialists searched INC headquarters, removed millions of dollars' worth of computers and communications equipment, and carted them off in sealed containers. Ninety-six Kurdish employees of the CIA and the INC were arrested during the course of this search.

All of them were executed in Qushtapa on the same day. There was no trial; the executions were carried out on direct orders from Qusay. From two to three hundred other INC employees were loaded onto trucks and brought to high security prisons in Kirkuk and Mosul. Qusay himself interrogated many of them. Qusay's intelligence specialists discovered detailed records of all of the CIA's activities over the previous several years. It was one of Langley's worst defeats in a long time.

Today, Saddam Hussein and his two sons appear to have recovered absolute power over Iraq. With the help of the CIA records, Qusay's Mukhabarat hunted down secret agents in Iraq and sleepers in Baghdad. A wave of violence flooded the country. The military was hit particularly hard. One hundred twenty officers were executed, and two members of the general staff, Nazar Omar al-Tikriti and Asaad Abdalhassan Falch, were arrested and tortured. What became of them, no one knows.

While these purges were going on, Saddam Hussein began to reorganize his security forces. Elite troops drawn from the Republican Guard, the Emergency Forces, and Saddam's militia were combined into the newly formed Holy Sea and Mother of All Battles, under Qusay's command. To what extent this new unit will keep the system of murder, persecution, and show trials intact is difficult to judge. In the past, Saddam's surveillance systems have functioned only because the elite troops, unlike everyone else in the country, are paid on a regular basis.

Be that as it may, on December 12, 1996, the Clan was again rocked by the unthinkable. It was a Thursday, the start of the Islamic weekend. Every Thursday, Uday would drive to the al-Mansur Club in Baghdad before going on to the exclusive al-Said. Usually he went by convoy and changed cars several times along the way. This time was different. He climbed into one of his Porsches and went alone to pick up his girlfriend Lubna, a young dancer. Then he drove from Lubna's parents' villa directly to the al-Said club.

Two blocks from the club, a group of six men stood and waited. Their leader was Ra'ad al-Hazaah, the nephew of General Omar al-Hazaah, a Sunni general from Tikrit, Saddam Hussein's native city. When Saddam Hussein attacked Iran in 1980, starting a war that would last eight years and cost a million lives, General Hazaah openly criticized the regime and left the army in protest. Afterwards he spent most of his time in a club for retired army officers in the Yarmuk district of Baghdad, where he also had his house. Whenever he was drunk, and that was often, he criticized Saddam Hussein.

In 1990, shortly before the invasion of Kuwait, General al-Hazaah was arrested in the officers' club. His tongue was cut out, and then he was shot. His son Farouk was also executed. The house in Yarmuk was razed by bulldozers.

Ra'ad vowed revenge. That Thursday the opportunity finally came. As Uday's speeding Porsche turned into the street to the al-Said Club, machine-gun fire erupted around it. The car itself was armored, but the bullets pierced the windshield. Uday was hit by fourteen bullets and gravely injured. Reports differ on whether Lubna died in the attack, or was hurt. While Uday was rushed to an operating table in Ibn-Sina Hospital, the most modern and well-equipped hospital in Baghdad, the assassins were able to flee. Followers of the banned Shi'ite Dawa movement under Ayatollah Mohammed Bakr al-Hakim, currently living in exile in Tehran, helped them reach the swamps of southern Iraq. From there, they crossed the border into Iran.

The day after the attack, in a statement to the press, Ayatollah al-Hakim claimed that "Uday's injuries are more serious than the regime is admitting." Uday's Shahab TV station had announced merely that "the son of the president was the victim of a cowardly attack and sustained superficial wounds." The truth about Uday's injuries leaked out only gradually: One bullet had lodged in his spine, another in his pelvis. As it became clear that the hospital's Iraqi surgeons were unable to help the president's powerful son, his uncle Barzan al-Tikriti tried to have him transferred to France. But France's authorities refused him entry to the country. Then Barzan, Iraq's UN ambassador in Geneva, made a personal call at the University Hospital in Lausanne. Here again, no one wanted to admit the president's son. Finally, Barzan arranged for two specialists from Germany, one from France, and Fidel Castro's personal physician to travel to Baghdad.

Uday underwent several operations conducted by the team of doctors, and some progress was made. His left leg, which had become gangrenous, was saved from amputation. But the end result fell far short of a complete rehabilitation. When he was released from Ibn-Sina in early June, he left on crutches. He struggled down the long corridor on the hospital's main floor, visibly straining to propel himself forward. He managed a tortured smile for the journalists who had been selected to attend. His left leg was completely stiff, and he seemed pale and weak overall. The event, which was to have been a kind of resurrection of the president's eldest son and heir, turned into an embarrassing spectacle. It was painfully obvious to everyone what an effort it cost him to drag his body the few yards down the hall. "He got what was coming to him," was what most Iraqis probably thought when they observed the scene on the evening news the next day.

"The bullets didn't just strike Uday's body," Latif Yahia claims. "They also broke a spell. In Iraq, a leader is not someone who is respected, but someone who is feared. Now the fear of Uday is gone, because the people have seen that he isn't invulnerable. They have seen that despite all his bodyguards and fidais, he is still not safe."

For years, people in Iraq credited Saddam Hussein and

his sons with superhuman powers. It was said they could capture, torture, and eliminate any of their enemies at any time they pleased, and that their doubles were everywhere, sowing chaos among their opponents. But suddenly everyone saw that a member of the ruling clan was in dire need of help, and that no one could give it to him; his injuries were incurable. Uday, the people realized, didn't know the secret of immortality after all. And if Uday didn't know, then neither did his father. Saddam Hussein, Uday, and Qusay—for the first time, Iraqis understood that they were all mortals like everyone else.

Before the attack, no one in Baghdad dared talk openly about the president's family. Now people were gossiping about the goings-on in the Clan, cracking jokes about those in power. Iraqis have quietly stopped going along with the authorities. Women are giggling about the scandals in the palace; the students are biding their time. Maybe they'll demonstrate again. Against Saddam.

Saddamism, the Arabic sickness par excellence, has been weakened, but its tenacity and pervasiveness cannot be overemphasized. For decades the people of Iraq have let themselves be swept up by this system. The words *corruption* and *fear* do not really do justice to it: corruption properly refers to a way of influencing an existing system, of speeding things along or of gaining an advantage by bribery. But in Baghdad corruption *is* the system; corruption is all that is left. It is not a means to end, but an end in itself.

Everyone grabs what he can. At the top are the members of the Clan from Tikrit: They embezzle, they looted Kuwait, they take a cut of all important transactions—including humanitarian aid. At the bottom it is no different. The customs agent collects a "fee" for opening your suitcase, the border guard for stamping your passport, the postman for delivering your mail, the secret police agent for leaving you in peace, the parking attendant for not stealing your rented car.

Cynics would call this the privatization of Iraq: Parents pay their children's teachers; a patient's family pays the doctors, the hospital administration, and then the funeral director. Those who want to feel safe pay the policeman on the beat.

There was never really a "state" of Iraq at all; there was just Saddam Hussein. He kept the country functioning by distributing and withdrawing favors, by praising, punishing, murdering—by being powerful. When Saddam seized control of the country, half of Iraq's current population had not yet been born. "The people get more out of pretending to love Saddam Hussein then they would by opposing him," Latif Yahia explains. "What use is it to them to rebel if their ration cards will have no value the next day?"

Latif escaped this system when he left Iraq. His escape may have saved his life, but it hasn't yet made him any happier. When he arrived in Vienna, he was very much in demand. The Austrian secret service kept him under constant surveillance, debriefed him, shielded him from the press. He was given a monthly expense allowance and installed in a little house on the outskirts of the city. Intelligence agents visited him almost daily to ask him about Iraq, and all this attention gave the former double a sense of importance that blinded him to the reality of the situation, putting him at an even greater remove from the real world than when he'd first escaped.

At the time, everyone was still talking about the Gulf War, and Saddam Hussein, the mystery man in Baghdad, had become a mythical figure—the devil incarnate. But when George Bush left the White House, the world forgot its fascination with Saddam Hussein. The two great rivals were gone, and nothing causes the world to lose interest faster than the disappearance of the enemy. The conflict between good and evil, the drama of two men locked in single combat—all of this had lost its relevance, and the key question for America, "Why didn't we finish the job?" didn't seem worth asking after Bill Clinton had assumed power.

The sudden loss of interest in Saddam and the Gulf War had particularly unfortunate consequences for Latif Yahia. In Baghdad he had had no identity of his own, but was the fidai, Uday's personal slave. His proximity to the summit of power had given him a privileged position that he never really wanted, but that he nevertheless began to enjoy. He had money, cars, and the most expensive suits, as well as the certainty that the system would continue to support him as long as he kept out of trouble.

In Vienna, everything was different. When he demanded a villa and a luxury car, a team of bodyguards, and diplomatic privileges, he failed to get anywhere with the Austrian officials, especially as the intelligence services gradually lost interest in him.

He was no more successful when he tried to approach the Iraqi resistance. "No matter who I spoke with," Yahia says today, "I always had the impression I was dealing with a copy of Saddam Hussein. They all carry on about him, think he's the devil, but they behave the same way he does. They even look like him. They wear the same mustache, they dress the same way; and like him they are all obsessed with power." For their part, none of the exiled dissidents ever fully trusted Yahia. All of them confirmed that he had been Uday's fidai, but many of them suspected he was now a double agent. "In a way, my fate was virtually identical to that of the Hussein sons-in-law," Yahia says. "I stayed in my little police hideout, and the only thing left for me to do was to talk to my wife, Bushra, about our daughter, Tamara, and her future."

Bushra is Iraqi. Latif has known her since childhood. After the Gulf War, she and Tamara managed to get out of Iraq. An international rescue agency gave the child a set of forged papers and smuggled her over the border to Jordan. In Amman, the Austrian embassy issued her a refugee passport that allowed her to enter Europe.

From the very beginning, Latif Yahia wanted to go public with his story. He hoped it would weaken the regime in

Baghdad, and he thought it would help show the Iraqi opposition that he was on their side. So he contacted the Austrian
magazine *News*. The resulting series of articles about corruption in the Iraqi ruling class caused a sensation. Almost all
the leading newspapers in Europe reprinted it. Overnight he
was catapulted into the spotlight of the world media. Iraq's
secret service tried everything to prevent the story from
being published or supported. Yahia was the target of an
assassination attempt on Stephansplatz, in the center of
Vienna. Two bullets were fired at him, both near misses; they
were later extracted from the façade of a nearby lingerie
boutique. Yahia went underground, moving from one apartment to another, but the Austrian authorities still refused
him police protection. In Baghdad, almost all of his relatives
were put in prison or placed under house arrest.

As would happen later to Hussein Kamel and Saddam
Kamel, Yahia received a verbal offer from the Iraqi embassy
in Vienna to return to Iraq, "with a full guarantee I would
not be punished," Yahia recalls. He refused, but Bushra
wanted to accept. "I just couldn't take worrying about what
was happening to my family in Baghdad," she explained.
Then there was the constant harassment of the covert agents
from the embassy: telephone threats, such as "We're going
to kidnap your daughter," and demeaning insults, such as
"Your wife is a whore."

It soon got so that Yahia and his family could scarcely
make a move in Vienna without being followed and observed. "We lived in constant fear for our lives," Yahia says,
describing a situation that was called freedom but was really
the continuation of his flight from Baghdad. "The stress
finally turned into real paranoia," he says. Then, late in the
summer of 1994, the game of hide-and-seek came to a dramatic end. Yahia had just stopped his car at a stoplight.
Alongside him waited another car with an Arab at the
wheel—an Egyptian, it was discovered later, who earned his
living as a taxi driver in Vienna. "The man rolled down his

window, spat on my car, and started shouting obscenities. He called me an 'Iraqi son of a bitch' and my wife a 'miserable whore.' " Bushra was sitting in the passenger's seat, five months pregnant with their next child. "The word 'whore' really hit me in the gut. If I had had a gun, I would have shot him on the spot." Yahia's rage still shows when he describes what he felt at that moment. He jumped out, dragged the Egyptian from his car, and pummeled his face.

Yahia didn't bother himself about the extent of the man's injuries. He got back in his car and left the scene. Under the force of Yahia's blows, the Egyptian had fallen and hit his head against the curb, fracturing his skull. In Austria, this constitutes "grievous bodily injury." The fact that Yahia drove away was an aggravating circumstance. In court, he was charged with grievous bodily injury and failure to aid a person in need. The judge sentenced the former double to a year in jail.

The sentence was later reduced to eight months. While he was in prison, Yahia's second child was born—Omar, a son. Shortly after his release, Yahia left Austria and went to London, where he set up a textile business with the help of other Iraqi exiles. But it was only a few months before Qusay's Mukhabarat tracked him down. "First they rammed my car, then they shot at me in a telephone booth just as I was trying to call someone in Iraq," Yahia reports. "Finally they found out who all my best clients were, and threatened them until they agreed not to do business with me."

Yahia left England and went to Norway, the country that has the most liberal asylum laws in Europe. "They promised us political asylum and gave us a small apartment. Tamara, who was already seven years old, was able to go to school," Yahia says, describing his attempt to recover a normal life for himself and his family. However, when he entered the country, he used an assumed identity and concealed his past—a naive attempt to start afresh. Just three months later his past caught up with him. "An Iraqi immigrant recognized me and told the police about my history," Yahia explains. Once again he was in trouble with the law. "Why did you conceal your past and use a false name when you entered the country?" the authorities asked. "Why didn't you tell us you held an important position in Saddam Hussein's regime?" Yahia and his family lost their right of asylum, and payments they received from the state emergency fund were cut off. "We were really at the end of our rope," Yahia says dejectedly. That very day, Bushra contacted the Iraqi embassy in Oslo to obtain reentry visas for herself, Tamara, and Omar. Twenty-four hours later, she and their two children were on a plane to Amman, and from there they took a car to Baghdad. Yahia found out only after they had gone. There was a note on the table in their apartment: "I can't go on like this. I want to go home." He has had no news of his family since. "Every time I try to call them in Baghdad, the line goes dead."

Today, Latif Yahia lives in Germany. Another Iraqi refugee, an old school friend, has taken him in, but Yahia isn't optimistic about his prospects: "I'll probably always remain a hostage to my past."

KARL WENDL
JUNE 1997